Pan Study Aids

GW01090520

Sociology

Paul Selfe

Pan Books London and Sydney
in association with **Heinemann Educational Books**

First published 1983 by Pan Books Ltd,
Cavaye Place, London SW10 9PG
in association with Heinemann Educational Books Ltd
1 2 3 4 5 6 7 8 9 10
© Paul Selfe 1983
ISBN 0 330 26684 5
Printed and bound in Great Britain by
Richard Clay (The Chaucer Press) Ltd, Bungay, Suffolk

PAN STUDY AIDS
Titles published in this series

Accounts and Book-keeping
Biology
British Government and Politics
Chemistry
Commerce
Economics
Effective Study Skills
English Language
French
Geography 1 *Physical and Human*
Geography 2 *British Isles, Western Europe, North America*
German
History 1 *British*
History 2 *European*
Human Biology
Maths
Physics
Spanish
Advanced Biology
Advanced Chemistry
Advanced Mathematics
Advanced Physics

Brodies Notes on English Literature

This long established series published in Pan Study Aids now contains more
than 150 titles. Each volume covers one of the major works of English
literature regularly set for examinations.

Contents

Acknowledgements

I am grateful to the exam boards for permission to reproduce questions. In addition I would like to thank Diane Lawley for her help in the preparation of the manuscript.

To the student

The aim of this book is to discuss all the areas on which O level candidates in sociology are regularly examined. You will be shown typical questions from past papers and guided through points you should consider in answering an examination question.

There are six boards that set O level papers in sociology or social studies. All the topic areas on which they examine candidates are discussed in this book. But it is important to remember that not all the boards cover precisely the same ground in their questions. Therefore you must be sure which topics do and which do not appear on the paper for which you are preparing.

Nevertheless, all the boards intend to test the candidates' knowledge and understanding of key sociological terms and concepts; their ability to interpret data and apply their understanding to questions about social behaviour and social organizations; and their ability to express their knowledge. Most of the boards assess candidates on their ability to write a structured essay or their ability to express some detailed knowledge in short answers. Only Oxford Board relies entirely on essays. The others include some short controlled response questions which test factual knowledge and an understanding of material presented in the question.

The exam boards

The addresses given below are those from which copies of syllabuses and past examination papers may be ordered. The abbreviations (AEB, etc) are those used in this book to identify actual questions.

Associated Examining Board, (AEB)
Wellington House,
Aldershot, Hants GU11 1BQ

University of Cambridge Local Examinations Syndicate, (CAM)
Syndicate Buildings, 17 Harvey Road,
Cambridge CB1 2EU

Jount Matriculation Board, (JMB)
(Agent) John Sherratt and Son Ltd,
78 Park Road,
Altrincham, Cheshire WA14 5QQ

University of London School Examinations Department, (LOND)
66–72 Gower Street,
London WC1E 6EE

Oxford Delegacy of Local Examinations, (OX)
Ewert Place,
Summertown,
Oxford OX2 7BZ

Welsh Joint Education Committee, (WEL)
245 Western Avenue,
Cardiff CF5 2YX

1 Preparing for the examination

When you begin your studies in sociology it is important that you are familiar with the syllabus that you are studying.

You are advised to read a copy of your syllabus early in your course. It is also important to become familiar with the structure of the question paper that you will be faced with in the examination. Past papers are always readily available at a small cost from the Boards and they will help you in your exam preparation.

The format of O level sociology papers by different boards

Board	Paper No.	Number of papers to be taken	Time allowed for each paper	Number of full essay questions to answer	Number of questions requiring short answers	Number of questions requiring essays or short answers
Oxford	2848/1 Sociol.	1	2½ hrs	5	—	—
AEB	022/1 022/2 Sociol.	2	2 hrs 1¾ hrs	— —	3 —	— 3
London	858 Alternative Ordinary	1	3 hrs	3	2	—
Welsh	4I 107 Sociol.	1	2½ hrs	3	7	—
JMB	Social Science	1	2½ hrs	2	6	—
CAM*	2250/1 2251/1 2250/2 Sociol.	2	2½ hrs 1½ hrs	— —	— —	4 3

*N.B. From 1984 candidates may undertake an optional project instead of Paper 2.

The aims of the syllabuses are also for the students eventually to be able to:

1 Develop the ability to make balanced judgements about the structure and institutions of society;
2 Develop some critical awareness of the dynamic nature of human societies, understanding how and why they develop and change;
3 Become more aware of the significance of roles, relationships and the effects of belonging to groups;
4 Become aware of the nature of their own social culture and the significance of the differences that exist between cultures;
5 Become aware of the sociological approaches and methods that are available to help people to be able to analyse and understand patterns of social behaviour and the ways in which social organizations work.

They also emphasize that the new student of sociology will not be expected to be familiar with sociological theory in depth, nor with the complex detail of methodology and research findings. However, they do require that candidates show an awareness of the nature of the society in which they live and a knowledge of relevant sociological studies or surveys. They should understand some of the different methods and approaches available to sociologists, and they should be familiar with the available literature.

This latter point should remind the students embarking on their studies in this subject that they are unlikely to do well by relying too heavily on one textbook. A list of recommended texts is on pp. 12–13. Both the list and the individual books and journals should be used in a selective way. The titles listed represent only a tiny selection from a vast number of publications in the discipline. The student will generally use such books purely for reference. It is unlikely that there will be sufficient time to read them from cover to cover – the books will contain some important details that can be used when researching answers. This detail can be obtained by careful examination of the contents and index sections of the books.

In preparing an answer it is a temptation to lift large sections from the work of the authors you are reading. This is a dangerous fault. Anyone who is familiar with marking essays will quickly recognize that the material has been used in an indiscriminate way. Direct quotations must be used sparingly and an acknowledgement of the source must be given. The second danger in taking large sections from the books consulted is that it is invariably impossible to recall the same detail when revising for the examination.

The answer is to read specific sections of books carefully. Make your own notes in words that you understand. Be sure to establish the central point the author is making and relate this to the argument that you are presenting. In this way you will be able to recall the point again when writing an examination answer. The idea expressed in the book will have become a part of your own thinking.

Success in the examination will stem from a clear understanding of the issues involved in the topic areas covered. If you find the explanations of one writer unclear then you must try reading another. The same author may have some chapters which you regard as adequate and others which are inadequate for your purposes. For these reasons you must become familiar with the available literature.

Remember, too, that sociology is concerned with a dynamic subject matter. Patterns of social life and behaviour are subject to constant pressures of change. The books that describe and account for these changes take several years to produce. By the time they appear in the bookshops and in your hands much of the statistical data will inevitably be dated as will information on other aspects of social life. The only way that you can overcome this difficulty is to read regularly a good newspaper and a weekly journal such as *New Society*, as well as watching documentary and other news programmes on television and listening to similar programmes on the radio.

Writing an essay in sociology

1 Remember that you are being asked to answer a question. You must answer it by referring to relevant material.
2 You are studying sociology. Therefore you will be expected to use sociological language and refer to sociologists and their studies in your answer. You are not likely to be asked to give your own opinions, those of your relatives or those you have obtained from the popular press.
3 You must organize and structure your answer so that you provide a clear and logical exposition. The London Board, for example, specifically states, 'Candidates are reminded of the necessity for good English and orderly presentation in their answers.'
4 To obtain the highest marks in a full essay question (in contrast to one that is broken down into a series of sub-sections) you must write a full essay answer and avoid note form.
5 You should develop a structure for your answers which will both guide you in revision (each part of your structure should remind you of what you need to know) and which will ensure that you present your information in the logical way required. The structure should be a simple one that you can impose on every question that you tackle.

Example

(a) Introduction – in about 50 words write a clear, accurate, non-controversial opening statement which should show the reader that you have read and understood the question and that you mean to answer it.

(b) Raise the key issues in the question. In about 100 words explain what the crucial problems are in answering the question. Define any terms that may be confusing or which are open to different interpretations.

(c) Write the main body of the essay. In about 200 words develop your answer. Discuss the work of writers who have put forward theories or who have researched the area. State some of their key findings and show how they relate to the question raised in the title.

(d) Write a summary in about 50 words. Emphasize the most crucial points that have been raised. Suggest the direction in which the evidence points.

(e) Conclusion – in about 50–100 words finally answer the question. The answer you reach should naturally follow from the points you have raised in the main body of the essay. If there is any doubt arising from conflicting evidence then state this as a problem. There may be no 'right' or 'wrong' answer, but the examiner will want to see that you are aware of the problems and that you appreciate the complexities of the question raised.

You should complete an adequate examination length answer in about 500 words. You will have little more than thirty minutes for each question you attempt at O level, and it is physically difficult to write much more than this in the available time.

6 Some boards break questions down into several sub-sections. Some state the number of marks awarded for each section. Take careful note of these. If, for example, section (a) offers two marks and section (b) ten marks, then it is clearly more important to write expansively on section (b) than on section (a).

7 Remember that writing a successful examination answer is a skill. It is not an innate ability which some people have and others do not. You must, therefore, practise frequently until you can write 500 words in thirty minutes. You are unlikely to gain a good mark for a too brief and concise essay. The question will be a complex one which requires wide-ranging discussion. You are likely to gain good marks for an answer which is comprehensive and therefore of good length.

Revision points

1 When you revise bear in mind the following points:

(a) **Always define the amount to be learned.**
Limit the boundaries of the area to be studied. Specify what it is that you want to learn. Specify the amount of time you have available in which to learn it. Break it down into reasonable sections.

(b) **Always define the amount of time to be spent on learning.**
You must establish how long your concentration span is and work within this limitation. It is best to stop work whilst you still feel relatively fresh. If necessary, have short breaks and then begin again. There is little point in continuing to work when you are feeling tired.

(c) **Always establish the right mental attitude.**
You must be in the right frame of mind for successful study. You cannot learn whilst watching television or if involved in other distractions.

(d) **Always spend some time in recall.**
Recall (remembering what you have learned) is helped by recalling frequently and by verbalizing what you have learned. It helps, for example, to discuss the facts or ideas you are studying with someone – not so much in a series of single-answer test questions, but in open discussion. Once you have verbalized some of the facts about the current trends in, say, divorce and its possible consequences, then you will find the details will become a part of your thinking.

2 When you are revising centre your studies on the question as a whole rather than on a mass of individual bits of material which may or may not be useful. Select a question to answer. Read it carefully.

(a) Underline or box the key words in the question:
Example:
'A sample survey attempts to gain an accurate picture of an area of social activity by representing as accurately as possible the group of people to be studied. Explain the ways in which sociologists attempt to achieve a representative sample .'

(b) Are you certain what the question is asking?
If you are in any doubt restate the question in your own words to make the meaning clear:
'When a sociologist draws a sample for the purposes of an accurate survey into some aspect of social life he must make

sure it is representative of the population. How (and why) does he obtain such a sample?'

(c) State briefly the answer to the question. If you know the answer then clearly you can proceed to tackle it. The answer will guide the way in which you structure your essay. You will know what material you require and the conclusion to which you are working.

Example:

'When sociologists are working in the scientific tradition of the discipline they draw samples of a representative type. They do so by using random procedures. They may use a stratified random sample, a multi-stage sample or a multi-phase sample. Where slightly less accuracy is required they may use a quota sample. But in each case the sample must include people of different sexes, ages, classes, areas of residence, etc. in the proportion that they appear in the total population in which the sociologist is interested.'

(d) It is useful to prepare a clear opening statement which would show that you have understood the question.

Example:

'Sociologists who work in the traditional scientific tradition emphasize the need for precision and accuracy in their results. When they prepare a research project they ensure that the sample they draw is of a representative type. There are a number of procedures by which this can be achieved. Failure to use them carefully would throw results into doubt.'

(e) If you are happy that you have understood the question and that you know the answer to it, then you should proceed. If you are still in the process of gathering information on the topic area, then your plan should reveal to you what further data you still require and the areas in which you have some confusion. You must then spend time checking these and in making notes from relevant books. When you have done this you should proceed to write your final answer to the question.

Some recommended texts

D. M. Carpenter and K. W. Ruddiman: *Looking at Society*, Pitman Publishing, £1.50

M. J. Davies and B. J. King: *Discovering Society* (Units 1–8), National Extension College, £6 for 3 vols

C. Hambling and P. Matthews: *Human Society*, Macmillan Educational, £3.35

K. Heasman: *The Study of Sociology*, Allen & Unwin, £1.65

G. Hurd (ed): *Human Societies*, Routledge & Kegan Paul, £2.95
O. Jones and S. Hill: *Sociology for O-Level*, Hart-Davis Educational, £2.25
K. Lambert: *Life in our Society* (vols 1 and 2), Nelson, £1.20 per vol
D. Lawton: *Investigating Society*, Hodder & Stoughton, £2.05
D. Lawton and B. Dufour: *The New Social Studies*, Heinemann Educational Books, £4.50
Longman's *Social Science Series* J. Nobbs, B. Hine and M. Flemming: *Sociology*, Macmillan Educational, £3.95
P. J. North: *People in Society*, Longman, £1.75
G. O'Donnell: *The Human Web*, John Murray, £2
J. Scotson: *Introducing Society*, Routledge & Kegan Paul, £1.50
P. Selfe: *Sociology*, Nelson, £2.35
J. L. Thompson: *Examining Sociology*, Hutchinson Educational, £3.75.
E. Wilkins: *Elements of Social Science*, Macdonald & Evans, £1.95

Authors	Content and relevance to syllabus	Clarity and style	Presentation, quality of illustrations, etc.	Skill development	Reading lists and glossary	Standard	Value for money
Selfe	●●●	●●●	●●●●	●●●●	●●	O level/CEE	●●●●
North	●●●●	●●●●	●●●	●●	●●●	O level/CEE	●●●●
Jones and Hill	●●●	●●●	●●	●●●●	●	O level/CEE	●●●
Nobbs	●●●	●●●	●●●	●●	●	O level/CEE	●●●
Scotson	●●●●	●●●●●	●●●	●●	●●●●	O-A level	●●●
Lawton	●●●	●●●	●●●	●●●●	●●●	O level/CEE	●●●
Davies & King	●●●	●●	●●	●●●	●	O-A level	●●
O'Donnell	●●●	●●	●●●	●●	●●	O-A level	●●
Heasman	●●	●	●●	●	●	CSE-O level	●
Wilkins	●●	●●	●●		●●	O level/CEE	●
Carpenter & Ruddiman	●●●	●●	●●	●		O level/CEE	●●
Lambert	●	●	●●	●		CSE	●
Thompson	●●●	●●●	●●●	●●●		CSE-O level	●●●
Hambling & Matthews	●●	●●●	●●●	●●●	●●	O level/CEE	●●
Hurd (ed)	●●	●●	●●	●	●	O-A level	●●

Key: (Rating according to suitability for average O level candidate. Hence lower ratings for sociologically superior but more advanced texts.) ● poor, ●● below average, ●●● good, ●●●● very good, ●●●●● excellent.

Source: New Society, 4 October 1979.

2 What is sociology?

Sociology is the subject that asks questions about life in society and seeks answers to them by particular methods which have been developed over the past 150 years.

It focuses on social questions relating to the organization of society, its structure and function and the interpretation of patterns of behaviour. The behaviour of people in groups as well as the social organizations that have been created in society are studied. It considers, too, the common social culture. Sociology is the discipline that seeks to understand the nature of social interaction and the kinds of associations which appear, develop and change over time. Sociologists are also interested in the beliefs and values that influence people's behaviour.

Sociological questions are those that concentrate on why people behave as they do and why particular events occur. This involves issues such as relating divorce rates, the causes of criminal behaviour, the effects of television, the explanations for racial prejudice and discrimination and so on.

Sociologists are trained to raise questions about the nature of life in society and to find the answers. This enables us to understand more clearly why things happen as they do, whereas before they were previously strange or baffling events which seemed to have no clear explanation.

The student of sociology must become familiar with the basic details of research studies because the examination questions will require knowledge of such information. Sociology is not just a matter of opinion. You will be asked to discuss and debate and explain aspects of social phenomena. The answers that you give must be based on the information that professional sociologists (and other social scientists) have produced from their studies.

The scope of sociology

Sociology does not set out to solve social problems. The aim is to reveal knowledge about social behaviour and the organization of the structures and institutions of society. (Some of the resulting knowledge may be useful in solving some social problems, but this is incidental.) In a nutshell, sociology helps people to understand the kind of society in which they live and the factors that affect the behaviour of all people (including sociologists) who live in it.

Scientific sociology

Sociology has very conservative origins. Its founding fathers (notably Auguste Comte) were influenced by the French Revolution. They believed that a science of society was possible in the same way that a science of the natural world was possible. Then, when the underlying laws that controlled society were understood, those factors that precipitated disharmony and conflict could be controlled and all revolutionary upheavals averted. These early thinkers are called **scientific positivists**. They emphasized the need for a positive scientific approach to all research into social life.

This scientific approach is the traditional school of thought in sociology. The majority of research is still conducted according to these positivist principles.

1 A problem is identified.
2 A method is selected to study the problem.
3 A hypothesis is suggested and data are collected.
4 The hypothesis is tested and the data are analysed.
5 A conclusion is reached. The hypothesis is supported or rejected.
6 A report is produced describing the procedures and results.

It is important to enter the examination room knowing at least one study that illustrates the way in which these steps have been followed.

Consider the following example:

In 1971, Ann Oakley began her research into the sociology of housework. In 1974 her book of that title was published. Most of the book is based on a research study of women's attitudes to housework, and uses material obtained in interviews with London housewives. The main sample of 40 women was selected at random from lists of two GPs in London, one in a working-class and one in a middle-class area. The names of the potential respondents were selected on an alphabetical basis: two names were selected for each letter of the alphabet. They were the first two names that were listed of female patients born between 1940 and 1950, with at least one child aged under 5. She wished to interview only Irish or British-born women, and so her sample was reduced from 71 to 65 names. She then visited the address given on the medical card explaining her aims and inviting cooperation.

Names were taken in alphabetical order, one from each letter in both class lists until a total of 40 interviews had been obtained. This sample was equally divided into working and middle-class groups (based on husband's occupation). Of the original sample of 65 she found that she was unable to trace 16; she failed to contact 7; and 2 were not interviewed because they offered an appointment too far ahead. The 40 interviews were each completed in one session using a tape recorder: they lasted about 2 hours.

Her questionnaire contained some open-ended questions ('If you could have the last ten years over again is there anything you would be doing differently?'), but the majority required short, factual answers (e.g. 'Do you know how much your husband earns?'). They were designed to elicit information about the respondents' satisfaction with housework, marriage, child-care, employment and life in general. These are some of the results:

(i) Do you like housework?

Class	Like (%)	Don't mind (%)	Dislike (%)	Total (%)
Working	60	10	30	100
Middle	20	10	70	100

(ii) The experience of monotony are fragmentation in work: housewives and factory workers compared

Workers	Monotony (%)	Fragmentation (%)
Factory	41	70
Assembly line	67	86
Housewives	75	90

(iii) Work satisfaction and identification with the role of housewife

Identification with the role of housewife	Satisfied (%)	Dissatisfied (%)
High level	43	57
Medium/low level	16	84

(iv) Do you like looking after the child/children?

Social class	Like very much (%)	Don't mind (%)	Ambivalent (%) Sometimes
Working class	20	5	75
Middle class	70	15	15

The general picture is one of dissatisfaction with housework; high levels of monotony and loneliness are reported. Housewives work long hours, they have low status, and it generally compares unfavourably with almost any other kind of work they may have had outside the home.

You will find details such as those given in this example in journals – New Society devotes a page each week to such summaries – in textbooks and in the original book or paper written by the sociologist concerned.

To produce a summary of the central details you will find it helpful to develop a simple system of analysis. You can use it for every example that you come across. Ask and answer the following questions:

1 Who is the author (or authors)?
2 What is the title of the study? When was it published?
3 What is the hypothesis or the area of social life under investigation?
4 What method (or methods) was used to obtain information (questionnaires, records and files, interviews, observation, experiment)?
5 What sampling method was used: random or quota?
6 Which of the statistical data are most relevant? Set this out clearly.
7 What are the key findings or conclusions? State these clearly and simply as a series of points.
8 What is the significance or relevance of the study?
9 What does it tell us that we previously didn't know?

Re-read the study by Ann Oakley. Look at the tables of statistics. Examiners often present such data and ask for an interpretation of their meaning. For example:

1 *Study the Tables (i), (ii), (iii), and (iv). Answer the following questions:*
   (a) What conclusions do you draw from Table (i)?
   (b) The phrase 'experience of fragmentation in work' means that some people felt that their work was broken down into a series of small and tedious parts. They had no overall feeling that they were doing a complete and unified job of work.
      (i) In what kinds of occupations might people feel low levels of fragmentation of work?
      (ii) Comment on the findings of Table (ii).
   (c) What are the attitudes of women with low levels of identification in the role of housewife towards work satisfaction indicated in Table (iii)?
   (d) What are the main differences in attitudes revealed in Table (iv) between working class and middle class mothers?

It is important to practise analysis of such tabulated data. Every year the government publishes a book entitled *Social Trends*. This provides a wide range of statistical data about the current trends in social life in Britain. You should be able to find a copy in the reference section of your library. You are advised to try and become familiar with it. Do not be frightened by the presentation of statistical details. If they are clearly presented the answers to questions based on them are usually straight-forward.

Other more general questions may be of the type:

2 *Explain (a) what sociology is;*
       (b) the kind of research sociologists do;
       (c) what more you now understand about your own society as
          a result of studying sociology.
What is meant by the statement that sociology is a social science?
Illustrate your answer with some examples of sociological studies.

The examiners may wish to test your knowledge and understanding of the traditional scientific approach adopted in some research projects. To answer such questions you must know the details of studies similar to those illustrated above.

They may wish to examine more precisely the finer details of your knowledge of the technical procedures a sociologist may use in the course of research together with your understanding of the kinds of problems that face them in the course of their work.

Sociologists undertake different types of study according to the kind of information they require:

Longitudinal studies

These are conducted over long periods of time. A group of people who have some particular feature in common are followed over a period of years to see how they develop and change. Various statistical analyses can be conducted on the information acquired to see the similarities and variations between particular groups. These studies are expensive, time consuming and very complicated, since large numbers of people must be involved. However, when successful the results can be very instructive. Examples include the work of J. W. B. Douglas and his colleagues who have followed the progress of a group of children born in 1945–6. Some of the results have been published in the books *All Our Future* and *The Home and the School*. The National Children's Bureau has been following the progress of 16,000 children born in the first week of March 1958 from which two reports have been published: *From Birth To Seven* and *Born to Fail*.

Case studies

Some sociologists focus their research on a particular phenomenon – a strike, an outbreak of racial hostility in a particular town or on events in a specific factory, prison or hospital. The features described relate only to that particular case and wider implications for the society as a whole are not drawn. Examples of case studies include the Lynds' analysis of Middletown and Benyon's report of work in the Ford Motor Company.

Attitude surveys or opinion polls

3 Outline the features and importance of all the following in social research:
(a) Survey population and sampling frame (8)
(b) Random sampling process (6)
(c) Interviewer bias (6) (AEB)

The purpose and aims of such surveys include:

1 the need for particular groups or agencies to know the opinions or attitudes of the public on certain issues;
2 to predict the outcome of particular changes in policy, of elections and of attempts to influence attitudes;
3 to give people the opportunity to express their feelings about issues in a democratic way.

Polling techniques have developed during the past 60 years as statistical methods of sampling have been perfected. This follows a series of errors and mistakes in which quite wrong results were predicted because information had been obtained from unrepresentative samples. (In 1936 an American magazine attempted to predict the outcome of a Presidential election by selecting names at random from a telephone directory. They overlooked the fact that at that time telephones were found largely only in middle-class homes.) The technique of using opinion polls efficiently was developed by Gallup who used much smaller but more representative samples.

The main problems are those of:

1 Who to ask. This is the problem of drawing a **sample**.
2 What to ask. This is the problem of **clearly stating** the questions.
3 What conclusions to draw. This is the problem of **interpreting** the results obtained.

Sampling

The sociologist has established his area of study. He has decided on the type of study he wishes to use. He must now select his sample. Clearly, he cannot hope to gain information about everyone in the total population. He therefore draws a sample and seeks information from and about them.

The sampling frame

This provides the source from which a sample can be drawn. It can be an electoral register, a school register, a doctor's list of patients, etc.

The type of frame used will depend on the type of information required. It is used when a random sample is required.

Types of samples

1 Random samples

In these everyone in the population to be sampled has an equal chance of being selected. It is a scientific procedure since it is objective and not open to bias. If all the names on an electoral register are consulted and 500 are drawn by random procedure (say, every tenth name from a register with 5000 names) this would constitute a random sample.

Whilst it is an expensive and time-consuming process to select and then locate the sample drawn, it does mean that the results can be subjected to statistical techniques to establish their level of significance. There are also refinements to the process of selecting random and other types of sample.

(a) Stratified random samples The sociologist divides the population according to factors that may be relevant to the outcome: for example, age, sex, class. Random samples are drawn from each stratum so that representative views of a cross-section of the public are obtained.

(b) Multi-stage sampling Where the survey is to cover a wide range of the population of a large geographical area the researcher may break it down into clusters. These could be districts, wards, roads and houses. Then a random sample of the clusters can be drawn, then random samples from within the clusters, and then a sample of households. This is a cheaper procedure and saves time in having to travel too widely in a large area locating respondents.

(c) Multi-phase sampling A random sample is drawn and respondents interviewed. Then a sub-sample is randomly selected and asked more specific questions. This enables the researcher to get some idea of the overall accuracy of his major study. Or it may be that different levels of knowledge are required for different parts of the survey.

2 Quota samples

These are the cheapest, simplest and most widely used types of samples that are drawn in research studies where high levels of accuracy are not required or not claimed.

Interviewers are assigned a definite number of people to interview who have the characteristics required by the researcher. The quotas are numbers not names. The weakness of the quota sample is that it is less scientific than a random sample. It requires an honest and efficient interviewer. Opinion polls and attitude surveys generally make use of this type of sampling because information is normally required quickly.

You may be asked questions of the following type:

4 *Explain what is meant by a longitudinal study. What kinds of useful information might it reveal? What are the main difficulties which arise in using this type of study?*

5 *Read the following passage carefully and answer the questions:*

'The National Children's Bureau has lost more than a third of the irre-placeable human guinea pigs it has been using for the past 23 years in one of the world's most costly and important continuing research projects.

The multi-million pound project is the national child development study. It has been following through the lives of 16,000 children born during the same week of March 1958. It has already yielded two reports . . . which produced evidence for the 'cycle of deprivation' theory adopted during the 1970s by both Labour and Conservative parties . . .

Among other things it wants to know is how childhood deprivation has carried over into their adult lives.

More than £1 million from more than five government departments has been set aside for this study alone. But in trying to set things up the Bureau has been embarrassed to discover that it has mislaid 6000 of the 16,000 sample . . . They cannot be replaced with other people . . . because this would destroy comparability with previous survey results.'

Adapted from report in the *Guardian*, March 1981

(a) *What kind of study is being described? (1 mark)*
(b) *Suggest three problems involved in a study of this type. (3 marks)*
(c) *Why would the results be endangered by the failure to locate all the members of the original sample? (6 marks)*

The main methods of collecting data for scientific sociology

Questionnaires

The researcher carefully drafts a set of questions designed to elicit details from which explanations of patterns of behaviour can be gained. The strengths and weaknesses of the questionnaire are usually tested in a pilot survey. Modifications can then be made if necessary.

1 Postal questionnaires

A questionnaire distributed by post ensures that a widely dispersed sample of respondents will all be reached quickly. But there are some potential problems in their use.

(a) If there are any complicated questions the respondents may not answer them. Non-response rate is often high.

(b) If the questionnaire is complicated and answered the researcher cannot be sure that the questions have been fully understood. Accuracy may be limited, thus casting doubts on the final conclusions.

(c) The postal questionnaire is best used when the questions are very simple and require a one-word answer. Complex and detailed research is seldom of this type.

2 Questionnaire and interview

In this case the researcher takes the questionnaire to the respondent who has been selected by either random processes or as part of a quota. The interview may be conducted in the respondent's own home if it is a lengthy one (see the details of the research by Ann Oakley, p. 15) or in the street if it is a brief and concise questionnaire.

The advantages of this approach are:

(a) The interviewer can be sure that the respondent has understood the questions.

(b) The non-response rate is likely to be much lower.

(c) The researcher can raise more complex issues with the respondent.

The disadvantages are:

(a) The interviewer must be skilled and trained. A poor interviewer may cause the respondent to feel hostile or that his time is being wasted.

(b) The costs are higher and it is a more time-consuming method.

(c) The rules of sampling state that where a respondent has been drawn by random methods and cannot be located the interviewer cannot substitute a person for the respondent selected.

The use of recorded statistical data; information on files

Some researchers make use of information that is already recorded: for example, court records, doctors' files, school records, census data or historical records.

Such information may only be available to bona fide researchers who can show that they have a professional interest and on condition that the anonymity of the names recorded is preserved.

The problems are that such records may be difficult to obtain; certain historical documents may not have been accurately recorded and other precise information may not be available because at the time of recording it was not considered important. It must also be remembered that although a correlation may appear to exist between two events this does not prove that one caused the other. Much repeated research would be necessary to show a causal relationship. However, the use of recorded data can often provide useful suggestions for further research programmes. Consider the following examples:

1 From: *The American Journal of Sociology*
Gary Kleck has found evidence of the relationship between gun ownership and homicide rates in America. In 1950 gun ownership in the USA was estimated at 38,000 guns per 100,000 residents. By 1960 this had increased to 43,000. According to a 1965 survey 48% of households had at least one gun and by the 1970s it was estimated that there were more than 100 million guns in private hands. But the author says that the situation is not likely to change unless gun ownership reduction programmes bring a visible decline in the rate of crime. Meanwhile, the homicide rates in the USA have increased.

2 From: *New Community*
Ceri Peach examined the monthly unemployment figures for each year from 1955 to 1974. He found that rates of immigration of West Indians into Britain corresponded closely with employment opportunities. Between 1951 and 1961 the immigration rate showed a positive correlation with demand for labour. Numbers declined as the British economy went into recession. His close analysis of the data suggested that West Indian immigration demonstrates a remarkable sensitivity to fluctuations in demand for labour.

Examples of examination questions you may face in this area of study include:

6 *Compare postal questionnaires with open-ended interviews as methods of gaining information for sociological research.* (AEB)
7 *What are the main considerations to be borne in mind when conducting research by post?*
8 *Some studies are conducted by examining recorded statistics. Give examples of studies that have made use of such data. What are the advantages and disadvantages of using this method?*

These questions require a full and detailed knowledge and cannot be attempted unless you can produce a sustained discussion of at least 450–500 words.

Non-scientific – subjective – sociology

Not all sociologists accept the need for an objective, scientific approach. There are some who argue that because sociology is a probing discipline which searches beneath the surface level of behaviour to locate the sources of action, other methods are necessary.

Sociologists who adopt this view argue that observational techniques are needed to gain an understanding of the everyday, common-sense world of people in society. The aim must be to see how people behave in relation to the meanings they draw from the situations in which they find themselves. They criticize the scientific approach because:

1 Some patterns of social behaviour are not open to scientific measurement. People may not know why they behaved as they did and so answers on a questionnaire would be meaningless.
2 Some groups whose behaviour is studied cannot be asked to complete questionnaires. For example, criminals, football hooligans, etc.

They use instead observational methods.

Participant observation

The researcher is a member of the group in which he is interested. He reports and records his observations. He can then see why a person responded as they did because he understands the relationships that exist between group members.

Non-participant observation

The researcher is not a member of the group being studied. He uses a variety of techniques. He may use a video or tape recorder, diaries, letters, or other methods to help him see the world through the eyes of those he is studying. Consider the following example from *Social Problems*.

Pamela Fisherman taped a total of 52 hours' casual conversation occurring between three couples in their separate homes. The analysis produced distinct differences in conversational structure between the women and the men. The women asked three times as many questions as men. Conversational compliments were also more frequently passed by women than men. She concludes that in a conversation women do the majority of the support work for men. Women were particularly skilled at inserting and encouraging appreciative 'mms' and 'ohs' at appropriate points in male conversation. The men, on the other hand, merely used the odd minimal response into the middle of female conversation. She also noted how the men tended to control the topics that were discussed.

This is a valuable method when used with care by someone trained in the techniques. Information is often obtained that might not be available by any other means. However, it is open to criticism in that:

1 The method relies on the honesty and thoroughness of the observer.
2 The observer may become so involved as a participant that he fails to see the events as a researcher.
3 He may be unable to record details as they occur and he may later forget to record significant details.

Nevertheless, there is now a large body of research in sociology which has been acquired by these methods and which has made an important contribution to the development of sociology. Sociologists in this school are sometimes termed 'symbolic interactionists', 'phenomenologists' or 'ethnomethodologists'.

Examiners will not expect O level candidates to be familiar with the complex theory that underpins non-scientific sociology. However, the method of observation is a popular area for questioning in examination papers.

You will be required to show how it has a valid place in sociology in those cases where information is not readily available by any other means and where the researcher is aware of its potential shortcomings and is trained in its techniques.

The study *Rules of Disorder* by P. Marsh, E. Rosser and R. Harré is an example of how useful observational methods were in gaining an insight into aspects of football hooliganism.

It must also be remembered that the scientific and non-scientific methods in sociology are not necessarily mutually exclusive. Many studies require a combination of methods to gain full understanding of patterns of behaviour. The method (or methods) used depends finally on the kinds of questions which the sociologist is asking and the kinds of information required.

An examination question might ask:

9 *Distinguish between participant and non-participant observation. Suggest the kinds of studies that a sociologist might undertake where it would be important to use one form of observation rather than another. What are the advantages and disadvantages of each?*

Or read the following passage and then answer the questions.

10 'Observation has been a basic part of the scientific method for hundreds of years. Very often the researcher may be a participant observer and his involvement in the group raises some interesting problems. Non-participant observation of a children's play session can reduce the mass of information to a more manageable quantity by the use of time-sampling.'

(a) Explain the meaning of participant observer.
(b) State any two problems with participant observation.
(c) State any two ways in which non-participant observation might take place.
(d) Describe what is meant by time-sampling. (WEL)

Key terms and concepts

It is important that you should be able to define or explain the key terms and concepts used throughout this chapter: for example, **sociology**, **sampling** (and associated methods), **methods of obtaining data**, etc. Others with which you should be familiar and which relate to questions about the theories and methods of sociology include the following:

correlation The measurable and testable connection or interrelationship between variables; for example, between crime rates and social class.
empirical Proof resulting from observation or experiment.
social institution Socially approved feature of society that affects the behaviour of those who come into contact with it. For example, the institution of marriage provides individuals with specific roles, it influences behaviour, expectations and a wide range of relationships. Other institutions include family and education.
science The search for knowledge and understanding according to logical principles and usually involving some form of experimentation.
social culture All those accepted ways of behaving (dress, food, pastimes, etc.) and of social organization (schooling, religious practices, etc.) that are common to a society and that are seen as 'traditional' to it and passed on from one generation to the next.
society Consists of all those individuals, groups and institutions centred around a particular culture and resulting in an organized pattern of social life.
social structure The interrelated parts of a society or social institution that comprise the framework within which it functions.

3 The institution of the family

Many sociologists who study the family emphasize its significance as a basic social institution. It is frequently described as 'a universal institution' and 'the most important unit of the social structure'. These comments indicate that the family is of great relevance for study because although it may take different forms (its structure may vary from one society to another) it is an institution common to every known society and as such performs important functions for its members and for society as a whole.

The traditional aims of sociological research have been to examine the structure and functions of different types of family systems both in the same and in different societies and to compare their similarities and differences.

It is then possible to describe the conditions in which different types of family system emerge; the form they take and the reasons why they develop and change. It is also possible to explain how the functions of families vary over time and place.

Whilst you are more likely to be asked to describe and account for changes in the structure and function of families in Britain a comparative knowledge of families in other societies would be useful. It would be important for exam purposes, therefore, to be familiar with the family structure of, perhaps, two other societies (see pp. 29–30).

You may be asked a question that refers specifically or by implication to British society only, such as:

11 *What sociological evidence is there that the extended family is important in modern British society?* (CAM)

Or, you may be asked to use comparative data in a question like:

12 *Compare the role of the extended family in modern British society with its place in any society you have studied where the wider, more inclusive kinship groups are dominant.* (CAM)

In order to answer such questions you must have a clear understanding of a number of key concepts used by sociologists. These include **structure, function, family, kinship, role relationships** and

socialization. It will also be necessary to have some detailed knowledge of the family structures of other societies as well as of the evidence that sociologists have produced to explain the emergence of one form of structure, the decline of another and their significance for social life.

What is meant by 'the family'?

Murdock has defined the family as a social group characterized by common residence, economic cooperation and reproduction. It includes adults of both sexes, at least two of whom maintain a socially approved sexual relationship, and one or more children, own or adopted, of the sexually cohabiting adults. Other writers have been critical of this view, pointing out that it is possible to use the term 'family' about groups of co-habiting people where there are not two adults of both sexes and where there are no children to be maintained.

In more general terms, a family may be described as any relatively small and fairly permanent group of people who generally (but not always) are related by blood or marriage, and who support and maintain each other socially, emotionally and economically.

Fletcher (*The Family and Marriage*) describes the family as a universal, cohesive and psychological unit. He says that family members share the same name, the same collective reputation, the same home, the same peculiar traditions of their own making and the same neighbourhood. They share the same joys, the same sources of conflict. The family, he concludes, is the educative group of the most fundamental kind.

Anderson (*The Sociology of the Family*) explains that the family is the most important unit in the social structure because its adult members are primarily responsible for the care, protection and socialization of the young.

For Farmer (*The Family*) it is of great significance because it constitutes our first experience of social life and for most of us it is the most permanent and enduring social group to which we are ever likely to belong.

It is generally agreed that whatever form the family takes it remains a family system in that it takes account of the basic needs of its members and it sustains the structure of society in that it helps to ensure that the young are socialized into the values and culture of the society.

What types of structures can be identified?

Sociologists, making much use of data from anthropological studies, have identified a variety of family systems. But for purposes of analysis two main types have been described. These have been related to two types of economically different societies. These have been distinguished as **industrial** and **non-industrial** (or agrarian or rural) societies.

Nuclear family	Extended family
Families in industrial societies	*Families in non-industrial societies*
1 They are generally small in size (husband, wife and a few children).	They are generally large in size (husband, wife, children and many relatives, living with or very close to each other).
2 The family has no long-term or permanent roots in the area. There are no particular traditional features of the area which bind them to it.	The family has long-term and permanent roots in the area (often based on agricultural work), and long-standing traditions have much significance.
3 Members are likely to move quite frequently in search of new jobs.	Members are unlikely to move from the area since every aspect of their lives is centred on it.
4 There is a strong emphasis on companionship and democracy in the relationships between husband and wife, each partner having approximately equal power in the running of the household.	Power is generally held by the eldest male (a patriarchal system).
5 The family exists independently of wider kin and has little economic dependence or even contact with them.	All family members rely on each other for economic and social support.
6 The typical relationship between husband and wife is that of 'joint conjugal roles', i.e. they share activities, friends, domestic duties.	The typical relationship between husband and wife is that of 'segregated roles', i.e. they have different roles in the home, different friends and leisure activities.

These descriptions are sometimes referred to as **ideal types**. They provide a starting-point for research. The sociologist can examine the real world and assess his findings against his **ideal model** to see how far it conforms to or deviates from the expected. The results of research gradually modifies and refines the concepts used. This indicates that there is no simple model which will always hold good. The more traditional models are being reassessed as research continues.

The nuclear family in Britain	The extended family in Yoruba Land: Nigeria
1 The small size of the family is related to economic considerations (i.e. income and housing opportunities, job prospects, etc.). Children are valued more for what they might achieve rather than for their economic value. The family is based on the concept of monogamy which is built into the Christian moral code and is supported by the legal system.	The large extended family is the norm (families can consist of over 100 members) with kin sharing residence or living closely together. The family structure is based on polygamy. This provides two advantages: (a) the people are mainly farmers and require a large cheap workforce; (b) a man who can support many wives and children has increased status.
2 The main advantages of this type of family structure are seen in terms of the economic structure of capitalist societies, with its emphasis on social and geographical mobility.	The extended family provides a wide range of security for all its members in a society that has no welfare state. Family members have a strong sense of attachment to a group and an area.

It is important to remember that the extended family may still exist in industrialized societies – even in urban areas. For example, Willmott and Young have shown the existence of extended families in Bethnal Green, which had the appearance of a small village in the centre of a great city. They noted that 43% of husbands and wives in their sample had seen their own mothers in the previous 24 hours.

There are, of course, likely to be other examples in rural areas of Britain of the existence of extended families which have long-standing roots in an area as a result of involvement in traditional occupations (especially agriculture).

Another form of family structure is to be found in the Israeli **kibbutzim**. These are forms of commune on which about 4% of Israel's population live. They operate in agricultural areas. Their aim is to produce a more community-centred society. Money plays no part in the internal economy of the kibbutz and, apart from some personal items, property is said to be owned by the kibbutz.

The family is of interest because children are generally looked after by the mother only for a short period of their lives. She quickly drops out of the daily care of her child and returns to work. The infant remains in a nursery with other children of similar age. They remain under the care of a housemother and they are later joined by a teacher. The children may see their parents only for a few hours each day and do not grow up in the same household with them. The role of the parents resembles that of relatives in British society.

You should now be able to answer this question:

13 *What is a family? Describe different kinds of family organizations you have read about. Explain why they are all families.*

The functions of the family

You may be asked to:

14 *Describe and comment on any three changes in family life that have taken place in western societies during the past 100 years.*   (WEL)

Or, having answered a question that asks you to explain what a family is and to describe different kinds of family organization, you may then have to say why they are all 'families'.

In each case you must spend some part of the essay in discussing the concept of function and explaining how the functions of the family have been of central interest to sociologists who research this area of social life.

What do sociologists mean when they describe the functions of an institution? A classical approach to understanding patterns of behaviour has been to look at the way the environment affects people. Some sociologists who have adopted this perspective have been called **functionalists** because they are interested in how the various parts of society interrelate and how these social institutions influence the behaviour of those who come into contact with them.

For example, the functionalist sees the continued existence of the family as a social institution in terms of the functions it performs for society and for the individual members of society. Functionalists see the effectiveness of the family in relation to its ability to carry out functions that are essential to the maintenance of the stability and perpetuation of society.

MacIver writes of the essential functions of the family. These are said to include the caring for the emotional needs of its members, the provision of a secure home, the socialization of the young, and the reproduction of the species in socially acceptable ways. The non-essential functions are those of teaching moral values, training for leisure and the maintenance of religious ideals.

Fletcher describes the major functions of the family in contemporary industrial society to be:

1 To legitimate and regulate **sexual behaviour**;
2 To ensure the **economic security** of the young;
3 To serve as a primary agency of **socialization**.

In summary it may be said that there are two broad functional areas that the family serves:

1 Those concerned with the biological, psychological and social needs of the individual (the satisfaction of human emotional needs and drives, for love, protection, self-esteem, etc.);
2 Those concerned with the social and cultural patterns of society itself. (People are given roles, statuses and a clear identity; they are socialized into the values of the society; the welfare of family members is catered for; the family is regarded as an important social institution and is protected by legal and often religious sanctions.)

Sociologists who have adopted this perspective

Talcott Parsons (USA) notes how the family structure of industrialized societies has been undergoing change. There has been:

1 An increase in divorce rates;
2 Changes in moral and social values;
3 A decline in birth-rate.

However, he argues that societies are able to adjust to these developments. There has emerged an isolated nuclear family which has become the basic unit of industrialized society because it provides a flexible and mobile unit. Two key functions of the family remain: **socialization** and the **stabilization of adult personalities**. Both are necessary for the long-term stability of society as a whole. Parsons believes that the nuclear family has become isolated in that it does not form an integral part of a wider system of kinship relationships. Family members remain independent of each other; contact between them is a matter of choice rather than duty.

The family, he argues, has lost most of its traditional functions as the state has taken over more and more of its previous roles. The family ceases to be an important economic unit. Nevertheless, an important functional connection remains between the family and the structure of industrial society. It is suited to the needs of such an economic system because its members are geographically mobile. There are increasingly strong bonds between husband and wife which also help to produce stable adult relationships, and so one may expect to find more stability in society as a whole.

Fletcher argues along similar lines to defend the family against many of the attacks that have been made on it. (Some writers such as Leach, Cooper and Laing have said that increasing rates of divorce, crime and psychological disorder in people can be related to the results of life in small, cloying and unhappy relationships in nuclear families.) He describes the modern British family as an improvement on the family of the past. It is now:

1 Smaller in size;
2 Longer in duration;
3 Economically self-providing;
4 Founded and maintained by partners of equal status;
5 Democratically managed;
6 Centrally concerned with the care and rearing of children;
7 Greatly aided by a wide range of public provision, both statutory and voluntary.

He agrees with Parsons that it seems likely that the degree of dependence of each family on its wider kinship relations will continue to diminish. The status of women and children in society will improve. He concludes by saying that industrialization will inevitably produce nuclear families because this type of family structure is most functionally appropriate for that type of economic structure.

Reasons for changes in the structure and function of the family
That is to say, the small nuclear family becomes the norm and its functions are different from those of the traditional extended family.

Industrialization	Secularization	Urbanization
1 More women enter the workforce.	The decline in the significance of religion in people's lives means divorce, contraception and abortion become more widely acceptable. Family size is more easily limited.	The growth of large towns and cities provides more housing and jobs. The population becomes more geographically mobile.
2 Having many young children in a family may become an economic burden. Also it is no longer necessary to have a large family to ensure the survival of a few.	Religion may no longer protect the family as it once did in traditional rural communities because of its loss of significance.	Better transport facilities also facilitate mobility and the break-up of traditional families.
3 An efficient education system has helped to produce a more socially and geographically mobile population and perhaps better prepared parents.	Whereas religion may once have functioned as a unifying force in family life, it no longer does so in modern secular society.	Urban life is more impersonal and there may be more strains on marriage, hence nuclear families are sometimes said to be less stable institutions.

4 The welfare state has taken over many of the traditional functions of the family, especially those of training in vocational skills and protection in times of hardship.

There are declining numbers of church marriages suggesting that it has less of a 'sacred' quality for many people; hence divorce becomes more acceptable and small nuclear families increasingly the norm.

The majority of the population now lives in large urban centres and in such areas the family unit becomes focused more precisely around the nuclear group.

A typical question for which you could make use of such data would be:

15 *Why has the nuclear family become the predominant type of family in Britain?* (OX)

NB: It would also be important to add some of the points made below.

Evidence that nuclear families exist in pre-industrial society

There is some evidence (especially from anthropologists) that monogamous marriage and nuclear families are found in hunting and gathering societies and it does not seem to be true to say that they all make use of a traditional extended family structure. Other criticisms of this view have been made by Laslett in his book *The World We Have Lost*. He has carefully examined Parish Registers in England from 1564 to 1821. These give details of the birth, marriages and deaths that occurred. From this data he has been able to reconstitute families to examine their structure. His conclusion is that nuclear families existed widely in pre-industrial England and that it may not have been industrialization which gave rise to the nuclear family, but rather the reverse. The existence of the nuclear family may have made the development of the industrial revolution possible by already having in existence the most functionally useful family structure.

Evidence that extended families continue to have significance

In their study of social life in Bethnal Green (1955), Willmott and Young found that localized extended family groups spreading over two or more nearby houses were the distinctive features of kinship in the East End of London. People were found to have long-established roots in the area, and there was little social or geographical mobility. They describe a high proportion of married couples in their sample as belonging to a combination of families who to some degree form one domestic unit.

In the USA Sussman and Burchinal argue that the views expressed by Parsons that the nuclear family has become the typical, isolated family structure in modern industrial society is not necessarily correct. They present evidence to show that a form of extended family continues to exist in such societies. They describe a 'modified extended family' in which family members may be living far apart from each other geographically but among whom there is frequent contact by visits, letters and phone calls. This is found to be true among all social classes and especially among middle-class families. They conclude, therefore, that the extended family has not disintegrated in urban areas; it continues to exist in slightly different form, and continues to perform important functions for all its members, both economic and social.

Rosser and Harris (*The Family and Social Change*) produce similar findings from their study of the family structure in Swansea. They also confirm that a form of extended family still exists centred on this urban area. They found evidence of a vigorous kinship grouping wider than the nuclear family and similar to that described in the Bethnal Green studies. Family members provided each other with support in times of need.

Conclusions

The classical distinction between nuclear and extended families must be treated with caution. It provides a useful model from which research can proceed. There is evidence, however, to suggest that alternative interpretations of the organization of family structures and functions are possible. Extended families may continue to exist, but in modified form, even in modern industrialized societies and in largely urban areas.

The functions of the family as agency of socialization and social control

By the term **social control** sociologists mean that there are certain agencies in society whose functions are to control the behaviour of the members of society. That is, there is a need for people to behave in certain socially acceptable ways. These ways of behaving are traditional to the society and are often a part of its culture. Society requires such controls since otherwise social disharmony may result.

Social control implies that there are **sanctions** which can be imposed on those who fail to behave in the correct ways. These may be formal sanctions (legal sanctions which have the support of law) or they may be informal, such as those sustained by pressure of public opinion or group pressure.

Every society has a number of agencies of socialization and social control. For example, in Britain children are trained by parents in the home and by teachers in schools; outside the home and the school control is formally in the hands of legal authorities. The pressure of public opinion is an important informal source of control.

The importance of the family as an agency of socialization

1 The behaviour of young members is shaped.
2 Members gain a self-image and identity.
3 They gain their values and attitudes.
4 The family teaches the wider cultural values of society.
5 Members gain a gender role (i.e. those roles appropriate to males and females).

Whatever form or social type of family a child has been born into it will have an enduring influence on his future life-style.

Role relationships in the family

Elizabeth Bott undertook a study to analyse different relationships between husbands and wives in relation to what she called their 'family networks'. She explains that the networks were the connections that they had with friends and acquaintances in organizations, places of work and in recreation; their attachment to particular areas, shopping precincts, churches, clubs, etc. All these went to make up the families network.

She distinguishes between two types of conjugal role:

1 **Segregated roles**   in which husbands and wives carried out most of their daily tasks independently of each other. They had separate leisure activities, different sets of friends and they saw this as being typical of their circle.
2 **Joint conjugal roles**   in which husband and wife share most activities and stress equality in all their dealings. In the home there is much division of labour; they share interests, friends and leisure activities.

Bott found that the two types of relationship were related to the family structure and network.

1 In the **dispersed network** there were few overlapping connections between the component units of the network (i.e. the people who the husband or wife worked with were probably not the same ones who they met socially in a local club; and those people were not the same ones that they met in church).

2 In the **connected network** there were many such overlapping relationships; that is, there was a wide circle of friends and acquaintances who were seen frequently.

Her conclusion is that the degree of segregation in the role relationships of spouses varied with the connectedness of the family network. The more this was connected, the greater was the segregation of roles. The more the network was dispersed, the greater was the likelihood of joint or shared roles between husband and wife.

Her data suggests that families with the most segregated roles lived in the most homogeneous and uniform areas of low population turnover (common among extended families). In contrast those with strong joint role relationships lived in areas of high population turnover and were more likely to be mobile nuclear families.

Your attention has been drawn to the fact that some exam questions ask for a discussion of a clearly stated topic area. You will either know the answer or you will not. Other questions are less specific and 'open-ended'; that is, it is for you to decide what is and what is not relevant and to draw on your own knowledge.

Although students are often wary of these less obvious questions there is no reason to avoid them if you have the requisite knowledge. In fact, they are very useful questions to attempt because you can select the material for the answer.

For example you may be asked to:

16 *Distinguish between separate (segregated) conjugal roles and joint conjugal roles within the family and offer a sociological explanation for each.* (WEL)

17 *(a) Some sociologists have argued that the modern nuclear family is isolated. What evidence have they offered for this?*

Clearly question 16 is the most specific one and requires precise knowledge. But question 17 would also enable you to make use of the same information in the course of your answer. If you have knowledge of a study such as that by Elizabeth Bott into different role relationships in families you could make good use of it in these questions.

Key terms and concepts

The following terms and concepts have been defined and used in this chapter. You must be able to use them and explain their meaning for examination purposes:

family; nuclear and extended family; family structures; function; kinship; role relations; ideal types; patriarchal; in-

dustrialization; secularization; urbanization; modified extended family; gender roles; family networks; segregated roles; joint conjugal roles; dispersed network.

Other definitions you may require include:

monogamy   one woman is married to one man.

polygamy   one woman or one man may be married to more than one spouse.

polyandry   one woman may be married to several men at the same time.

polygyny   one man may be married to more than one woman at the same time.

4 Changing role relationships in the family

A **role** is a pattern of behaviour directly associated with a person's social status or social position in a group or in society. The individual behaves in accordance with what is expected of someone in that position.

The way that people behave is affected by their role in that their behaviour is in accordance with what they believe is appropriate for someone of their status, and it accords with the expectations of others who 'know' how a person in that position ought to behave.

In some situations roles may be informal; in a group one person may have adopted the role of 'mother', another the 'joker', another the 'intellectual', etc. In other situations roles are more formal: for example, those of doctor and patient, teacher and pupil, shop assistant and customer, etc.

Role conflict or **role strain** can arise where a person finds that their relationships with others are affected by a clash of interests resulting from the codes of behaviour expected from the roles they play. For example, a teacher may find such conflict between trying to be friendly with his or her students and judging their work impartially.

The roles that people play vary in their importance and in the extent to which they influence patterns of behaviour. Some are particularly significant, especially those learned at a young age and subject to constant reinforcement and supported by a wide consensus of acceptance in society at large. Roles learned and adopted in the family are of this type since they have a far-reaching influence on long-term behaviour patterns.

It is important to recall here that the family is an important agency of socialization. Whether you are concerned to answer a general question, such as:

18 *Explain why the family is such an important unit in the social structure.*

Or a more general question such as:

19 *In what ways have the roles of women changed over the past one hundred years.*

you must be able to discuss the significance of the socialization processes that occur in the family. You need to be able to explain how people learn to adopt particular roles as a result of growing up in particular types of family structure.

The changing role of women

The biological view

Some writers have suggested that there may be biological explanations to account for why women have traditionally looked after the home and the children and where they have taken jobs outside the home to have generally avoided those of a technical or scientific nature. They argue, for example, that:

1 There are major differences in brain structure which cause males to have superior spatial skills, which explains their dominance in scientific fields. On the other hand, the left-hand side of the brain predominates among females to give them superior skills in use of language; hence there are more women in occupations requiring this particular facility.
2 There may be significant hormonal differences between males and females which encourages male aggression and competitiveness and female sociability and cooperation.

The sociological view

Many sociological critics of this view argue that emphasis on the biological model is dangerous because it does not take account of:

1 The significance of cultural and social factors in affecting attitudes. That is, it does not recognize that people are socialized into particular roles according to the cultural values of their society. In Britain, there is a strong image of a scientist being 'a quiet man in a white coat'. This may divert many women from a field which they perceive to be a predominantly male domain.
2 The fact that many of the suggested biological differences are based on animal studies and it may be unsafe to draw conclusions about human behaviour from them.
3 Acceptance of a biological view may lead to the conclusion that things cannot be changed and that the roles in which people find themselves are natural and inevitable.

The sociological view, therefore, is that the roles that people adopt are derived from the social culture. That is, they are related to the needs of the society in which they live. They are representative of the values of that society. So that in a society in which survival is precarious it may be that no distinction is made between who hunts, who cooks and who looks after the children. In a society in which survival is comparatively easy such distinctions in role are much more likely.

In light of these points consider how you would answer the following question:

20 'The Mbuti pygmies described by Colin Turnbull in *Wayward Servants* have a social structure in which the role of biological sex as a determinant of social role and status seems to be negligible. Hunting and gathering are the main activities on which they depend for survival, and both sexes take part. They also share political decisions and have the same social status. There is very little division of labour by sex; men often care for even the youngest children. Pregnancy is no bar to hunting. The Mbuti language distinguishes between the sexes only in terms of parenthood: they have words for "mother" and "father" but not for "girl" and "boy", "woman" and "man". Where other societies in their rituals emphasize the distinctions between the sexes, Mbuti rituals emphasize the lack of them.'

Ann Oakley, *Sex, Gender and Society*

(a) What is the significance of the fact that the Mbuti pygmies have no words for 'boy' and 'girl' – e.g. does it mean that they are unable to perceive *any differences between boys and girls?* (4 marks)

(b) In the light of the information presented in the passage, comment on the claim that 'the roles of wife and mother are the natural roles of women'. (6 marks)

(c) What changes seem to be taking place in women's roles in modern Britain and how would you explain them? (10 marks) (CAM)

Consider carefully whether the passage supports or casts doubt on the biological view.

Notice in (a) the word 'perceived' is emphasized. What does it mean?

In (b) are you being asked, is it natural for women to bear children? or is it natural that they should play a particular role in relation to them?

The answers to these questions will emerge from a careful reading of the passage.

Sociologists of the family have been particularly concerned with the ways in which **gender roles** are produced and reproduced in societies. In Britain the changes in the role of women since about 1857 have been of great interest. These constitute one of the greatest changes to have taken place in family life.

Consequently, this is a favourite topic area in examinations. For example:

21 *What have been the major changes in the social position of women in the twentieth century?* (OX) (See p. 45.)

Anna Coote has said that in Britain girls are encouraged to accept their traditional female roles in society. They are given dolls, dolls' houses, little housewife cleaning sets, toy kitchens containing utensils for the modern miss to cook just like mother. Their sights are set firmly on the home while their brothers play with mechanical toys which turn their attention towards their masculine roles. School reading books reinforce the distinction between the roles expected of little boys and little girls.

Consider the following examination question:

22 In this country, most children learn to read by working their way through one or other of the popular reading schemes – the 'Janet and John' series or the 'Ladybird' series for example. The passages below are all taken from one such reading scheme. Those in section (i) are taken from the first version of the series which was published in 1964. In 1972, the series was rewritten and the passages in section (ii) are taken from this more recent set of books.

(i) 'Jane likes to help Mummy. She wants to make cakes like Mummy. "Will you let me, please? I can make cakes like you." "Yes," says Mummy. "You are a good girl." "We will make some cakes for Peter and Daddy" says Jane. "They like the cakes we make."

The children have to work. Peter has to help Daddy work with the car. Jane has to help Mummy work in the house. She likes to help Mummy work.

Here are the two girls. They have some flowers to take home. "Mummy likes flowers," says Jane. "Yes, my Mummy likes me to take flowers home" says the other girl. The children walk by the trees. The girls look at the flowers as they go by. The boys look for rabbits and fish.'

(ii) 'Peter likes to play with toys. He plays with a toy station and a toy train. Jane says, "Please can I play?" "Yes," says Peter, "I have the train. You play with the station."

Peter and Jane like to help Mummy. They go to the shops for Mummy. "Come on," Peter says, "we have to go to the fish shop." Peter and Jane like to help Daddy. They help Daddy with the car. Jane is in the car. Daddy and Peter have some water (to wash the car).

Jane and Peter want some flowers. "Some flowers for you and

some for me," says Jane. "Get some flowers, Peter. Get some for
Mummy and Daddy."'

(a) *Apart from learning to read, what else may children be learning
from passages like these? (Give examples)   (3 marks)*

(b) *On the basis of the evidence in these extracts, what changes seem
to have been made when the series was rewritten in 1972? How
would you account for these changes?   (4 marks)*

(c) *It could be said that the pictures of family life presented in the
earlier and later extracts reveal far more similarities than
differences. Would you agree with this view? (Give reasons)   (3
marks)*

(d) *Using the passages above and any other evidence you think
relevant, discuss the extent to which sex-role differences may result
from social rather than biological influences.   (10 marks)*   (CAM)

In answering the question, especially part (d), consider other points
from the article by Anna Coote:

She went on to say that few girls' schools ever have adequate facilities for
teaching science; boys seldom learn to cook, make beds, wash or iron
clothes.

In 1974 (when the article was published) it was commonplace to find
that the head-teacher was usually a man, as was the doctor; the TV news
was most frequently read by a man and God is a man. So it was not
surprising that children developed the idea that authority was naturally
vested in the male of the species. Girls were encouraged to be passive,
responsive, eager to care for children. They were widely taught that their
goal in life was a man. As a result most girls regarded employment as a
stop-gap between school and marriage and few bothered with higher
education. Whilst almost as many girls as boys took and passed O levels,
the proportion of girls taking A levels dropped to just over a third.

Her argument is that the role that women adopt in seldom challeng-
ing men for equality or for positions of power is the result of the early
process of socialization.

Notice, too, how the concepts of socialization and social role together
with the comments of writers such as Ann Oakley and Anna Coote also
help to answer a question like:

23 'Beer has developed as a man's drink. It takes some getting
through and long practice. Women who plunge in and order a pint
give reckless, if unconscious challenge to the man's right . . .'
                              Ann Garvey, Women in Pubs, *New Society*

What does this extract suggest about the traditional roles of men and

*women in modern Britain? How are these roles supported and
reinforced in modern Britain and to what extent are they changing?*
(AEB)

The work of Tessa Blackstone is also relevant to this question: in an
article (*New Society*, 21 February 1980) she explained why there are so
few women scientists and engineers. She argues that sex differences in
learning abilities have no biological basis since they are susceptible to
training. Also, differences within each sex are greater than those
between them. She concludes that there are few women scientists as a
result of environmental influences on attitudes. She produces some
significant findings:

1 Girls are less likely to take sufficient A levels to enable them to get
  on to courses in higher education.
2 They see arts subjects as feminine and science subjects as
  masculine.
3 Girls attribute any success to luck or 'extra effort'. Any failure is
  attributed to 'lack of ability'.
4 Boys are more likely to find 'failure' a challenge, whereas girls are
  discouraged by failure.
5 Teachers tend to have stereotypes as to what girls can and can't do.
  They do not see them as potential engineers.
6 The quiet, conscientious girl probably gets less attention than the
  more extroverted boy.

The results of these (and other) differences in treatment and attitude on
the part of parents and teachers are that children are socialized into particular roles and perceptions of themselves. Girls come to have lower expectations about long-term careers; they are less likely to see themselves
as scientists, engineers or even graduates. These images are reinforced by
the mass media, advertising, parents and teachers.

Recent legal changes

1 The Equal Pay Act 1970   is meant to do two things:

(a) It seeks to ensure that women who are doing broadly similar work
    to men (work rated the same under job evaluation) get paid at the
    same rates.
(b) It makes it illegal for wage agreements to discriminate against
    women by containing provisions that apply only to men.

Property rights	Political rights	Educational opportunities	Recent legal changes
1857 Matrimonial Causes Act. Divorce procedures simplified and made cheaper. Women were given some limited property rights. 1880 Married Women's 1882 Property Acts: gave a wife a right to (a) Property belonging to her; (b) Earnings from her work; but (c) She remained liable to support a pauper husband. 1970 Matrimonial Proceedings Act: all assets to be divided equally on the basis of a half share to each partner following a divorce. 1977 A common-law wife is given the same legal rights as a married woman.	1869 Women were given the vote in municipal elections. 1888 They were given the vote in county council elections. 1918 All women over the age of 30 could vote in general elections. 1928 Women were entitled to vote in general elections at 21. 1972 The voting age was lowered to 18 for both men and women. N.B. the number of women MPs fell from 27 in 1974 to 19 in 1979. The Conservative representation increased from 7 to 8. The Labour number fell from 18 to 11.	1840 Queen's College and Bedford College were established for women in London University. 1870 Women's colleges were 1880 established in Oxford and Cambridge. (Full degrees not granted until the 1920s.) 1870 A national and 1880 compulsory system of education was established. 1902 There was an increase in the number of training colleges for teachers. 1980 48% of A level students were girls; 36% of university students were female.	1970 The Equal Pay Act. 1975 The Employment Protection Act. 1975 The Sex Discrimination Act. 1975 The Equal Opportunities Commission is set up and empowered to enforce and monitor the workings of some of these acts.

2 The Employment Protection Act 1975 is meant to do two things:

(a) It gives some women the right to paid maternity leave. A woman who has worked for an employer for two years can get six weeks' maternity pay; this is 90% of full pay less the National Insurance maternity allowance.

(b) It enables a woman to return to work with the same employer after her child has been born providing this is within 29 weeks of the birth.

3 The Sex Discrimination Act 1975   Sex discrimination is conduct which involves actual or inferred intention to treat a person less favourably on the grounds of his or her sex. This act makes sex discrimination unlawful in employment, training, education, housing and the provision of goods and services. This means that:

(a) In employment it is unlawful to discriminate by sex in the recruitment of employees or in the treatment of existing employees. (There are some limited exceptions, for example where a person's sex is a genuine occupational qualification for the job e.g. where an actor is required to play Hamlet).

(b) In education it is unlawful to discriminate in the provision of facilities. Girls must have the opportunity of doing wood work and boys domestic science if they wish.

(c) In the provision of goods and services it is unlawful to discriminate in the provision of loans, mortgages, entertainmnent, etc. Exemptions include single sex hospitals, in religious orders, or where a question of decency or privacy arises.

Where individuals wish to make complaints under these acts direct access is available to the courts and to industrial tribunals. Remedies include damages and a declaration of rights and injunctions to remedy the situation.

The Equal Opportunities Commission 1975 This body has powers to identify and deal with practices of discrimination. It can issue notices to offenders requiring them to comply with the law. It assists and represents individuals if necessary, conducts research and takes action to promote equality of opportunity.

In 1976 the EOC received 8255 complaints, in 1977 4074. In 1977 they conducted research entitled 'Equality between the Sexes: How Far Have We Come?' The major findings were as follows:

1 Women had not yet achieved equal pay. On average they continued to earn less than two-thirds as much as men each week.

2 The rate of progress towards equality was decreasing.

3 In general, women remained concentrated in the ten worst paid occupational groups.

4 They remained lower on the promotional ladder.

5 A high proportion of firms found loopholes in the acts which they exploited. They tended to segregate women into new areas of work so that they were no longer doing 'broadly similar work to men'. Also they created more part-time work (less than 30 hours a week) which can legally be paid at a lower rate.

6 Of the 575 firms they sampled they found that only 2% had taken positive action to increase opportunities for equality.

7 They found that there was also much resistance to this from many male workers on the shopfloor and from some trade union groups.

Some of these changes, particularly the most recent package of legal rights, have not yet had their full effect on social life. There is still much debate as to how they will affect the position and role of women in the future. They are, therefore, frequently the subject of examination questions. Some detailed knowledge of the legislation will be required and the ability to refer to the work of authors who have begun to research this area, in order to answer such questions as:

24 *Do men and women have equal opportunity in the field of education and employment?* (OX)

25 'Once at work, women tend to be concentrated in the relatively unskilled jobs, not necessarily because they lack ability but because they are not interested in self-advancement. They regard industry as a man's world and they enter it simply as a means to an end; perhaps for this reason, they are difficult to organise in large numbers. Very few will join a trade union, and those who do will invariably be passive members; they develop little sense of comradeship and "belongingness" in the firm, and no interest at all in such matters as joint consultation. On the other hand, women possess a greater sense of loyalty towards their employers and will obey orders more readily than male employees. They like routine and are frightened of change, because of what Zweig calls their "innate conservatism", yet this may be an advantage to a firm which requires them to do simple but repetitive tasks – for which, so it is said, women are admirably suited.'

E. A. Johns, *The Social Structure of Modern Britain*, 1965

(a) *Is it true to say that women 'tend to be concentrated in the relatively unskilled jobs'? (Give examples of the main areas in which women are employed.)* (4 marks)

(b) *Does sociological evidence support the statement that women are 'passive', 'conservative' and 'not interested in seeking advancement'?* (4 marks)

(c) *The passage implies that women are non-political. Is this so, and if so, why?* *(4 marks)*

(d) *How far does either the educational system or the media reinforce the views expressed in this passage?* *(8 marks)* (LON)

26 *How have changes in the role of women affected their work patterns?*

In answering a question such as 26 it is necessary to explain the changes that have occurred since 1857 to show how they have affected status and opportunities. It is also necessary to know how women's work patterns have been changing and some of the details of relevant research.

Women in total labour force, 1901–79

Year	Women as % of labour force	Married women as % of women in labour force
1901	29.1	–
1911	29.8	12.6
1921	29.5	12.9
1931	29.7	15.2
1951	30.8	38.2
1961	32.5	50.2
1971	36.5	63.1
1976	40.6	65.5
1979	41.4	66.0

Source: Social Trends

The three main points to emerge are:

1 The number of women in the workforce has increased significantly since 1961, but especially since 1971 with the proposals to introduce new legislation for greater equality for women in work.

2 The legislation which has been introduced has helped in this respect; but as the EOC has shown, it has not been entirely successful.

3 The number of married women in the female workforce has also increased dramatically since 1961.

Research findings

1 Ann Oakley, 'Mothers and Children in Society' (*Nursing*, 1981)

Oakley argues that despite legislation, substantial differences remain between the roles and opportunities of the two sexes. The labour force is largely segregated into 'women's jobs' and 'men's jobs'. Two-thirds of all women workers are found in the ten least well-paid occupations, especially shop assistants, office workers and nurses. Few of the top jobs are held by women (despite having a queen and a female prime minister). She suggests that girls are not encouraged to think in terms of 'a career' because it is still assumed that being a mother and housewife is their natural role. Work outside the home is always of secondary importance. However, an increasing number of women are taking on dual roles of housewife, mother and paid employee.

2 R. and R. Rapaport, *Dual Career Families* (1971)

The Rapaports undertook a study of families in which both husband and wife had a career. They noted how increasingly conjugal role relationships are changing (see pp. 36–7). There is a greater emphasis on democratic relationships and more companionship in marriage. In their study they noted:

(a) In such families there was an increase in the number of dilemmas (relating to work-sharing in the home, etc.).
(b) There were some additional strains in the marriage, especially when one partner found compromise difficult.
(c) Where couples were able to cope with the problems the marriage and family life was generally judged to be a success.

3 Foggarty *et al.*, *Women in Top Jobs*

Foggarty and his colleagues found little evidence of many women in top jobs. Among their conclusions are the following points:

(a) Women seemed to be less competitive and ambitious for high levels of success.
(b) Employers tended to see women as 'less reliable' than men. It was widely assumed that maternity would end a young woman's career prospects.
(c) Most of the women who had been successful said that it had been very hard to get to the top. Many said that they did not think all their male colleagues treated them as equals.
(d) There was a strong anti-femininist feeling among many of the males questioned about working with or in subservient positions to women.
(e) Few of the women who reached top positions also had families to look after.
(f) They believe that there were few women in top jobs because few were recruited, few applied and few were selected. The image remains that most of the top jobs are men's jobs.

4 Heath, Women Who Get On In the World (*New Society*, 12 February 1981)

Heath notes that most women workers are concentrated in the low-skilled manual jobs and low-level white-collar occupations. If jobs are ranked according to their overall status and returns, then the occupations in which women are concentrated are almost all in those at the bottom of the hierarchy. He notes that the 'helping professions' have been a definite ladder of upward mobility for many career-minded women, e.g. nursing, teaching and social work. The average working-class home is now more likely than at any previous time to have one of its members in a white-collar job.

5 Ann Oakley, The Failure of the Movement for Women's Equality (*New Society*, September 1979)

Oakley comments that men and women cannot be equal partners outside the home if they are not equal inside it. Housework hours have increased this century (despite domestic technology) because standards have risen. The rearing of children has become a more complex and demanding exercise. If women under-achieve in public life, men under-achieve in domestic life. She concludes that there is a male-dominated culture which is difficult to reverse. Thus, only 1% of bank managers, 2% of accountants and 5% of architects are women. Female unemployment rates increase much faster than male rates. Only 5% of MPs are women and only 6% of cabinet ministers in 1978 were women. There were none in Mrs Thatcher's cabinet. (A report in 1981 stated that only 2% of married women earn more than average male earnings.)

Consider how you would answer the following questions.

27 *What does Oakley mean when she says that women and men cannot be equal partners outside the home if they are not equal inside it?*
    Suggest some sociological reasons to explain why there are so few women in professional occupations. (See pp. 46 and 49.)
28 *Oakley also argues (p. 48) that the labour force is largely segregated into 'women's jobs' and 'men's jobs'.*
    (a) Why should this be so?
    (b) What evidence is there for this view? (See pp. 46–7.)
    Suggest some of the ways in which boys and girls are prepared for different roles in society.

Key terms and concepts

The following terms and concepts have been defined and used in this section. You must be able to use them and explain their meaning for examination purposes:

role; biological view; stereotypes; discrimination; role conflict (role strain); socialization; social culture; gender roles.

Other terms which you may require:

social change   When there are changes in a part of the social system following reform, new attitudes and values or ways of behaving as a result of new laws or innovations by opinion leaders who help establish new trends.

conformity   Behaviour acceptable to the group or society as a whole.

norms   Patterns of accepted behaviour in a group or in a society to which members are expected to conform.

5 Marriage and divorce

Statistics published by the Office of Population Censuses and Surveys (OPCS) indicate that 95% of women and 91% of men have been married by the age of 40. An increasing number of divorced people are remarrying. In 1976 three out of ten marriages were remarriages for one or both partners.

Marriage

Marriage is a social institution that formally legalizes the relationship between husband and wife. The ceremony of marriage imposes certain duties on each person and provides them with specific rights. In Britain it has been described as 'a voluntary union of one man with one woman for life' (*Report of the Royal Commission on Marriage and Divorce*, 1955).

It is an important institution because it is central to the family system. It proves to be a turning point in the lives of most people because it marks a change in role (from 'boy-friend and girl-friend' to husband and wife); the partners generally set up a new home and take on new responsibilities. The wide-ranging set of rituals and ceremonies that mark the transition from engagement to marriage to homemaking indicates the significance of the institution of marriage in society.

The number of marriages in Britain (thousands)

1901	1911	1921	1931	1951	1961	1971	1972
300	310	360	340	400	390	460	470

1973	1974	1975	1976	1977	1978	1980
450	425	420	400	360	400	415

Source: Social Trends

The figures in the table indicate that marriage has remained a popular feature of social life, although some commentators (e.g. *The Royal Com-*

mission, 1955) suggest that matrimony is no longer so secure as it was in the past and that there may be a tendency to take the duties and responsibilities of marriage less seriously. Dominion (*Marital Breakdown*) makes similar points and suggests that people are increasingly 'divorce minded'.

The number of divorces in Britain (thousands)

1901	1911	1921	1931	1951	1961	1971	1972
1	1.5	3	6	30	25.4	79.6	119

1973	1974	1975	1976	1977	1978	1980
106	113.5	120.5	126	135	140	158.8

Source: Social Trends

Most of the questions that are raised about attitudes towards marriage and the current state of the family in Britain are related to the trends in divorce. There is frequently a question of the nature:

29 *Does the increase in the divorce rate during this century show that the institution of marriage and the family are in decline?* (OX)

Or:

30 *Recent divorce statistics are a reflection of the state of marriage in Britain. Does this mean that the modern family is less stable than in the past?* (AEB)

To answer such questions you must:

1 Know the statistics for marriage and divorce for the period specified. (You would need data for perhaps six years taken at intervals from the time period under consideration.)
2 Know some arguments for and against the view that marriage and the family have become less stable institutions.
3 Also be able to discuss the problems of assessing 'stability' or 'decline'.

The statistics

Some people find it easier to recall data such as are in the tables in graph form rather than in tabulated form. It may be helpful, therefore, if you are able to turn the same information into graphs.

Obviously, you would still have to know some of the numerical detail in order to construct the graph; but as long as you can state the first, last and a middle figure and then recall the shape of the graph, you will be able to demonstrate sufficient knowledge for the purpose of the question.

Are the institutions of family and marriage less stable now?

Some arguments to suggest they are	Arguments to suggest they are not
1 There has been an increase in the number of divorce decrees from about 1000 in 1901 to 140,000 in 1979.	More than 90% of men and women marry and a high proportion of divorced people remarry.
2 People seem to be more divorce-minded since divorce is easy to obtain and carries less stigma than in the past.	It is true that unhappy marriages are more easily ended now; but in the past unhappy and unstable marriages may have remained intact.
3 The increasing rate of abortion suggests lack of family stability.	Although the abortion rate may have increased we do not know whether the result has been to make existing families more stable since family size is limited.
4 Writers (such as Fletcher) suggest that couples are placing more emphasis on companionship in marriage: if this attitude persists it may be that formal marriage will become redundant since its main function in the past has been child-rearing and the legitimization of a mating relationship.	Marriage is an integral part of the social structure of Britain and it remains as popular as ever. Childless couples are always in a small minority and so its main function to legitimize a relationship socially and legally remains.
5 Traditionally, the Church has been closely associated with marriage. The decline in the relevance of religion in the lives of many people suggests that marriage has lost its sacred quality. There are increasing numbers marrying in registry offices.	Fewer people may be marrying in churches – but the vows remain as valid and significant, and the roles imposed on each spouse are the same.
6 There are increased strains on marriages in urban industrial society making breakdown of marriage more likely and family life less stable.	There have always been strains on marriage – but the ceremonials and rituals associated with it help to give it more security: a dimension lacking in the relationship of unmarried couples.

The problem of assessing the 'stability' or 'decline' of the institutions of family and marriage

When we say that something is **stable**, we mean it is firmly fixed and not easily moved, changed, destroyed or altered. It withstands pressures that might otherwise undermine it.

If the family and marriage are less stable we would need evidence to show that they were in the process of rapid change. We would need some way of measuring the effects of the processes. These might include:

1 Rate of divorce;
2 Rate of abortion;
3 Rate of illegitimacy;
4 Rate of delinquency.

We would have to argue that as these rates increased, so the stability of family life decreased because these are signs of pathological disorder.

The defenders of family and marriage must argue that these are inadequate measures. This is because we do not know enough about family life in the past when families may have been under equally severe pressures (e.g. from war, famine, economic depression, etc.). So that family life and marriage was potentially just as unstable even though divorce, abortion, illegitimacy and crime rates were lower. The instability may have taken different forms such as family violence, separations, unhappy relationships between family members, etc. In other words, it is difficult to establish whether families and marriages are more or less stable in modern society since it is difficult to find comparable measures.

There is a similar problem in assessing whether or not the family and marriage are in **decline**. It is the difficulty of deciding what measures are to be used.

Two writers who have attempted to make such an assessment are Edmund Leach (an anthropologist) and Ronald Fletcher (a sociologist). They present two extreme views:

(a) Leach In the 1967 Reith Lectures he argued that the modern nuclear family is a dangerous institution because its members live in small, isolated households often having little direct contact with other kin or even neighbours. Stress, he thinks, is inevitable in daily life in urban society, and this leads to conflict between parents and children. It does not, therefore, provide the basis of a harmonious society, but rather it is the source of all social disorders. His answer is to abandon the nuclear family for an extended or communal type of structure, in which children would grow up in larger and wider units with more emphasis on the community than the individual family.

(b) Fletcher In *The Family and Marriage in Britain* he strongly opposes this view and defends the modern family in industrial society. He argues that there is no evidence of decline or lack of stability. Standards of parenthood have improved and so have the material and moral standards of life. He says that the functions of the family have actually increased in recent years because there are greater demands on the family to ensure the welfare, education and control of family members than in the past. Fletcher concludes that in many ways the modern family is in a stronger position than at any period in our history.

Changes in family size

Statistics about the changes in family size that have occurred in Britain over the last 100 years can be presented in a number of ways. They present a fruitful area for exam questions and answers to them are usually straightforward.

You may be asked a question in which you have to present the relevant statistics and explain the changes that have occurred. For this question you must be able to quote some of the details shown in the table.

1900–09	1920–24	1930–34	1940–44	1950–54	1960–64	1970–74	1974–79
3.3	2.2	2.1	2.0	2.3	2.2	2.0	1.9

Source: Social Trends (adapted)

31

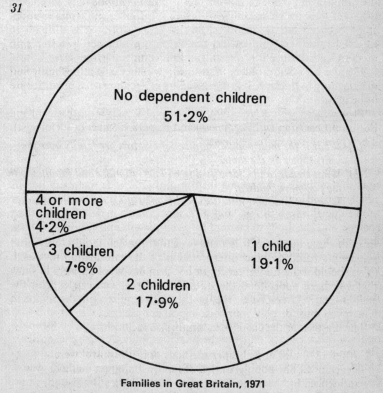

Families in Great Britain, 1971

Source: Social Trends 4, 1973. (Taken from G. O'Donnell, The Human Web, 1975)

Or, you may be given some detailed statistics and asked to answer specific questions about them. For example:

(a) *What does the chart tell you about the distribution of family size?* *(4 marks)*

(b) *What is meant by families with 'no dependent children'?* *(2 marks)*

(c) *Are large families necessarily 'deprived'?* *(6 marks)*

(d) *Account briefly for the trend towards smaller families in this century.* *(8 marks)* (LON)

A similar question is:

32

Family size distributions after 10 years of marriage, England and Wales (%)

	Year of marriage					
	1951	1956	1961	1963	1964	1965
Number of liveborn children:						
0	14	11	8	9	9	10
1	27	22	18	17	17	18
2	35	38	44	46	48	49
3	16	19	22	21	19	18
4 or more	8	11	9	8	6	5
Total	100	100	100	100	100	100

Source: Adapted from Office of Population Censuses and Surveys

(a) *What is the most popular number of children per family over the years shown in the table?*

(b) *What trends can be identified in childless families and families with four or more children?*

(c) *What explanations have sociologists offered for the trends towards smaller families since 1900?* (AEB)

In both these questions it is parts (a) and (b) which require only brief statements based on your interpretation of the information provided. (You should write full sentences rather than one-word answers to show that you have understood the question and that you can express the answer clearly.) In each case the final sections require a full discussion in which you must display your sociological knowledge.

The reasons for the changes in family size include:

1 After 1870 new and cheaper methods of birth control were developed. The popularization of family limitation methods was influenced by the prosecution of an MP, Charles Bradlaugh, and Annie Bessant for publishing a book on the subject.

2 The Education Acts of 1870 and 1880 made school compulsory and children were less of an economic asset.

3 Industrial legislation limited the employment of children.

4 Improvements in medicine meant improved life expectation and so it was no longer necessary to have a large family to ensure the survival of a few children.

5 The suffragette movement and the gradual improvement in the rights and opportunities for women meant that more entered the labour force. It was more convenient to have smaller families. The 1975 legislation has been effective in this respect.

6 Family size was affected by changes in social norms and fashion. As the upper and middle classes began to have smaller families, the trend followed among those further down the social scale.

7 During times of economic depression, i.e. 1870s, 1920s, 1930s, 1970s, the fear of poverty and unemployment discouraged large families.

8 Two world wars had a similar effect.

9 In the period 1950–65 there was a slight increase in family size. This is attributable to:

(a) Economic affluence. People could satisfy their material wants and increase their family size.

(b) The introduction of the Welfare State in 1948 and the improvement in provisions of nursery schools, child benefits, etc.

(c) The increase in the number of marriages after the war and the reuniting of families.

10 The decline in average family size since 1965 is related to the development of an efficient oral contraceptive.

11 The Abortion Act and the Family Planning Act were passed in 1967.

Working mothers

There are an increasing number of married women in the female labour force. (Try to recall the number of women in the labour force for 1951, 1961 and 1971. What proportion of them were married? Check your answers on p. 48.)

Research has been done to see the effects on young children of working mothers.

In the examination you may be asked a question of this type:

33 *Are children whose mothers go out to work necessarily neglected? What evidence is there to support or contradict this opinion?*

Research by Yudkin and Holme: *Working Mothers and Their Children*

Yudkin and Holme examined research in this area and conducted their own study. They suggest that the factors that increase the tendency for mothers to take jobs outside the home include:

1 The increase in equality and democracy within marriage;
2 Earlier marriage and smaller families;
3 Increased incentives: the ability to earn a high wage and the desire to increase the standard of living of the family;
4 The increasing number of women with professional qualifications who wish to make use of them.

Attitudes of employers

Generally, mothers of young children are not regarded by employers as the best sources of labour because it is believed they will have high rates of absenteeism. However, they are considered to be useful as sources of temporary and part-time labour.

The effects on children of having working mothers

1 Most of the mothers in their sample of pre-school children made adequate arrangements for the care of their children whilst at work. Usually a grandmother or other relative looked after the child. About 20% used a playgroup. About 20% were 'latchkey' children.
2 They say that a review of the literature about the effects of working mothers on children shows 'dogmatism and relatively little real evidence of long-term effects'.
3 There was some evidence that fathers were taking a more significant role in the care and attention of the children in such dual career families.
4 The greatest pressure was on a mother to work when there was no other breadwinner in the home (i.e. no father or the father was unable to work). In such cases provision for the care of the children was often not as good. They were more likely to be cared for by a succession of different caretakers or childminders. This could have a disturbing effect on the child.

Mothers most likely to take full-time work

1 Where there is no other breadwinner in the home;
2 Those with only one child;

3 Those with a child (or children) over the age of 5 (only 15–20% of working mothers in their sample had children under the age of 5);
4 Those able to make adequate arrangements for their children while they worked;
5 Where the family was on a low income and extra finance was needed.

Some of their conclusions

1 In the short term there may be some emotional disturbance in pre-school children if their mother works. But children can adapt themselves fairly quickly – providing arrangements for their care are satisfactory.
2 Among school children there was some evidence to show that they developed more maturity and independence when their mothers worked.
3 There was no correlation with rates of delinquency and working mothers. Where delinquency did occur this related to lack of overall adequate care and attention.
4 They suggest that full-time work is less advisable for mothers with children under the age of 3. Such children require much constant attention from an adult with whom they feel particularly secure.
5 The most important factor is the kind of care that can be arranged for the child. Where this is of high standard there are few problems and the child will not suffer.

Yudkin and Holme are generally optimistic about the effects on children whose mothers work outside the home. Latchkey children may actually become more mature and independent as a result of having a working mother as well as being in a home with higher living standards.

Mia Kellmer Pringle (Director of the National Children's Bureau) writes in her book, *The Needs of Children*, that it is not so much the mother working outside the home which affects the development of a child so much as the quality of the substitute care. More recently, she has modified her view. She now thinks that only a full-time mother could give a young child all the full-time love and care it needs. She advocates the payment of a wage to housewives in recognition of the important work they do in child-care and child-rearing.

Divorce

Divorce is one of three categories of marital breakdown. It means the legal termination of marriage. A petition is filed stating the grounds for the divorce. The case is heard in the divorce court and generally the marriage is nullified. **Decrees Absolute** finally terminate the marriage and free the parties to remarry if they wish (see p. 64).

Another category is **legal separation**. The partners separate, but the marriage continues to exist. If reconciliation proves to be impossible, divorce usually follows.

A third category of breakdown is that of **desertion** in which one partner simply walks out or disappears from the family home. The marriage remains until divorce petitions are filed and a decree absolute is granted.

Reliable figures for separations and desertion are difficult to obtain, but there is some evidence to suggest that like the divorce rate, they are increasing. (Chester, *Divorce,* suggests that the number of recorded separations may have increased by more than 65% between 1960 and 1970.)

A popular question is one that asks you to discuss and explain the changes in the divorce rate during a particular time period. For example:

34 What factors have caused the changes in the divorce rate since 1957?

It is helpful to answer this kind of question by referring to the factors shown in the table opposite.

Some other factors associated with divorce rates (and about which you may be asked) include:

1 **Age** at which marriage is contracted.
2 **Length** of marriage. Statistics indicate that 40% of marriages that end in divorce, do so within the first ten years of married life and more than 75% within twenty years.
3 **Number of children** in the marriage. Divorce rates are highest among those with few children.
   (N.B. There is some debate as to the significance of children for a marriage. Dominion (Director of the Marriage Research Centre) says that children bring out many positive characteristics from parents and so increase the stability of a marriage. Abrams (*Report by Social Sciences Research Council,* 1980) suggested that it may be a myth to believe that children help cement a marriage. His findings indicate that there is a sharp fall in levels of happiness among many married couples following the birth of the first child – which may not be recaptured. Recently, there has been an increase in the numbers of divorces in which children were involved.)

You may be asked questions of the following type based on a more precise analysis of some of the statistics.

Changes in legislation	Industrialization	Urbanization	Secularization
1857 Matrimonial Causes Act. This made divorce more widely available. It also introduced legal separation.	(a) Growth of factory system may have helped reduce importance of the family as a productive unit. Family members may come to rely less on each other.	(a) City life is associated with higher divorce rates than rural. In urban life there may be more sources of conflict and tension.	(a) The decline in the significance of religion in the lives of the majority of people may mean that divorce has become more widely acceptable.
1878 Matrimonial Causes Act. This introduced maintenance. A wife could gain custody of children.	(b) More women work outside the home and are less economically dependent on their husbands.	(b) There may be stronger controls over social patterns of behaviour in village communities.	(b) People may be less concerned about the sacred aspects of marriage. In 1977 there were more civil
1909 Royal Commission on Divorce. This recommended that men and women should be treated equally before the law.	(c) With more women at work the birth-rate declines. Divorce rates are higher among childless couples.	(c) Families in urban areas are likely to be more geographically mobile which may reduce their contact with other kin members who	weddings (in registry offices) than church weddings for the first time since records started in 1832.
1923 Matrimonial Causes Act. A wife could gain a divorce on grounds of her husband's adultery.	(d) Young people may also become economically independent at an earlier age. Divorce rates are	may be able to support a marriage in difficulty.	(c) In secular societies divorce carries less stigma, abortion is more widely accepted and rates of illegitimacy increase.
1937 The Herbert Act. The grounds for divorce were widened – but no divorce before three years of marriage.	highest for those who marry under 21. They are also high for marriages where the bride is pregnant.	(b) In urban areas marriages are more likely to occur between partners from different cultural backgrounds – which may result in less compatibility.	
1949 Legal aid introduced. **1950** Matrimonial Causes Acts. **1965** Consolidated existing legislation.			
1969 The Divorce Reform Act. Introduced 'irretrievable breakdown of marriage'. Non-cohabitation for two or five years.			

35

Divorce statistics: decrees absolute granted in England and Wales, 1961–76

	1961	1966	1967	1968	1969	1970
No. (in thousands)	25.4	39.1	43.1	45.8	51.3	58.2
Rate (per thousand*)	2.1	3.2	3.5	3.7	4.1	4.7

	1971	1972	1973	1974	1975	1976
No. (in thousands)	74.4	119.0	106.0	113.5	120.5	126.7
Rate (per thousand*)	6.0	9.5	8.4	9.0	9.6	10.1

*of married population
Sources: Social Trends, No. 8, 1977 and Annual Abstract of Statistics, 1977

(a) How would you account for the sharp rise in the divorce rate in the early 1970s? (2 marks)
(b) There is evidence that the divorce rate is higher among those who marry at a younger age. How might this be explained? (6 marks)
(c) With what justification can it be argued that the statistics in the table illustrate 'the decline of the family' in British society? (12 marks) (CAM)

36

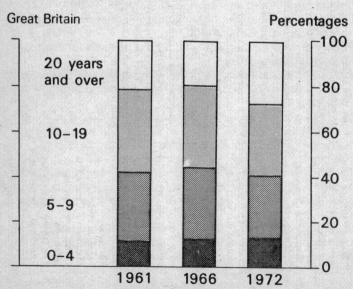

Great Britain   Percentages

20 years and over

10–19

5–9

0–4

1961   1966   1972

Divorce: by duration of marriage
Source: Social Trends, 1975

(a) *What changes does the chart show in patterns of divorce over the period 1961–72?*

(b) *What effects have changes in divorce law had on marriage stability in modern Britain?* (AEB)

Notice how in 35(c) you are asked to comment on 'the decline' of the family; and in 36(b) you are asked to comment on 'the stability' of marriage in light of divorce statistics and changes in divorce law. Try to recall the problems of assessing whether or not the institutions of marriage and family are less stable or in decline. Check your answers with the points already made on pp. 55–6.

Remember that you will gain credit in an exam answer for being able to refer to specific authorities, authors, books and other sources to support your arguments. Try to include some of the following details in an answer on the topic of marriage and divorce. But if you come across other details from your reading – especially of current developments – make a note of them and include them in an examination answer. This will indicate that you are keeping abreast of events.

1 Data from *Social Trends* indicate that in 1980 more than £5 million was paid out each week in supplementary benefits to about 250,000 families unsupported after separation or divorce.

2 Legal aid costs more than £50 million p.a. The average cost of a divorce per parent is about £400.

3 Women are filing an increasing number of petitions for divorce (more than 70% in 1976).

4 Richards (Medical Psychology Unit, Cambridge) says that more than 50% of fathers lose touch with their children completely following a divorce.

5 In 1979 a conciliation agency opened in Bristol. The aims are to safeguard the interests of children in a divorce by trying to help resolve conflict between parents. Also to increase the lines of communication between the divorcing couple. This is normally done through solicitors which is expensive and time-consuming.

6 In 1980 an eminent lawyer (Sir George Baker) said that divorce should be made easier. He advocated a one-year separation to show irretrievable breakdown of marriage.

7 In 1981, Mia Kellmer Pringle, an eminent child-care expert, suggested that there should be two forms of marriage: **simple contract** for those not intending to have children and a **binding contract** to ensure a long-standing marriage (of at least ten years) for those wanting children. She is particularly concerned to protect the interests of children and she is keen to discourage marriages at young ages.

Do children suffer who come from homes broken by divorce?
Illsley and Thompson make the point that the term **broken home** must
be used with care. There is no general agreement as to what constitutes a
broken home:

1 Homes may be broken in many varied ways: by the death of a
   parent, by desertion, separation, imprisonment, hospitalization, or
   by divorce.
2 Some homes may be broken permanently and others for brief
   periods.
3 Little is known about the extent and significance of these different
   forms of broken homes in the general population.
4 Few studies have looked at the different effects on children of the
   different forms of broken home.
5 Few studies have been conducted in terms of the differences in
   effect according to age and sex of children in 'broken homes'.
6 There is little information about the significance of the events on
   children which precede and follow the break.

As far as the effects of divorce are concerned, some of their conclusions
are that:

1 Broken homes of this type do not possess a monopoly of childhood
   unhappiness.
2 Some children may be better off when removed from an unhappy
   home atmosphere into a stable one-parent family.
3 Young male children may be more at risk. There is some evidence
   to suggest that male juvenile delinquents are more likely to have a
   weak or defective relationship with their father.
4 In general, where parental relationships are disturbed then those
   between parents and children are also likely to be unsatisfactory.

Herzov (child psychiatrist) says that whether or not children are
affected by divorce depends on:

1 How well they can adjust to new social and economic circumstances
   (parents may remarry or remain as single-parent families).
2 Their age, sex, temperament and the way they can cope with the
   stresses of the divorce processes. (Young, pre-school children may
   be at greater risk and so more vulnerable, since they may become
   more confused and distressed. Older children may be able to cope
   better.)
3 How the children are treated by the parents during the divorce
   proceedings. Often a child becomes a pawn or scapegoat in the
   battle between the parents and suffers as a result.

His conclusions are that there is a proportion of children who are at risk, but the result of a recent American study suggested that after five years two-thirds of the children in the sample were not adversely affected by the experience of parental divorce. He speculates that it may be that an absent parent is less of a danger to the emotional stability of a child than one who is permanently present but who is unable to fulfil the child's needs adequately.

Wallerstein and Kelly in their book *Surviving the Breakup* are less optimistic. They argue that parents must be more aware of their significance for their children. They remain vital to a child's development (even if separated). For this reason they advocate the increased use of **joint custody**. This would discourage the attitude of 'having won the children'. This often contributes to the bitterness between parents and so harms the children. At present in England and Wales only 2½% of such children are the subject of joint custody orders. The authors point out that in the USA about 80% of children requiring psychiatric help are from homes broken by divorce.

Consider the following question which combines a discussion of both marriage and divorce.

37 'There has been a fall in the age at which people get divorced. This is reflected in the increase in the proportion of divorcing wives under 35 years, from 50% in 1961 to 58% in 1969. The Registrar General has shown in his commentary for England and Wales 1964 that the time between divorce and second marriage for wives aged between 25 and 29 is well under two years.

For some three-quarters of divorcing couples, divorce is a temporary condition between the dissolution of an unhappy first marriage and the beginning of a more hopeful second marriage. Such a high rate of remarriage when linked to the rising divorce numbers shows modern morality opposes the idea of continuing a defunct marriage, but does not reject the actual institution of marriage.'

C. Gibson, Social Trends in Divorce, *New Society*, 5 July 1973

Comment on the stability of the family in modern Britain.

To answer the question:
1 Read and re-read the quotation carefully.
2 Rewrite it simply in your own words – one short section at a time. Make sure you explain what point is being made.
3 You should end up with one central point supported by a number of related facts.
   Write down this central point in capital letters so that it is clear in your mind.

   List the four related facts which are stated in the quotation,
   (a)–(d).
4 Re-read the question that you have been asked to answer.
5 Notice the key parts of the question: **stability, modern Britain,
   above information, other evidence.** Underline these so that you
   do not forget their importance.
6 If you are in any doubt about the meanings of any of them clarify
   them before you go any further. For example, for the purpose of
   your answer you may decide to take modern Britain to mean
   'Britain since 1970'.
7 Plan your answer on the following lines:

   (a) **Introduction**   Explain what you are being asked to do in order
       to answer this question (see point 2) (about 50 words).
   (b) **Key factors** in this discussion: definitions of terms   Notice
       particularly the problem of assessing 'stability'. Show that you
       have understood the details in the quotation by stating the main
       points in a clear and simple way (see your answers to point 3
       above) (about 100 words).
   (c) Develop the **main body** of the essay   Present relevant marriage
       and divorce statistics from, say, 1970. Comment on these
       explaining the changes that have occurred. Present details from
       relevant authorities and sources. Be sure that you work towards
       a particular conclusion. Is the family less stable as a result of the
       changes you are discussing? Answer this section in about 250
       words.
   (d) Reach a **conclusion**   Summarize the key points you have made
       and show how they help in reaching your final answer. Try to
       write between 50 and 100 words on this part of your answer.

Key terms and concepts

The following terms and concepts have been defined and used in this
section. You must be able to use them and explain their meaning for
examination purposes:

**marriage; divorce; family stability; homogeneous; industriali-
zation; secularization; urbanization; broken homes.**

You should also be certain that you are very familiar with the statistics for
divorce and marriage rates.

6 Stratification

The questions that are asked on the topic of social stratification (sometimes termed **social differentiation** or **social differences**) divide into two main types. There are those that deal with the theory of social stratification. These are concerned to test your understanding of the concepts of social class and status. They may ask you to

38 *Describe any four determinants of social class in Britain.* (WEL)

Or a question may state:

39 *Marxists believe that modern industrial societies are divided into two major classes according to ownership or non-ownership of capital or property. Other writers say that this is too simple a distinction. They point to the various differences in status which exist, based on factors other than occupation.*
   How useful are the above ways of looking at stratification in modern Britain?

Such questions require detailed knowledge of the theoretical issues.
   Other questions deal with the significance of class for understanding other aspects of social behaviour. Frequently there are questions which ask you to explain the relationships between class position and voting behaviour or educational performance. For these you need to know the theoretical details together with facts from relevant research studies.
   Both types of question require clear definitions of terms. If **class** or **status** are mentioned in a question you must be able to show that you understand their sociological meaning. Never take any such key words for granted and certainly *do not* answer as a layman might. (They generally talk of three classes, variously described as upper, middle and lower, or rich, average and poor.) There are frequently questions that test this ability to distinguish between complex concepts.

40 *Explain the meaning of and use examples to show the difference between power and authority.* (WEL)

Social stratification is a particularly important area of the syllabus because there is so much research that connects class background to so much of everyday social behaviour.

Social stratification refers to the way in which a society is divided into different social groups or strata. In contemporary Britain the division is based on class and status. In other societies or in other historical times the basis of stratification may be different. For example, the social ranking of groups may be based on caste, slavery, estate, etc.

In modern industrial societies the terms class and status are most frequently used to describe the different broad social groups which exist.

Social class   When they use this term sociologists are referring to such groups that can be ranked in superior and inferior positions according to particular criteria. Studies have shown that members of each group tend to share similar features in common. Although there are distinctions between each class group there is no suggestion that one class is better or worse than another; it is just that they are different from each other.

It has been found that class is a useful tool of social analysis (when looking at crime, voting behaviour, educational achievement, etc.) since research shows that correlations exist between social class membership and such aspects of life in society.

Karl Marx

Questions in the exam sometimes refer directly to the contribution of Marx to the discussion of social class. He was a German writer (1818–83) who lived in exile in Britain where he wrote many of his books. His work is generally very complex and contains a strong philosophical and economic basis. You would not, therefore, be expected to have a detailed knowledge of his ideas. He is important in discussions of some areas of sociology because he was one of the first writers to make an analysis of the social structure of society. Many of his ideas are open to criticism, but his work has been influential and therefore you need to be able to refer to some of his arguments. One of his major contributions was the attempt to clarify the nature, origin and significance of social class.

Marx described the existence of two class groups based on economic distinctions. The **bourgeoisie** are those who own the means of production and sources of wealth. They are the capitalists, the landlords, the factory owners, etc. The inferior class is the **proletariat**. They have only their labour to sell to the owners of the places of work. The mass of working people belong to the proletariat.

He argues that to own the means of production is to be in possession of great power. The owners have control of the economy of the society and the lives of the workers. He said that the economic organization of society shapes and influences all other major social institutions. For example, the political organization of society is said by Marx to reflect the interests of the bourgeoisie and to give power to that class.

In his analysis of history he emphasizes the constant struggle that has always existed between classes. He sees such struggles as the source of social development and change. Societies based on inequalities give rise to conflicts. In this way he explains how societies have progressed through a series of stages, from **ancient**, to **feudal** to **capitalist**. It is part of his argument that the central conflicts of interest inherent in capitalist society are those of class antagonism. He says that when power is transferred to the subjugated class (the proletariat) society will be remodelled on a fair and just basis. Ownership will be collective and not individual. There would be no class divisions, but rather total cooperation among all members of the society and the gradual elimination of any form of organized government as the state eventually 'withered away'.

Some criticisms of Marx's arguments

1 He claimed to have a scientific analysis of historical and social development, but in fact his ideas are hard to test.
2 He predicted the polarization of classes into two major groups in capitalist societies. This does not seem to have occurred in Britain. Some writers (for example Roberts *et al.*) argue that there is a fragmentation of the class structure going on at present (see pp. 77 and 166).
3 Marx also predicted increasing class conflict which does not seem to be the case.
4 Some societies (e.g. caste) are very unequal but they have not been subject to revolutionary change.

Marx's work has been useful in that it has drawn attention to the possible significance of the economic organization of a society. He presents a view of how economic structures can give rise to social divisions.

Many writers argue that it is necessary to take account of more than just economic factors in order to explain and understand the nature of social stratification.

Factors affecting a person's social class

(1) Occupation

Much sociological research uses a simplified system of assessing class. It is based on a person's occupation. This is because there has been found to be a correlation between this feature and other factors, such as a person's status, life-style, life-chances, etc. The scale most frequently used is that of the Registrar General's classification. He has a list of more than 20,000 separate occupational titles and these are grouped into occupational units, each one having a social class classification. In their (1972) study *From Birth to Seven*, Davie, Butler and Goldstein made use of this scale and presented the data (based on a sample of 14,495 people) shown in the table.

Social class	Typical occupations	% in the class
1	Higher professionals: accountants, architects, doctors, lawyers	5
2	Other professional and technical: managerial/intermediate: aircraft pilot or engineer, manager, nurse, fire-brigade officer, teacher	14
3a (non-manual)	Other non-manual occupations: lower white-collar workers, sales representatives, supervisors	10
3b (manual)	Skilled manual workers: where person has gained qualifications through apprenticeship, etc.	44
4	Semi-skilled workers: agricultural worker, postman, telephone operator	17
5	Unskilled manual: kitchen hand, driver's mate, window cleaner, labourer	6
% in their study of households with no male head		3

It is interesting to note that membership of these categories does change slightly from time to time, when the Registrar General makes some revisions to his classifications. These tend to occur mainly at the lower end of the scale so that those classified in one census as class 5 may be listed as class 4 (or vice versa) in a later census. Some researchers also make use of knowledge of a mother's occupation in order to assess the class of the family. However, people do tend to marry someone of a similar social class.

Other, more refined systems of classification have been devised but they are all based mainly on occupation. The Hall-Jones scale uses the following categories:

1 Professional and high administrative;
2 Managerial and executive;
3 Inspectional, supervisory and other non-manual, higher grade;
4 Inspectional, supervisory and other non-manual, lower grade;
5 Skilled manual and routine grades of non-manual;
6 Semi-skilled manual;
7 Unskilled manual.

On the basis of the Registrar General's classification classes 1, 2 and 3a are generally considered to be the 'middle classes' and 3b, 4 and 5 to be the 'working classes'. Clearly most of the population (more than 65%) falls into the latter category.

It has been said that occupation remains the backbone of social grading because no better method has been discovered; but in reality it is one of a number of possible measures.

(2) Income and wealth

These are important indicators of a person's status in the community. They help determine a person's possessions and life-style. They are often wrongly assumed to be the only index of class membership.

(3) Attitudes and values

Many studies show that people in different social classes have different perspectives with regard to the way the social world is organized. These beliefs affect their patterns of behaviour. Lockwood and Goldthorpe report:
(a) Most people have a clear image of how their society is socially divided on the basis of the distribution of wealth, power and status.
(b) The typical **working-class view** is that the division is between those who have power and those who don't. The typical **middle-class view** is that society is like a ladder which can be climbed by anyone who wishes to make the effort.

(4) Life-style

The cultural values of a class inform members about taste, patterns of expenditure, leisure activities, etc. Styles of living are related to class membership to some extent.

(5) Life-chances

Studies show that there are differences in life expectation, chances for obtaining medical care, or a particular job. There are also differences in the chances people have for obtaining power and status in society. These differences all relate to class membership.

(6) Family status and social background

People obtain a self-identity according to their social background. This results from their patterns of socialization. The status a family has, the kind of education members enjoy, the qualifications they gain, the home they live in — all help identify the class of the family.

(7) Power and authority

(a) Power   Refers to the ability a person has to influence the behaviour of others in accordance with his own wishes. It is one of the benefits of high social class.

(b) Authority   This is the legitimate power invested in someone, usually as a result of the formal qualifications of their occupation. The social authority of those in high-status occupations derives from the power that this confers and again is likely to be a product of their social class.

Conclusions   Social class has a number of dimensions. There is generally found to be a correlation between a person's occupation and the other features mentioned. This is therefore taken as a simple guide to a person's class.

The significance of social class

There are frequently questions that ask you to explain, with examples, the ways in which social class background influences patterns of behaviour. There may be general questions of the type:

41 *'An understanding of social class is essential in explaining the working of British society.' How far is this true?* (LON)

This requires a broad knowledge of a number of areas. Or there may be a specific question which directs your attention to a particular area of social life. For example:

42 *Is juvenile delinquency more common amongst the working class than amongst the middle class? Discuss with reference to studies.*

The important areas in which questions are asked and which illustrate the relevance of social class on a person's life-style and life-chances are listed below. They are dealt with again in more detail in following chapters in which the specific topic areas (of crime, education, etc.) are discussed.

1 Education (see pp. 216–17)
2 Health and welfare (see pp. 250–51)
3 Voting behaviour (see pp. 164–5)
4 Crime and delinquency (see pp. 184–5)
5 Occupational choice and work attitudes (see pp. 108–9)
6 Leisure choice (see p. 137)

For further examples of research which shows the connection between a person's social class and other features of their life in society, see chapters on leisure, mobility, distribution of income, poverty, trade unions, youth culture and race relations. You need to select from such detail in order to answer a question such as:

43 Select examples to show how a person's occupation influences his whole way of life.

The embourgeoisement thesis (the affluence thesis)

Some questions may ask you to define a number of concepts, among them **embourgeoisement**. Or you may be asked a question in which, although the term is not used, an understanding of it is central to the answer. For example:

44 Discuss the suggestion that there has been a decline in the importance of social class differences in Britain since 1945.

The embourgeoisement thesis claims that the more affluent sections of the working class are losing their identity as a social stratum and are becoming merged into the middle class (i.e. they are becoming more bourgeois).

This is a suggestion which gained popularity when it was put forward by Butler and Rose in 1959 to explain why the Conservative Party had managed to win three consecutive general elections. Since there are more working-class than middle-class voters and since most people are influenced in their voting by their self-identification of class, these writers suggested that as people became more economically prosperous they came to see themselves as middle-class and voted accordingly.

The thesis was tested by Lockwood and Goldthorpe (*The Affluent Worker in the Class Structure*). They were critical of the thesis and said its supporters had not taken account of all the factors that contribute to a person's social class. Lockwood and Goldthorpe believed that a person's class position was affected by other factors as well as income. They said the other factors to be considered were:

1 The **economic aspects** of social class. There are many subtle differences to consider. Manual workers have less job security, less chance of promotion, and fewer fringe benefits.
2 The **relational aspects** of social class. They defined this as 'the extent to which workers are accepted on equal terms by middle-class

people in formal and informal social relationships'. In their study they found that manual and non-manual workers did not eat their meals in the same places, they did not mix socially after work and they did not live in the same areas.

3 The **normative aspect** of social class. They defined this as 'the extent to which manual workers acquired a new outlook and new standards of behaviour which resemble those of the middle classes'. They found little evidence that this was the case. They seldom looked for high levels of promotion; they found low levels of job satisfaction; they formed most of their friendships within their immediate circle of work mates and relatives.

There were some similarities with the middle-class respondents in their sample. A high proportion were concerned to acquire more material goods and they had high aspirations for their children. They suggest that there may be a new working class emerging who have some direct contacts with white-collar workers and who have some influence of aspects of their life-styles.

Their conclusions   They do not think that there is a process of embourgeoisement related to increasing affluence among traditionally working-class people. Nor is there much evidence that the Labour Party has lost its image as a party of the working class. Where the working-class voter was voting Conservative it was generally because they had some middle-class attachments (relatives who were white-collar workers, etc.) and not simply because of their higher wages and increased number of material possessions.

The main area of convergence between the classes was in terms of their shared preferences for increased 'privatization'. That is, many working-class members in the sample were more home- and family-centred than previous research had suggested. They also emphasized the significance of companionship in marriage. To this extent the behaviour of both middle- and working-class respondents was similar. They favoured a more 'private' life-style rather than one based on a wide circle of acquaintances and friends outside the home.

Proletarianization

This term is sometimes used in conjunction with that of embourgeoisement. It has been used by some writers (e.g. Westergaard and Resler) to suggest that there are some groups of workers whose class position is difficult to identify because they are in an intermediate position between the two main class groups. This is particularly true of some white-collar workers. Are they becoming more 'proleterian' (working-class) or more 'bourgeois' (middle-class)?

Marxists would say that there is no doubt they are proletarians. They do not own the means of production. To think otherwise is to be deluded by 'false consciousness'. Westergaard and Resler take this view.

Some writers have suggested that such workers generally see themselves as being middle-class, and there is evidence to suggest that there do remain differences in life-style, attitudes, values, etc. which confirm the more middle-class status of the majority of low level, white-collar workers.

Weir and Mercer conducted a study in Hull to try to resolve the dispute. They defined white-collar workers as those who spent most of their working day in an office environment; they wore normal clothes; they had staff status; they were not part of the management; they had a salary; they had pension rights and a secure job.

For many of the women in Weir and Mercer's sample there was evidence of increasing proletarianization. That is, they were workers with low levels of qualifications; they were generally from working-class backgrounds; they were often working in large and noisy offices which were not unlike factory conditions; they were often employed to operate machines and their work was impersonal and the pace of their work outside their own control. Such women workers tended to get the more fragmented work tasks; they had little contact with management or high level white-collar workers. Although they may have had middle-class aspirations and may have described themselves as middle-class, the authors suggest that they remain closer to a working-class position. For male white-collar workers the reverse was true. They had better chances for upward mobility and could be more accurately described as middle-class workers. For them there was less evidence of proletarianization.

David Lockwood has also said that the proletarian view which causes people to perceive society as divided into competing social classes based on economic and social inequalities generally occurs when large numbers of manual workers are bound together in close-knit occupational communities. They are set apart from other social groups and they share similar life-styles. He believes that the traditional deferential and proletarian workers are concentrated in industries and communities which are increasingly backwaters of industrial and urban development.

Roberts, Cook, Clarke and Semenonoff (*The Fragmentary Class Structure*, 1977) also refute the embourgeoisement thesis and say that their evidence implies that it only ever affects a small minority of manual workers. However, they do see some changes occurring in the class structure of modern Britain. They argue that the middle class is increasingly dividing into a series of different sub-groups. Each one has a distinctive place in the social hierarchy. They conclude that the middle class is becoming more fragmented; some white-collar groups are more unionized, others are more professionalized, etc.

Halsey (*Origins and Destinations*) and Goldthorpe (*Social Mobility and*

Class Structure in Modern Britain, 1980) show that there has been some upward mobility out of the working class and into the middle class among their respondents (1918–72). This is because there is more room at the top. But those working-class people who have not been socially mobile have become more homogeneous as a group, whereas those who have been upwardly mobile have helped to make the middle class more hetero- geneous. They also agree that there is an increasing lack of solidarity among the middle-class groups in society.

You may be asked to

45 *Explain what social and economic changes have occurred in the class structure of modern Britain since 1945.*

To answer such a question you need to consider the following points:

1 What kind of economic and social changes need to be considered?
2 What are their implications for the class structure?
3 Which authorities can be cited to support your argument?
4 What conclusions can be reached?

Here are some of the points that help answer these questions:

Economic changes	Social changes
1 There has been improvement in general living standards as rates of pay have improved.	Standards of working-class housing have improved.
2 People have had more access to material goods, especially cars, televisions, etc., in all social classes.	There has been widespread urban development.
3 Working people have gained greater legal protection of their jobs, redundancy pay, etc.	There has been a decline in many of the traditional working-class industries, especially cotton, coal, etc., which may have caused a decline in working-class community life.
4 The economic boom of the 1950s and 1960s tended to raise people's expectations about the quality of social life. These have not been seriously deflated by the economic depression of the 1970s and 1980s.	There may be a widespread view among many people that class differences have largely disappeared, so that people are less class conscious.

The implications of these changes

Some writers have suggested that class is of less significance in shaping patterns of behaviour:

For example, **King** (Professor of Political Theory) has argued that people are now less influenced by class identification in their voting behaviour. Voters are beginning to look more closely at what the parties offer, rather than being influenced by their traditional images. He thinks people do not favour extremist politicians, and this may cause more working-class voters to turn away from the Labour Party.

Dahrendorf (Director of the London School of Economics) also argues that major social and economic changes have caused a collapse of traditional class allegiances. He says that traditional class divisions have been eliminated. There are fewer social groups who have identical demands and needs in common. Dahrendorf concludes that the concept of class is having an increasingly limited influence on people.

However, there are other sociologists who argue that although there have been many significant social and economic changes, class remains a very important factor in people's lives. In explaining how this may be the case it would be useful to refer to the work of some of the authors previously mentioned – especially Lockwood and Goldthorpe, Halsey and Goldthorpe, and Roberts *et al*.

There is also research by **Townsend** (Inequality in the Workplace, *New Society*, October 1979). He produces much objective evidence to show that class inequalities continue to exist. People also subjectively perceive differences between various social groups; although living standards have improved, class differences remain. Townsend concludes that his evidence confirms that many manual workers continue to have low expectations of their positions in work. They feel that they have little control over the pace of their work. Because they do not expect much they do not press for greater equality of treatment. Unemployment and re- dundancy are seen as inevitable parts of life. He thinks that changes in laws concerning employment provisions have prompted commentators to reach complacent conclusions about progress in the workplace. In- equalities have not narrowed – on the contrary the gap between white- and blue-collar workers has widened.

Also **Sennet and Cobb**, two American authors, reach a similar con- clusion and refute the idea that social and economic changes have diminished the significance of class. In their book *The Hidden Injuries of Class* they look at the subjective aspects of class membership: that is, the feelings and perceptions of members of low social class groups. They uncover and define the emotionally hurtful forms of class differences. Their findings are based on long-term intensive interviews with ordinary members of the public. These reveal how deeply their lives and life- styles, attitudes and values have been influenced and shaped by the class to which they belong.

What conclusions can be reached?

If you have been asked simply to state the kinds of economic and social changes that have occurred in British society since 1945 and to illustrate the possible effects on the class structure, then your conclusion will be more of a summary of the key points you have raised.

If you have also been asked to say whether they have changed the class structure, so that class differences are of less significance, then the conclusions you reach must be based on your interpretation of the evidence used in your answer.

(Remember that in any question it is important to reach a conclusion if you have been asked a question. Your final answer to it must appear in the final section of your answer.)

In this case, if you think that the weight of the evidence points to the continuing significance of class on life-styles, attitudes, values, etc., then you must say so. If, on the other hand, you think that the authors putting this view have overstated their case and have ignored the deeper effects of social and economic change, then you must make this point in your concluding remarks.

Sometimes examination questions ask you to distinguish between different types of social stratification systems. For example,

46 *Show that you understand the meaning of the following terms: (a) stratification; (b) caste; (c) status; (d) slavery; (e) serfdom.*

Frequently, you are asked to distinguish between class and status. In order to deal with such questions you should re-read the present chapter and look carefully at the notes in the table opposite.

Key terms and concepts

The following terms and concepts have been defined and used in this chapter. You must be able to use them and explain their meaning for examination purposes:

Marxist perspective; Registrar General's classification; class; status; social differentiation; stratification; bourgeoisie; proletariat; capitalism; socialism; caste; power; authority; privatization; proletarianization; Weberian perspective; slavery; serfdom; affluence; manual worker; professional worker; white-collar worker; blue-collar worker; life-style; life-chances.

Other terms you may wish to use:

hierarchy Ranking in order of superiority according to some criteria (e.g. headmaster, deputy head, senior staff, other staff, prefects, sixth formers, other pupils).

Types of social stratification

Social class	Social status	Caste	Feudalism–serfdom	Slavery
Marx was the first to make an analysis of stratification by class. He argued that class divisions arise in industrial capitalist societies when there is a clear distinction between the owners of the means of production ('bourgeoisie') and the non-owners ('proletariat'). The distinction is based on the relationship of the individual to the means of production. Class distinctions are heightened by the sense of alienation that workers feel when they are employed in dangerous and tedious forms of work. Distinctions are manifested in different life-styles, life-chances, and attitudes and values. Mobility is possible in a class society although the amount seems to be greatest within class groups (e.g. from 5 to 4) rather than across class lines (e.g. from 4 to 2).	Weber (1864–1920) opposed the views of Marx. He said it is important to distinguish between class and status. A person's status is the standing or prestige they have in the community or in the particular social groups. People are treated in accordance with their status since it designates social position. It is argued that a person's chance of obtaining particular scarce resources relates more to their status than to their class. For example, a white worker in class 4 may have higher status than a black semi-skilled worker. Therefore he has a better chance of gaining a good home and a job. Class is less significant; it is a more fluid concept and open to greater mobility than would be accepted by Marx. Two important types of status are identified: (a) Ascribed; (b) Achieved (see p. 82).	This is an example of a closed, rigid system of stratification in which no mobility is possible. It operates in parts of India and is related to the Hindu religion. There are five main caste groups. Membership is fixed at birth. (i) Brahmins: priests and nobles. (ii) Kshtriya: rulers and administrators. (iii) Vaisya: merchants and farmers. (iv) Sudras: manual workers. (v) Untouchables: outcasts who perform the menial tasks. Caste membership determines every aspect of social life: occupation, marriage partner, dress, education, etc.	In Britain feudal society was characterized by a hierarchy of authority headed by the king and nobility. Next came members of the church, followed by the freemen. These groups formed 'estates': (i) They were legally defined: members were subject to rights and duties. (ii) They had definite functions. (iii) They were political groups. The serfs had minimal rights and lacked power. They did not form an estate. This system of estates gradually transformed into a class system as feudalism fell into decline. This was facilitated by the growth of capitalism and the emergence of a new merchant middle class who required a mobile labour force.	This represents another extreme form of social stratification in which there is great inequality. The slave has no legal or social rights. He is bound to a master who has unlimited power over him. Slavery existed in ancient Greece and Rome and in the Americas until the late nineteenth century. It fell into decline because it is an inefficient method in an industrializing society.

ideology   A set of interlocking beliefs which governs the behaviour and attitudes of the group which holds the values. These beliefs help to explain the world and the behaviour of people in it. Some people have a religious ideology, others political ideologies.

ascribed status   People can gain initial status from the family into which they have been born. Those born into high social positions have better opportunities than those born into low status families, regardless of their levels of ability. People may also obtain ascribed status by having connections with particular groups or individuals who themselves have high status. Some ascribed statuses are permanently fixed, such as a person's gender or aristocratic title.

achieved status   People can obtain different status levels according to their efforts and achievements. Where they have worked for qualifications, obtained scarce resources or married into an eminent family, then others in the community will confer high status on them. This is based on their respect and recognition for their abilities. (We may say that a person has had every chance but has achieved nothing, so that low status is conferred.)

7   Social mobility

Social mobility is closely associated with social class and status as a topic area.

Questions in this area are generally straightforward. An answer to a question on mobility is likely to require reference to and discussion of at least one or more of the following:

1 A clear definition of **terms** that relate to the concept of mobility;
2 The key **variables** that affect rates of mobility:
   (a) the occupational structure;
   (b) the economic structure;
   (c) the educational structure;
3 The **methods of measuring** and establishing the extent of mobility;
4 The **processes** of mobility: how and why some people are more mobile than others;
5 The **consequences** of mobility.

A typical question is:

47 *What do sociologists mean by social mobility?*
    What are the methods involved in measuring social mobility?

1 Definition

Sociologists are interested in discovering the extent to which people in society can move up or down the social scale.

The analysis of social mobility is the investigation of the causes and consequences of the movement of individuals or families up or down the social scale in terms of increased or decreased social status.

2 The key variables

Occupational structure	Economic structure	Educational structure
(a) It is a convenient way of measuring changes in class and status levels to compare either a person's occupation with that of his father or his job at the start of his career with that he has at the time of the study.	(a) Changes that occur in the economy affect opportunities for mobility. Where the economy is expanding, chances of mobility increase.	(a) Job choice is related to the level of qualifications obtained in school.
(b) Rates of mobility are affected by the extent to which access to particular occupations is made easier or more difficult. (More professions may require degrees for entry into their ranks.)	(b) Changes in methods of production may be significant. For example, automation and the microchip may have helped to de-skill certain occupations and limit the chances of mobility for some workers.	(b) 1870–1944: Chances of upward mobility were limited because of the restricted nature of the educational system.
(c) There is widespread consensus in our society about which occupations have high, intermediate or low-status ranking. Movement from an unskilled background to a professional one would indicate high levels of mobility.	(c) Some occupations may be under pressure to become more 'professionalized' so that entry to them becomes more restricted.	(c) 1944: Tripartite System: More working-class children entered grammar schools. Only small proportions reached university (25%, 1938–68). Children from middle-class homes had best chances of upward mobility (Douglas, Dale and Griffiths). Public school background remained an advantage and reinforced ties between status of parents and their children.
	(d) The economic policies of the government may affect mobility. For example, cuts in expenditure on education, health services, etc. may cut off some of the traditional routes of mobility for some workers.	(d) 1964–81: the Comprehensive system was developed on a national scale.

(d) A person's occupation relates to their status, life-style and life-chances. Mobility is increased where people can easily re-train or change jobs.

Neave (1973) showed they were successful in gaining more university places for working-class children.

Forde (1969) is pessimistic and says that in her study she found no strong evidence of increased social mobility.

Halsey (1980) is also pessimistic and suggests that there has been little change in the relative chances of reaching the top jobs for those born into different social classes.

3 Methods of measuring and establishing the extent of mobility

There are two methods that are generally used:

(a) Inter-generational mobility   The occupational status of a son is compared with that of his father (or grandfather) at the time of the study. Reference is made to an occupational classification of class (usually the Registrar General's). It is then possible to measure whether or not a person has moved up or down the social scale.

(b) Intra-generational mobility   A comparison is made between a person's occupational status at the start of their career with the position they have achieved at the time of the study.

The first major study of mobility levels in Britain was carried out in 1949 by Glass. The main findings were:

(a) There were fairly high levels of inter-generational mobility. Approximately two-thirds of the respondents were in a different status group from that of their father's. About one-third had moved up and one-third down.

(b) Most of the mobility that occurred was of a short-range type; that is, sons tended to be in occupational groups either just above or just below that of their fathers.

(c) There was little evidence of much long-range mobility in either direction (that is, movement beyond more than one class up or down).

(d) There was a high degree of self-recruitment both at the top and bottom ends of the social scale (that is, a high proportion of sons of professional or manual workers were themselves in the same occupational groups).

(e) The study revealed a significant level of social inequality in that it appeared to be quite difficult for people to move from their class of origin into a higher status group.

(f) On the level of intra-generational mobility, the greatest opportunities for movement among those born into families of manual workers were those who themselves started work in skilled occupations (namely those who had obtained technical qualifications).

(g) Workers who had such skills were more likely to be able to move into white-collar administrative occupations. Those born into families of white-collar workers themselves had greater opportunities for upward mobility into professional groups.

The main conclusion to be drawn from this large-scale 1949 study is that there was more movement *within* class groups (i.e. within working-class categories and within middle-class occupational groups) than between them. There were limited opportunities to cross from a working-class group into a middle-class one. Where this did occur it was most likely to be from a skilled manual occupation into a low-level white-collar group.

Later evidence from other studies into the social background of members of elite groups tend to confirm some of these findings. Those born with high levels of ascribed status tend to have more opportunities of obtaining such socially powerful and valued positions than those born into low status families. For example:

(a) Glennester and Pryke (1964) found that public schools (used predominantly by middle-class parents) produced a disproportionate number of people in the top positions in society. These included 87% of Conservative cabinet ministers, 70% of ambassadors, 66% of bishops, and 64% of top business executives.

(b) Willmott and Young (1970) showed that of their sample of managers 83% were the sons of managers.

(c) Giddens (1971) found in his study that only 1% of the company chairmen that he interviewed had working-class origins.

(d) Boyd (1973) confirmed the importance of a high status educational background for mobility: 80% of judges, bank directors and Governors of the Bank of England had a public school education.

(e) In 1979, Mrs Thatcher appointed the Cabinet of the new Conservative Government. Of the 22 members only two (including Mrs Thatcher) did not attend a public school. Six attended the same public school (Eton), and 17 were graduates of Oxford and Cambridge.

The Oxford Mobility Study (1980)

This study, under the direction of Halsey and Goldthorpe, produced some of the following information:

(a) Long-range mobility increased in Britain from 1949. About 7% of sons born into the lowest social class were, at the time of the study, in the highest class group.

(b) High rates of self-recruitment remained in class 1: 45% of the sons of fathers in class 1 were themselves in this class.

(c) The authors suggest that there is now 'more room at the top'. There has been an expansion in the occupations making up class 1, and this has enabled more people to enter this group, especially because class 1 parents tend to have smaller families and therefore cannot fill the places themselves.

However, their overall conclusions remain rather pessimistic. They suggest that despite the economic and social changes that have occurred in recent years, the class structure of modern Britain continues to inhibit mobility. They confirm that a child born into a white-collar background has at least four times more chance of becoming upwardly mobile and reaching a top position than a child born into a working-class family.

In addition to a direct question about the nature and extent of mobility in Britain an exam question may ask you to distinguish between different types of mobility. For example:

48 Distinguish between sponsored and contest mobility.

If this question is a short answer question or a part of a longer one, then the detail included in your answer needs to be adjusted accordingly. You may be asked to explain the meaning of any three of the following pairs of terms:

(a) Class and caste (see p. 81);
(b) Achieved and ascribed status (see p. 82);
(c) Bourgeoisie and embourgeoisement (see pp. 70 and 75);
(d) Inter-generational and intra-generational mobility (see p. 86).

In order to answer part (a) of the question you must refer to the ideas of Turner (1960). He described two types of mobility:

(a) Sponsored mobility This describes the way in which some people have obtained high status by being recommended (or 'sponsored') on the basis of their ascribed status; that is, a person achieves a particular job or privileged position through his contacts or because he is seen to have the qualities desired by those who are in a position to make the selection. He has the right family background, the right type of education, etc. Their personal achievements (in terms of paper qualifications) may be minimal, but this does not affect their chances of selection to join elite groups.

(b) Contest mobility This describes the way that some people obtain higher status positions on the basis of open competition. Their achievements are more relevant than their ascribed status. People compete on even terms. Those with the best qualifications or the most relevant experience or the most drive and ambition will gain the highest rewards.

In Britain, mobility takes place by both methods. There is evidence to suggest that sponsorship remains a relevant factor in the upward mobility of some people in British social life.

4 The process of social mobility

This involves analysing how and why some people become more mobile than others. Research has produced some of the following findings:

Family background

Douglas (*The Home and the School*) suggests that children from home backgrounds where they are encouraged and motivated are more likely to do well in school and so have more potential for mobility.

Dale and Griffiths (amongst other research) suggest that children who have mothers who have had a high level of education are more likely to receive encouragement to do well in school and work. This may be a particular advantage for female children.

Carter notes in his study (*Into Work*) how some families train their children for independence at an early age. This is more characteristic of middle-class families who tend to emphasize the importance of 'deferred gratification'. These attitudes provide an advantage for such children since they encourage mobility.

It may be inferred from the work of Lockwood and Goldthorpe (see pp. 75–6) that working-class families with middle-class connections (e.g. having some close relative or friend in a white-collar occupation) are more likely to encourage mobility in their children.

Himmelweit found that working-class children from small families tended to be more successful in school than those from larger families (and so have more chance of upward mobility). This factor of family size was not significant among middle-class children. It is suggested that family size and birth order are important because first-born children or those with few brothers or sisters spend more time in the company of their parents and so develop maturity more quickly.

Peer group attachment

Downes has shown how attachment to a peer group culture can be an important influence on behaviour. People tend to accept the norms and values of their friends. If these are norms of 'success' and 'getting on', then the individual may benefit from such attachments as far as mobility is concerned.

Marriage and mobility

Berent undertook a study of the relationship between mobility and marriage. He found a high correlation between the status of marriage partners; but there was a tendency for women to marry into a social class above their own (e.g. the nurse who marries the doctor, the secretary who marries the director, etc.).

5 The consequences of social mobility

The process of mobility requires the capacity to leave behind one environment and adapt to a new one. It requires the ability to adopt new attitudes and values and to form new social relationships.

(i) Merton (*Social Theory and Social Structure*) has said that among the consequences of mobility may be an increase in the sense of **anomie**. That is the feeling that one no longer feels a part of a group with which one can identify.

(ii) People like to make use of a reference group as a guide to appropriate patterns of behaviour. This is known as **anticipatory socialization**. The upwardly mobile tend to adopt the patterns of behaviour relevant to the group they hope to join. One possible consequence of this may be that individuals or families are seen as 'deviant' within their traditional friendship groups (e.g. they may be viewing different TV programmes, reading different newspapers, etc.).

(iii) Increases in social mobility may affect the structure of the family system. Family members may become more geographically as well as socially mobile. This may hasten the break-up of the traditional extended family structure.

Some of the general conclusions about mobility in Britain

1 Education is probably the most significant of the variables affecting rates of mobility. Those with the highest qualifications have greatest occupational choice where there is a contest.

2 There is evidence that sponsored mobility remains a significant factor.

3 Changes in the economic and occupational structure will affect rates of mobility in that depression or increasing professionalization of jobs may limit chances of mobility.

4 There is no absolute agreement about how much mobility there is in Britain. The 1949 study suggested that most mobility was of a short-range type, with little long-range mobility across class lines.

5 The 1980 (Oxford Study) indicated that there was more long-range mobility (about 7%) and that there was more room at the top. Nevertheless they conclude that there has been little change in the relative chances of reaching the top of those born into different social classes.

6 All the evidence shows that it is easier for those born higher up the

social scale to increase their mobility into top positions than for those born into lower social classes.

7 All factors that increase a child's involvement with adults rather than with other children will increase their chances of becoming upwardly mobile. But these chances are related to the kind of social background from which they come and the motivation and encouragement which they receive.

8 Of the mobility that takes place in British society most seems to occur within class groups (movement from an unskilled to a skilled manual occupation, for example, or from a low level, white-collar occupation into a profession) rather than across class lines.

49 What factors determine changes in the rate of social mobility?

Key terms and concepts

The following terms and concepts have been defined and used in this chapter. You must be able to use them and explain their meaning for examination purposes:

mobility; inter-generational; intra-generational; sponsored mobility; contest mobility; anticipatory socialization; anomie.

You should also be able to define these terms:

economic structure   The kind of economic system which operates in the society. In Britain there is a mixed economy (both public, state-controlled and private enterprise). It is based on the principles of capitalism.

capitalism   An economic system in which the means of production is in the hands of private individuals who are free to employ labour and accumulate profits. It is possible to obtain unearned income through investments.

educational structure   The kind of educational system that operates in the society. The values and demands of the economic system will influence the educational structure.

the occupational structure   The occupations available in the society, their relative status and the access that people have to them.

reference group   The group with which a person compares his or her standing, behaviour, etc.

deferred gratification   The decision which some people make to put off until later in life the gaining of certain pleasurable rewards (e.g. preferring qualifications rather than high pay at the start of their working life).

8   Youth culture

The mass media and other commentators often refer to 'a youth culture' or 'a pop culture' or sometimes to 'an adolescent culture' or even to 'a counter culture'. This gives rise to several types of related questions in the examination papers. For example:

1 What is meant by the concept of a culture associated specifically with young people? (Also what do the terms culture and sub-culture mean?)
2 What are the possible explanations for the emergence of youth cultures?
3 What forms do youth cultures take?
4 What general conclusions can be drawn about the patterns of behaviour of young people in society in relation to those of older generations?

A typical question is:

50 'It is unclear when youth begins and ends. No clear dividing lines separate the varying stages (of life). . . . Modern society has few, if any, of those "rites of passage" which in many other societies mark the thresholds between clearly defined stages in the individual's progress through life. . . .'
   Berger and Berger, *Sociology: A Biographical Approach*, 1976

   (a) *What does the extract mean?*   *(5)*
   (b) *What is meant by 'youth culture'?*   *(5)*
   (c) *What arguments are offered relating to the possible existence of a youth culture in modern Britain?*   *(10)*   (AEB)

The term **youth** has no precise meaning. It is generally taken to mean that period between childhood and adulthood. The culture of youth refers to the accepted values, attitudes and patterns of behaviour associated with this youthful, adolescent section of society, which tends to be different in significant ways from the older, adult section of society.

The term **youth culture** implies the existence of a single all-embracing culture which is common to all young people because of their youthfulness. In fact it is more useful to consider the existence of many youth cultures. Some writers tend to use the term in its former sense (especially journalists in the mass media) whereas most sociologists use it in a more analytical way.

Milson (*Youth in a Changing Society*) provides a useful typology of youth groups in society in his analysis of youth cultures.

1 The **assenters** (the conforming members of youth)
   (a) The privileged (successful youth)
   (b) The unreflecting conformists
   (c) The ritualists (they are sometimes critical of aspects of society)
   (d) The strivers (the socially mobile youth)
   (e) The hedonists (those searching for pleasure and enjoyment)
2 The **experimenters**
   (a) The political revolutionaries (e.g. student protesters)
   (b) The personal revolutionaries (e.g. hippies)
3 The **socially rejected**
   (a) Delinquent youth
   (b) The escapists (e.g. drug-takers)
   (c) The disgruntled (the anti-social youth)

Milson argues that these types describe the various forms that the youth culture can take in society.

Possible reasons for the emergence of youth cultures

Different writers have put forward a variety of possible explanations. They include the following:

Hemmings writes of the period of adolescence as one when young people are questioning and criticizing. He says that every society has to absorb the effect of generation after generation of adolescents. This is good for society since they help to question and test pre-conceived values. Their basic needs are:

1 To establish personal independence;
2 To seek peer group acceptance;
3 To establish a sense of personal identity and if necessary to challenge authority.

He believes that youth turn to supportive cultures in order to cope with particular problems and find solutions to particular needs. The form they take depends on the kind of peer group to which the adolescent is attached.

Sugarman shares this view and suggests that the reason why the values and norms of youth are often in conflict with those of an older generation is because there are strong social pressures enforcing conformity among youth to the norms of their peers in preference to those of an adult culture.

Wilson (*Youth Culture and the Universities*) suggests that the youth culture has become more prevalent in Britain since 1945 as a result of major economic and social changes. It may be that the generation growing up in the 1950s was more idealistic, more economically independent and had greater access to influential literature and other sources as a result of the expansion of education than previous generations. There were more causes with which to identify (CND, Vietnam, race, etc.).

Jupp argues that young people were becoming more politically aware in the 1960s and 1970s, and many of the disruptions that occurred in the universities and colleges were the result. There was major student unrest in the USA in 1964, in Paris in 1968 and this spread to Britain in the 1970s.

Roszak (*The Making of a Counter Culture*) points out that the youth culture took another form among that section of youth who were looking for more personal solutions. Many young people in the 1960s and 1970s were increasingly opposed to the widespread materialistic philosophy of the time. They searched for alternatives and many tried new religious movements, drugs, etc.

Cohen (*Folk Devils and Moral Panics*) suggests that the concern about youth cultures may have emerged in recent years as a result of the way the mass media tend to make widespread use of the behaviour of youth as 'news'. This is because such behaviour tends:

1 To fit into their patterns of news values;
2 To fit in with the general public's expectations about 'how young people behave these days'.

It may be that to some extent the mass media have helped to create the youth cultures which they later come to report.

On the basis of this data consider how you would answer the following question:

51 *Not rebelliousness, but mass consumption and the mass media have created the youth culture.* (LON)

(NB: See also details on pp. 157–60.)

The significance of different types of music for youth cultures

One of the most important factors in almost every example of youth culture is a type of **music**. Often the music carries the culture in the sense that particular values are embodied in the lyrics and those who share the values also share a liking for the musical idiom and style and performers.

The hit parade was invented in the USA in the 1930s. Since then the pop market has become a phenomenon of almost every industrialized society. Many research studies into the forms of youth cultures illustrate the significance of music in the lives and life-styles of young people.

1 Murdock and McCron wished to see whether the generation that someone belongs to is more important than their social class in shaping their social behaviour or whether youth cultures vary according to the social class of the young people concerned.

They interviewed a national sample of secondary school children. They found the pupils divided pop music into four main categories: (i) top twenty pop; (ii) progressive music; (iii) reggae and soul; and (iv) family pop.

The researchers found that the mainly working-class children who did less well academically in school chose reggae and soul music whilst the more successful middle-class children preferred progressive music.

For both groups music was found to be an important expressive outlet denied by usual school values. They concluded that choice of music between the two groups was different and reaffirmed class divisions. They argue that social class factors remain very important in shaping their life-styles. The underlying attitudes and values of youth continue to be influenced by their class background. Rather than creating a classless society of the young, the authors find that different types of pop music emphasize the existence of class distinctions among youth.

2 Hebdige describes the emergence of Tamla Motown as being an important feature of the youth culture of working-class black Americans in the 1960s. It was an attempt to capture a particular market. Soul music was identified with hardship and life in the ghettos. Tamla Motown took up this theme and through the lyrics and the artists used made reference to black power and black causes. It advocated participation and involvement on the part of those who became absorbed in the music. Later, it became increasingly commercial in theme and output. The record producers made use of a formula so that all the music fitted a particular sound and rhythm which made it easily identifiable. Some commentators argue that Tamla Motown reflected the plight of black people in the USA at a

particular time: others argue that this music was simply a matter of commercial exploitation on the part of the media, who realized there was more money in dance music than almost any other kind.

3 Hall explains the relevance of reggae music for black youth in particular. This stemmed from the musical sub-culture of Jamaica. It is a product of poverty and deprivation. The music grew out of the context of slavery and colonization, and it makes constant reference back to these roots. There is a strong connection between reggae and Rastafarianism. This is the religious movement, founded by the Jamaican Marcus Garvey in the 1920s, which makes use of biblical prophecy to explain how eventually they will return to their homeland in Africa.

Reggae music takes up these themes and offers a means of critical commentary on the life-styles of poor blacks as well as promising salvation and the chance of a happier future.

52 'The main social division . . . was between the academically unsuccessful pupils who wanted to leave school as soon as possible, and the successful pupils who wanted to stay on, or had already done so. As might be expected, the "failures" were predominantly working class, while the "successes" were mostly middle class, with a smattering of working-class aspirants. The bulk of the early leavers preferred reggae and soul records, particularly the funkier versions. Also high up on the list were Motown performers and hard pop groups like Slade. Most of the actual and prospective sixth formers, on the other hand, said they preferred progressive records. . . . In our view, most commentators have seriously under-estimated the importance of class inequalities in shaping adolescents' lives and in limiting their responses. Although pop has undoubtedly extended the range of expressive styles open to adolescents, we would argue that their underlying values and definitions continue to come from class-based systems, rather than from pop. Our findings so far suggest that . . . pop is reaffirming class divisions.'

G. Murdock and R. McCron, Scoobies, skins and contemporary pop, *New Society*, 29 March 1973

(a) What view of 'pop' culture are the authors of this passage arguing against? *(4 marks)*
(b) What sort of evidence would be put forward in favour of the view which these authors reject? *(7 marks)*
(c) How could you investigate whether the claim that 'pop is reaffirming class divisions' is valid in 1979? *(9 marks)* (CAM)

A question like this one must be answered with care.

1 You must avoid allowing your own personal preferences from entering your answer. You must not get side-tracked into a discussion about the merits and weaknesses of particular groups. (You must allow for the fact that tastes change over time and the groups mentioned in the question may long since have disappeared.)

2 You must answer each part of the question by making the necessary deductions and inferences from the data provided.

In (a) are they arguing *against* the view that pop music is classless? In (b) you must consider the view they *reject* and offer some points that they may not have considered. For example, are young people aware of class differences? Do they tend to make use of them in their dealings with each other? Are there some groups made up of people from widely different class backgrounds that you can name? Do most pop groups seem to appeal to an audience across class lines? You must put your answers forward as speculations or as possible hypotheses about what may be the case.

In (c) you must suggest ways of undertaking a study into how you could actually find out whether or not pop music reaffirms class divisions. You must, therefore, bear in mind the methodology of sociology (see pp. 18–25).

    (a) What kind of method would you adopt?
    (b) How would you select your sample?
    (c) How would you test the hypothesis?

Notice that there are a lot of marks to be gained for this part of the question and so it must be answered in a careful and methodical way.
    Consider this more direct question:

53 *'Youth is classless.' Discuss using sociological evidence.* (LON)

Read pp. 99–101 carefully. Much of this detail can be used in your answers to these questions.

54 'The reaction to the growth of jazz in America from the 1920s onwards has been well-documented. Jazz was resisted because of its identification with the Negro, a low status group in society, and because of further identifications with crime, vice and greater sexual freedom. In addition, traditionally trained "classical" musicians opposed jazz because it appeared to violate both "classical" music standards and "classical" cultural standards, since it was not performed in concert halls. . . . The reactions of the musical establishment to the "rock revolution" were similar in that not only was the 1950s rock and roll seen as a gross violation

of traditional musical values, but also as a moral threat to the young people who represented the major part of its audience.'

G. Vulliamy, *What counts as school music?*, 1976

(a) *What evidence would you use to support the argument that 'classical' music still has a higher status in our society than other forms of musical expression?* *(8 marks)*

(b) *Only certain styles of popular music seem to be treated as a 'moral threat' to the young. Suggest reasons for this, using actual examples from the 1960s or 1970s.* *(12 marks)* (CAM)

Notice how the extract that forms the basis of this question also refers to the class divisions that arise in musical tastes.

In your answer to (a) you must be careful not to generalize about snobbishness in musical taste. Do not make use of anecdotes about the kinds of people you know who like classical music or certain kinds of pop music. You must relate your comments to sociological ideas about the significance of social class and status. You must comment on the ways that class membership informs people about how to behave and even what to think in certain situations. You must make the point that social class provides people with particular values and gives them a perspective on the world (see pp. 70–74).

For further ideas about answering section (b) read pp. 95–9 carefully.

Why is some music treated as a moral threat to the young?

1 Young makes the point that most pop music has its roots in black music, especially 'the blues' which was the music of slavery. As a result both youth and black people tend to be treated as 'a threat' to the established order. They are viewed, he says, with the same ambivalence, as happy go lucky, lazy, hedonistic – always searching for simple pleasures and as potentially dangerous. Loud, rhythmic, vivacious music is seen to epitomize the values of rebellion by an older generation.

2 Some musical idioms have become associated with deviant youth. Often this is the result of the use of stereotypes in the mass media of what such youth is assumed to be like. For example, jazz was associated with the use of drugs and a promiscuous style of life. Punk music became identified with rebellious anarchistic youth who wished to abandon all the acceptable rules of social behaviour. When rock and roll films were first shown in the 1950s there was some vandalism in cinemas. The music then became associated with destructive behaviour. But, there are many young people who enjoy all of these musical styles and who are not deviant in their social attitudes or behaviour.

3 In the eyes of some people in society reggae music has become
   identified with delinquent black youth. This is because of the
   connection with Rastafarianism whose members wear their hair in
   dreadlocks and may use drugs for religious purposes. In fact
   Rastafarianism actually preaches peace and equality to its adherents.
   Reggae music has developed from its original religious roots into a
   commercial form which is enjoying a large white following and a
   new interpretation by many white groups.

The forms that youth culture can take

Becker argues that people who share a culture share a body of knowledge
and understanding about how to behave and what to think in certain
situations. They share interpretations and solutions which arise from
their interactions as a group. Therefore, on this view, a culture can arise
where people come together for any length of time so that they develop
shared meanings and ways of coping with the situation in which they find
themselves. Thus, for children in school the exam system, teacher–pupil
relations, etc. all constitute 'a problem' which must be dealt with. The
culture that arises provides the solutions. These cultural interpretations
will vary between groups, school classes and across school years.

1 Hargreaves (*Deviance in Classrooms*) has taken up this idea and
   investigated the ways in which particular types of cultural values
   can arise in a school. He studied the cultural characteristics of a
   streamed secondary modern school, and found that from a
   knowledge of the stream it was possible to predict some of the main
   values held by the pupils.

   (a) The higher the stream, the more committed were the pupils to
       the values of the school. They were more regular in attendance
       and participated in more activities in school.
   (b) Movement towards the lowest stream reversed this trend.
   (c) The greater the distance between streams, the lower the
       proportion of friendship ties between streams.

2 Student culture: Joan Abott argues that identifiable cultural
   activities develop around students who:
   (a) Have a strong social conscience and who wish to work for a
       specific cause. These are **idealists**.
   (b) Wish to work within the existing social structure in a particular
       way. These are the **politically motivated**.
   (c) Have a clear view of their future careers and so work within the
       existing system to that end. These are the **vocationalists**.

3 Leech (*Youthquake*) writes about that section of youth that is specifically concerned with a spiritual quest. He notes how many young people are seeking a new life style based on religious values. He accepts that these are not always of an orthodox kind. But he argues that the search for salvation seems to be attracting a growing number of western civilization's alienated youth. He notes the prevalence of pop songs and musical shows with strong religious themes and how the young are increasingly attracted to new sectarian movements.

4 Frith describes the emergence of punk culture in the 1970s. He says that it was a largely working-class youth movement which arose in the art schools. Art schools have always been the source of most of the British youth cultural symbols. They have encouraged the questioning of traditional forms, values and beliefs. As a result they have encouraged the bizarre hair styles and clothes, etc. Frith believes that punk culture uses middle-class Bohemianism as its model – the view that life is for living in your own individual way without recourse to the norms of everyday society. The cultural significance of punk derives, therefore, not from its articulation of the experiences of unemployment, but from its attempt to become a working-class interpretation of the leisure activities of the traditional middle-class Bohemian rebels.

5 Roszak (*The Making of a Counter Culture*) argues that a section of youth is coming increasingly to oppose and reject the impersonal technocratic base of modern society. This is the source of much radical dissent among young people. He claims that in the 1960s and 1970s there was a generation of youth who were profoundly alienated from the parental generation. They have been intent on founding a counter culture which opposes traditional values.

Wilson sees the hippy culture of the 1960s and 1970s to be an example of these attitudes. He describes them as being largely non-political. Their slogans were focused on the war in Vietnam, the power of the police and restrictions on personal freedoms.

6 Cohen (*Folk Devils and Moral Panics*) explains how some sections of youth come to be associated in the eyes of the public with a deviant youth culture. He says that from time to time societies become subject to periods of moral panic. A condition, a person or group emerges to be defined as a threat to the main values of society. The mass media report the event within their news value system. The problem becomes exaggerated and the public more sensitized. Ways of coping are evolved and the condition eventually disappears – soon to be replaced by another.

He suggests that one of the most recurrent types of moral panic in Britain since the war has been associated with the emergence of various forms of youth culture. The result is that any young people who happen to be seen behaving in unusual or anti-social ways are quickly labelled as 'hooligans' or 'delinquents' and are categorized together in negative ways. He concludes that in the gallery of types that society erects to show its members which roles should be avoided and which emulated, these groups of youth have occupied a constant position as 'folk devils'; that is, visible reminders of what we should not be.

It may be that the majority of youth do not easily fit into any one of these categories. The numbers involved in such cultures are perhaps very small whilst the majority of youth generally conforms to the central values of society. Notice how Milson in his typology (see p. 93) has several categories of assenting youth. However, most writers agree that adolescence is a time of experimentation and of questioning and of establishing a sense of identity and future purpose. To this extent there are inevitably differences in patterns of behaviour between the younger and adult generations. Hence you would need to draw on all the foregoing discussion in a question such as:

55 *Newspapers often refer to the generation gap. How acceptable or useful do you find the phrase?*

Consider also some of the conclusions reached by Wilson (pp. 102–3). He suggests that to understand why youth cultural movements have predominated in recent years it is necessary to examine some of the processes of social change. These relate to changes in the social structure, in the work order, in the family and in wider social attitudes.

56 (i) 'For boys in the high streams, life at school will be a pleasant and rewarding experience, since the school system confers status upon them. The peer group values reflect the status bestowed on such boys by the school. Conformity to peer group values is thus consistent and rewarding.

In the low streams, boys are deprived of status in that they are double failures by their lack of ability or motivation to obtain entry to a grammar school *or* to a high stream in a secondary modern school. For boys in the low streams, conformity to teacher expectations gives little status.

There is a constant movement of boys between streams. Those with positive orientations towards the values of the school will tend to converge on the higher streams and those with negative orientations will tend to converge on the low streams. On every occasion that a boy is promoted or demoted, the greater becomes the concentration of the two opposing sub-cultures.'

Adapted from D. H. Hargreaves,
Social Relations in a Secondary School

(ii) 'In Hammerton Boys it was quite clear that oppositional groups had emerged under streaming by the end of the third year. However, after mixed ability grouping was introduced at the beginning of the fourth year, the counter school groups developed and hardened in exactly the same fashion as may have been expected under streaming. And those verging towards the anti-school outlook were, if anything, aided by the new forms of mixed ability grouping, topic centred teaching, and the obvious confusion caused by the high number of group changes during the course of the day.'

P. Willis, *Learning to Labour*

(a) *What do you understand by the term 'sub-culture' as used here? (4 marks)*
(b) *With reference to the extracts above and other relevant information, explain how the formation of sub-cultures among school pupils may be influenced by (i) factors internal to the school and (ii) factors beyond the school. (8 marks)*
(c) *Describe and account for the development of any one sub-cultural group you have studied. (It need not be a group formed within an educational institution.) (8 marks)* (CAM)

Notice how the ideas of Becker (p. 99) are useful in answering this question. Although at one level this seems to be a question about the educational structure, in fact the concept of culture and sub-culture is central to it.

In (b) (i) you are asked to consider how the organization of the school itself can give rise to cultural differences in attitudes among pupils. In (b) (ii) you must consider some of the other points that have been made about how youth cultures are shaped and influenced by factors relevant to the wider society (see pp. 93–4).

In (c) you are not presumed to have made a personal study of a particular youth group. You are being asked to discuss an example of *one* particular group which you have read about and about which you have some fairly precise detail. For example, the work of Cohen, Leech or Frith would be useful here. Ideally, you should look at their books and articles for details. They are readable and they should be accessible in local libraries.

Wilson considers some of the following factors to be significant:

1 There have been more liberal child-rearing practices.
2 There have been more child-centred teaching methods.
3 There has been much social legislation with an increasing emphasis on social justice.
4 There has been an economic boom and decline accompanied by some national demoralization.

5 There has been an increasing emphasis on hedonistic attitudes among young people. They have become more economically independent.
6 There has been more idealism among some sections of youth in recent years, and they have enjoyed improved educational opportunities.
7 The mass media are an important element in moulding contemporary modes of disenchantment and social unrest. The new agents of acculturation have become a professional body of communicators whose interests are to arouse the emotions rather than to inform the mind.
8 Work has become more routinized and rationalized which may have served to diminish the intrinsic levels of interest young people have in work. As a result they turn to their own activities in their free time.
9 There may have developed a breakdown of trust between the younger and older generation – who are seen by the young to have caused most of the problems that face them in a modern world.
10 He acknowledges the extent to which people can be pressured and guided into patterns of behaviour by processes of which they are largely unaware: by peer group pressure, by the influence of the media, etc.

Key terms and concepts

The following terms and concepts have been used and defined in this chapter. You must be able to use them and explain their meaning for examination purposes:

youth culture; adolescent; typology; poverty; deprivation; norms.

Other terms which you may wish to use:

deviant Person who does not conform to the norms of the group or society to which he or she belongs.
hedonist One who searches all the time for the most pleasurable experiences.
counter culture A culture that is in opposition to the values of the dominant social culture.
sub-culture The culture of a specific sector of society which differs in certain ways from the culture of the rest of society.

9 Work

Work is a central feature of life in a modern industrial society. This is because **wage labour** is the basis of the economic system: work is a source of income and of physical survival. It may also serve to satisfy other social needs.

Sociologists who study this aspect of social life are interested to find answers to such questions as:

1 What are the factors that influence a person's choice of work?
2 What factors determine a person's attitude to their work?
3 Where people are dissatisfied in work how can they be motivated?
4 What influence does a person's work have on other aspects of their day-to-day behaviour?
5 What effects do changes in work structures and technologies have on workers?

Examination questions tend to focus on these general areas.

57 *How do sociologists explain why some people dislike their jobs whilst others enjoy theirs?* (LON)
58 *What are the major factors which produce low job satisfaction?* (OX)

These questions require you to make a careful analysis in terms of

1 The meaning of work;
2 An explanation of the term 'job satisfaction' and its relationship to people's expectations about the nature of work;
3 The concepts that sociologists use to describe the different attitudes people have to work;
4 The meaning of industrialization; division of labour;
5 The attempts made to motivate dissatisfied workers.

What is meant by work?

Parker (*The Future of Work and Leisure*) explains that work is an activity involving contractual obligations between an **employer** and an

employee. The employee accepts particular constraints and obligations in the process of earning his or her living. In return they get an agreed rate of pay. In the same way the employer is also bound by the **contract**.

Work is a relative term which is definable in a society according to its norms and accepted cultural standards and practices. There may be no universally accepted definition of what constitutes 'real' work.

In general terms work may be said to be a social activity with the functions of producing:

1 Goods required by society;
2 A more stable and integrated society as a result of the interactions and interrelationships that develop among working people so that they become dependent on each other.

Brown (*The Social Psychology of Industry*) makes the point that work is an essential part of man's life since it is that aspect of his life which gives him status and binds him more closely into society.

Industrialization

The **industrial revolution** began first in Britain in the eighteenth century, then in Western Europe and later in the USA. Production is taken from the home or small-scale group and conducted in a factory or in workshops. These become the specialized economic institutions. In the twentieth century many other societies have had industrial revolutions, including the USSR, China, Japan, parts of Africa and South America. Industrialization has several important consequences for a society's economic structure. In Britain they have included the following:

1 The **division of labour** has increased.
2 The **size** of industries has increased.
3 Impersonal, secondary relationships have come to predominate in work.
4 There has been an increase in **industrial conflict**.
5 Mass employment has meant that workers have insisted on the right to be able to combine together into powerful **trade unions**.
6 People have more access to goods and services so that living standards are raised.
7 There has been an increase in levels of affluence.
8 New technologies and methods of production are constantly being developed in order to maximize production efficiency.

The division of labour

A modern economic system needs to be efficient in the production of goods. The division of labour means that instead of many workers producing a variety of goods to satisfy their own needs they are employed to produce only a small part of the total product. For example, many thousands of workers may be involved in the construction of a very complicated product by each contributing in a different way to its completion. A car assembly line is a typical example of this process.

The advantages of the division of labour

1 The work is generally very repetitive, therefore it is not necessary to employ workers with high level skills or qualifications.
2 A highly complex item can be produced comparatively cheaply and reach a wide number of consumers.
3 Mass production helps to raise living standards.
4 At times of economic boom specialization of labour helps ensure high levels of employment.

The disadvantages of the division of labour

1 The work is generally repetitive, uninteresting and does not require specialized qualifications. The skills are learnt through brief training or by repetition over time.
2 When mass production techniques are used, as in the production of cars, televisions, etc., the work is normally based on a conveyor belt system. This sets the pace of the work and controls speed of output. Workers may come to see themselves as being controlled by the machines.
3 Industrial conflicts, disputes, strikes, etc. are more frequent in such working environments.
4 There may be a loss in traditional skills associated with cottage industries since products are mass-produced. The work of craftsmen are in less demand, their products take a long time to complete and they are more expensive than similar ones produced by machine.
5 Where labour is divided in the production of a particular item many of the workers involved may not see the finished unit, for it may pass through many workshops before completion. They do not have any particular pride in their work if they are responsible for only one particular component.

Mechanization

This term is used to describe the techniques of mass production in a factory based on the division of labour around conveyor belts. Henry Ford invented the assembly line system in the early part of the twentieth century. He disciplined young boys with little knowledge of the technical details of the product to repeat simple tasks as the skeleton of a car passed them on the conveyor belt. It is a method which has been developed in every highly industrialized society since that time.

Job satisfaction

Many sociologists who study the social structures, relationships and problems associated with people in work are interested to know why so many seem bored and disillusioned. It is generally true that each year more days are lost through sickness and absenteeism than through strikes. Some writers suggest that each of these factors is a symptom of dissatisfaction with work.

Herzberg (*The Motivation to Work*) says there are five factors which give workers a sense of satisfaction in work:

1 Where the worker obtains a sense of pride in his job;
2 When he obtains praise and compliments for his work;
3 When he obtains special trust or responsibility;
4 When it is possible to obtain promotion or a new challenge;
5 When the work is intrinsically interesting.

Attitudes towards work

Sociologists have identified three different attitudes towards work:

1 **Intrinsic satisfaction**   This is where a person gains enjoyment for its own sake from the work. It satisfies the worker's expectations. It is most likely to occur where the job is freely chosen and it meets most of the points made by Herzberg. High pay may not be crucial to the individual because the job itself is felt to be worth doing. It is an attitude found most strongly among white-collar workers.
2 **Extrinsic satisfaction** (or an instrumental attitude)   This arises where the individual has no real interest in the work itself. It is only undertaken for the rewards it offers beyond the job. It may offer high pay, much free time, etc. Those who hold such attitudes seldom have much choice in selecting a job and so are less likely to gain intrinsic satisfaction from it. It is therefore more common among lower level blue-collar workers.

3 **The Protestant Ethic** Some people may not gain much intrinsic satisfaction from their work and may not only seek extrinsic reward. They feel that it is morally virtuous to work; failure to work is socially degrading. It is the view that everyone should work to the best of their abilities regardless of the nature of the work in order to prove their worth as a citizen of the society in which they live. This view reflects the teaching of Luther and Calvin in the sixteenth century who established the 'Protestant Ethic'. It is epitomized in a maxim like 'the devil makes work for idle hands'.

Factors affecting attitudes towards work

Generally, jobs that have high levels of social status provide wider scope for obtaining intrinsic satisfaction than those with low status.

Fox (*A Sociology of Work in Industry*) makes the point that the goals a person seeks are taken from the groups of which they have been members. People learn particular responses, accept certain values and live up to the expectations which others have of them. The individual learns to want and seek those things they come to see that they are 'supposed' to want according to the standards of their family, friends and reference group. Three important factors affecting attitudes, therefore, are:

1 **Social class background** This helps to determine a person's horizon of expectation, which fixes an estimation of worth and potential. It helps specify the kind of work the individual believes they ought to do and would be capable of doing; that is, the kind of work that a person of their social background should aim at. Some occupations are seen to be unsuitable because they are associated with others of a higher (or lower) social class than themselves. For example:

Social class of medical students, 1966 (%)

Class 1	Class 2	Class 3	Classes 4 and 5
39.6	36.2	21.7	2.5

Source: Social Trends

2 **Education** One of the significant norms of social classes 4 and 5 is that education has a largely extrinsic or instrumental worth. Whereas to obtain high level, professional qualifications it is necessary to see education as having some intrinsic worth. This is one of the dominant values of class 1 and 2. Proportions going into semi and unskilled work declines steeply as age of leaving school increases.

3 The work experience The employee who finds intrinsic
satisfaction in work will develop more interest and enthusiasm
because there is more personal satisfaction and fulfilment. High pay
is not necessarily a key factor in determining level of interest. The
work tends to give more scope to develop the individual's
personality and social skills.

   The employee who finds work distasteful, monotonous and
routine is likely to develop extrinsic attitudes. They cannot develop
all their abilities and aptitudes. High pay becomes important as a
means of justifying tedious work.

You should now have the basis of the answers to the following
questions as well as those on p. 104.

59 *What do you understand by the term 'division of labour'? Illustrate
   your answer with reference to any one industry or occupation.* (OX)
60 *Discuss the suggestion that the division of labour is the main cause of
   dissatisfaction at work.* (OX)
61 *Explain what is meant by the division of labour and comment on any
   four of its disadvantages.* (WEL)
62 *'I work in a factory. For eight hours a day, five days a week, and I
   begrudge every precious minute of my time that it takes. My
   working-day starts with that time-honoured ritual known as
   'clocking in'. After clocking in one starts work. Starts work, that is,
   if the lavatories are full. . . . After the visit to the lavatory there is
   the tea-break to look forward to; after the tea-break the dinner-
   break; after the dinner-break the 'knocking-off' time. Work is done
   between the breaks, but it is done from habit and is given hardly a
   passing thought. Nothing is gained from the work itself. . . . The
   criterion is not to do a job well, but to get it over with quickly. . . .
   People who speak grandiosely of the 'meaning of work' should
   spend a year or two in a factory. The modern worker neither gives
   anything to work nor expects anything (apart from his wages) from
   it. Work, at factory level, has no inherent value. The worker's one
   interest is his pay-packet.'*

                                                        R. Fraser, *Work*

   (a) *What evidence is there in the passage that the writer has a purely
       'instrumental' attitude towards work? (2 marks)*
   (b) *What aspects of industrialization are usually considered to have
       reduced the amount of satisfaction which people get from their
       work? (9 marks)*
   (c) *Production line workers are often thought to have less job
       satisfaction than other workers. In what ways might this situation
       be altered? (9 marks)* (CAM)

The details that are required in the answers to parts (a) and (b) have been discussed. In order to answer part (c) you should consider the following points:

How can workers be motivated?

A report by the Office of Health Economics (1973) said that one of the most significant factors associated with sickness absence is lack of job satisfaction. The key to overcoming the problem is in the hands of management. Studies by the Work Research unit, set up in 1974, and by researchers such as Daniel, Fox, Lupton and Benyon have resulted in many suggestions for making tedious work more interesting.

The key factors have been identified as the need to increase the worker's sense of responsibility, achievement and variety of skills as well as being able to control the pace of work where possible and to develop more intrinsic satisfaction in work. Some of the ideas that have been tried include:

1 **Job rotation scheme**   Workers are trained to tackle a variety of jobs rather than one repetitive routine. It is a method pioneered by Volvo in Sweden.
2 **Worker participation schemes**   These include having men from the shopfloor elected to the Board of Directors so that they have a voice in the decision-making process. They may also include profit-sharing schemes and cooperative undertakings where the workers themselves run the firm. These have met with varying levels of success in Britain. One attempt in Spain, in Mondragon, has been successful over a long period.
3 **A four-day week and 'flexi-hours'**   These systems provide the workers with more free time and more control over the length of their working week.
4 **Improved work conditions**   These have helped to make the experience of work more pleasurable for some workers. They are provided with better eating, sporting facilities, etc.
5 **Changes in technology**   These have been introduced in recent years in an attempt to replace the assembly line with systems that place more emphasis on individual involvement. In some Swedish car factories men work in small teams in order to complete an entire car. All the parts are brought to their section of the shopfloor for construction. There has also been increasing emphasis on automation as a method of production. There is much debate about whether this does rehumanize tedious work or whether it makes work even less interesting.

There is some evidence to suggest that some of these attempts have been successful: absenteeism and sickness rates have diminished and rates of industrial conflict lowered. Other attempts have been less successful. Job rotation schemes may be expensive for a firm to introduce and less efficient results may occur. Few of the cooperatives in Britain have survived for long. However, such moves are regarded as helpful attempts on the part of managers who generally enjoy their work to understand the problems of many shopfloor workers who often do not enjoy theirs.

A further set of questions arise from discussion of the significance of the introduction of new technologies. These generally relate to their effects on the attitudes and patterns of behaviour of the workers to experience them. For example, consider the following questions:

63 *What effect does automation have on job satisfaction?*
64 *The division of labour and automation may make for more efficient production but only at the cost of more boring work and dissatisfied workers. Discuss.* (OX)
65 *How would you distinguish between mechanization and automation?*
66 *Outline and comment on any three social consequences of technological change in British society.*   (WEL)
67 *'Automation is the name given to industrial processes which use machinery and computers not only to make goods but also to control, by "feed-back" mechanisms, the rate of production, the input of raw materials and the coordination of separate processes. In automated factories less manpower is needed, but workers have to understand the whole process and their responsibility is much greater.' Is automation a curse or a blessing?*

Notice how this last question provides you with a good deal of important information as to what **automation** means. Although there is a lengthy quotation which you must read carefully this is certainly a question which you should consider answering in an exam since it provides you with so many important pointers as to what should go in your answer. The question reminds you (in ways that the previous questions do not) that:

1 There is a special definition of automation.
2 There are some advantages to automated processes.
3 There are some disadvantages.
4 The question focuses on the debate about the merits and weaknesses of the system.

The effects of new technologies on workers

Ogburn (*Social Change*) says that each technical invention has an effect on those who use it and the society must adjust to it. The long-term effects of new technology may have significance for every feature of the social structure.

Woodward has developed a typology in which she analyses the behaviour of workers in terms of the technology used. She describes these as (i) **craft or unit methods**, in which there is little or no division of labour. The initial craftsman is responsible for the construction of the whole item; (ii) **mass production**, in which goods are produced by the conveyor belt system, (iii) **process** or **automated production**.

She draws attention to the fact that mechanization is not the same thing as complete automation. **Automation** is a recent piece of terminology to describe the production and control of output by a machine with minimum human supervision. In an ideal case automation implies the complete control over its own actions from beginning to end. Automation is prominent in many kitchens where fully automated washing machines and central heating systems operate.

The term was coined in 1946 by Delmer Harder who devised an automated process for the Ford Motor Company to manufacture car engines. One engine was produced in less than 15 minutes whereas before it had taken 20 hours. By 1972 they claimed to have the fastest and most automated production line in the world.

Daniel has conducted research into the effects of introducing automation into a factory on the attitudes of workers. He notes that there is much debate as to the advantages and disadvantages. They include the following:

The advantages

1 Workers who were previously involved in repetitive, monotonous work may find automation an improvement because they are no longer tied to one point on the factory floor.
2 The worker does not have to repeat one simple set of tasks.
3 The worker is not controlled by the pace and rhythm of the production line.
4 The worker may become a part of the production team. If there is a problem it may require team work to solve it.
5 In such circumstances the worker may have more responsibility than before.
6 In automated processes workers are generally relieved of particularly dangerous or unpleasant tasks since these are now completed by machine. Nevertheless, the worker must be alert to crisis and problems.

The disadvantages

1 The worker may have very little to do throughout the day or night whilst on duty, other than watch dials and press buttons.

2 Some workers may find that they have become de-skilled; that is, the automated processes may not require employees who have been highly trained or those with specialized qualifications.
3 Such workers may have little pride or interest in their work since all the construction is done by machine.
4 Fewer employees are required in automated industries.
5 Many workers may feel less sense of involvement in the work since the machines may be regarded as largely infallible. Also the workers may have little knowledge of the technology which they are supervising.
6 Automated industries may require more shift-work than other forms of production which may not be to the liking of employees.

Daniel's conclusion was that the men he interviewed who lacked formal educational and work qualifications found automation an advantage for them. The work was richer in intrinsic reward than any other kind that they might have had. On the other hand, he found that for those workers who had previously been employed in skilled occupations or who had ambitions to make use of other qualifications which they held, then the automated production system offered them less. They tended to emphasize the disadvantages.

The microchip

This is sometimes known as 'the integrated circuit' or 'the silicon chip' (silicon is the chemical element which forms the basis of the microcircuits). There has been a great deal of debate about the significance of the development of the microchip in recent years.

Some possible disadvantages

1 Guest (in a *New Society* article) has said that in the 1980s electronic microprocessors are on the point of causing a technological revolution. He showed concern about the possible increase in unemployment. As many as five million people could be put out of work by the turn of the century. The point is made by critics that the reprogramming of a robot on an assembly line may be cheaper than retraining a worker. Many office jobs would also be under threat.
2 The microchip may de-skill workers in that it becomes unnecessary to have high-level technical skills in fields where microprocessors are used. A semi-skilled maintenance man may be required to replace new printed circuits where necessary.
3 Daily life may become less interesting. A host of services previously requiring the individual's personal attention may be done without

leaving the home by operating simple computers: e.g. ordering goods from shops, paying bills, obtaining news, etc.
4 Less social interaction may result. Some writers have predicted that more daily work could be conducted from homes using microprocessors. Indeed, some have concluded that the results could be to produce a race of home-bound, slack-muscled mental defectives, since so few demands would be made of individuals to negotiate and think deeply about normal problems of daily life.
5 The large urban city that resulted from the industrial revolution may change. The increasing use of the microchip in work could result in smaller workforces, smaller firms requiring fewer of the immediate facilities of large cities. The move away from urban centres of sources of work would cause de-population, a falling off in available revenue for local authorities and a change in the social and economic structure of the city.

Some of the possible advantages

1 A report from Manchester University (1980) suggests that fears about large-scale unemployment resulting from the use of the microchip are probably exaggerated. Some industries may be more adversely affected than others (e.g. textiles may require 40% fewer employees; in mechanical engineering it may be less than 10% fewer workers required by the end of the century).
2 Johnston (*Who's Afraid of the Microchip*) says that the new technology will also create many new jobs.
3 Freeman (Sussex University) suggests that the values of the microchip in schools, the home and in work outweigh the disadvantages. There will be increased efficiency wherever they are used. Any job that relies on information can be done more easily and accurately through microelectronics. In the home, for example, there would be increased efficiency. Fuel use, bills and costs could be monitored; there would be better security systems available, etc.
4 Work may become more interesting and stimulating when the computer is used to deal with the repetitive office tasks. Children in schools may find lessons using computers more valuable, etc.
5 Where there is urban de-population and rural growth there may develop a greater sense of community spirit and a falling off in social problems associated with life in crowded cities.

Conclusion

Freeman has said that no one has really produced a clear model of all the possible effects and consequences of the new technological change associated with the microprocessor. Much more research is needed and people need to be better informed through the mass media as to the possible outcomes.

When revising this topic of the sociology of work it is helpful for you to see how there is one important theme which frequently gives rise to examination questions. This is a discussion of how people's **attitudes** to their work and their **behaviour** outside work are related to the ways in which the work is **organized**. Hence the significance of (i) the division of labour and (ii) the effects of new technologies. There is a third related factor: that is the concept of **alienation**. This relates to the negative experience which many people have of their formal day-to-day work.

These three factors often overlap. Sometimes questions require specific knowledge of one part or sometimes the other concepts are related in the question and a wider discussion is required. For example:

68 *Explain the difference between automation and alienation.*
69 *What are the factors which produce low job satisfaction? What is the relationship between the division of labour and alienation?*

Alienation

Marx was among the first to discuss the concept of alienation. Subsequent sociologists and other social scientists have attempted to make a more careful analysis of its implications.

Marx described two social classes: those who owned the means of production (the **bourgeoisie**) and those who had only their labour to sell (the **proletariat**). He said that the labourer received a means of subsistence in exchange for his labour. The capitalist owner received the productive work of the labourer. It was his argument that few of the proletariat could hope to gain any real satisfaction from their work since they were always employed by others who controlled their means of existence.

His concept of the alienation of workers stems from this view. It is the idea that mundane and unpleasant work alienates the worker from his true noble nature and from a sense of his own worth and ability as a member of society. For him alienation consists of the following:

1 The worker gains no sense of personal value or worth from work.
2 The worker has a constant sense of misery, unhappiness or futility in work.
3 The worker has no driving physical or mental energy in work and little motivation to work hard or efficiently.
4 The worker doing menial work is debased and humiliated.

5 The greatest satisfaction comes during leisure time.
6 The work is not done out of a sense of interest and is seldom a voluntary choice. It is more frequently taken out of necessity and is therefore a form of forced labour.
7 The work does not provide intrinsic satisfaction but is always of instrumental value in satisfying other needs.
8 The alien character of such work is shown by the fact that when there is no compulsion it is avoided like the plague.
9 For Marx work is alienating for the worker because at the work place the worker belongs to another person.
10 He concludes that it follows that man's existence in society is regarded purely as an economic factor. He saw private property as the product, the result, the necessary consequence of alienated labour and, in the alienation of man from man, the germ of class division.

Marx went on to say that the man of modern industrial society remains imprisoned for the greater part of his existence by his reliance on others for employment and by the specialized nature of work resulting from the division of labour. This causes him to leave unused a number of aptitudes and abilities. Labour for Marx was alienated when it became a commodity sold to others. When it was not a form of self-expression the worker lost his sense of individual identity. However, he sees alienation as a temporary condition associated with the nature of capitalist society.

Many writers have subsequently criticized the Marxian notion. They argue that it is too vague, it is not open to quantification or precise definition. For example, Fox says that it cannot simply mean 'lack of fulfilment in work' since this would also make the eager young executive who is frustrated in his ambition an alienated worker.

Blauner (*Alienation and Freedom*) has attempted to overcome some of these criticisms. He attempts to give the concept more precise definition. He argues that it is helpful to analyse the term with reference to five factors. Do the workers appear to feel a sense of:

1 **Powerlessness**   When the worker becomes manipulated by others or by an impersonal system of authority and control. Then he feels he is a cog in a machine. He cannot control the pace of work or the quality of production.
2 **Meaninglessness**   The worker lacks a sense of purpose or value in the work. It could be done by machine. There may be no finished product to see. The individual's part in the production of the goods is small and gives no sense of satisfaction.
3 **Isolation**   The worker feels no real sense of commitment to the firm. There is no pride in being an employee. The worker may also

be physically isolated from fellow work mates by distance or by noise.

4 Normlessness   The worker does not share the goals of the employer. He is not committed to the same values or aims and his own normative values may be in conflict with those of the employer.

5 Self-estrangement   The worker feels debased by the limited nature of the work. It does not express anything of his true abilities. He feels unhappy and disgruntled. The work has only extrinsic worth.

Key terms and concepts

The following terms and concepts have been used and defined in this chapter. You must be able to use them and explain their meaning for examination purposes:

work; job satisfaction; division of labour; mechanization; intrinsic satisfaction; extrinsic satisfaction; the Protestant Ethic; worker participation; automation (process production); mass production; microchip; alienation; self-estrangement; technological change.

10   Trade unions

Questions on this area of industrial relations are not asked with great regularity by all the examination boards. For example, questions appear very frequently on the Oxford papers whereas there are seldom any questions on the nature of trade unions or the extent of strike activity on AEB papers.

However, where they do appear, questions are centred on four main areas:

1 the nature and function of trade unions;
2 the role of the shop steward;
3 changes in trade union membership over time;
4 the causes and extent of strike activity in Britain.

The following two questions are examples from the first area.

70 *What services do trade unions perform for their members? What part do trade unions play in the British system of industrial relations?*
    (OX)
71 *What is a trade union? Describe and comment on any three functions of trade unions.*   (WEL)

Definition

Trade unions are organizations of workers who join together (usually within a particular industry or type of occupation) for the purpose of taking **collective action** when their interests are threatened.

They are concerned with problems of **working conditions**, **wage rates** and other **internal disputes**. The effectiveness of a trade union depends on its **size of membership**, the **nature** of the work around which the union is organized and the ability of its officers to **negotiate**.

The Webbs (1920) defined a trade union as 'a continuous association of wage earners for the purpose of maintaining or improving the conditions of their working lives'. A Royal Commission (1968) said a trade union was 'a combination of employees, the principal activity of which is the regulation of relations between employees and employers'.

The origin of trade unions

Williamson (*The Trade Unions*) says that although combinations of workers have existed since medieval times, modern unions essentially resulted from the spread of the industrial revolution and the growth of the factory system in the nineteenth century. The dominant features of work during the early years of industrialization were long hours, low wages and poor conditions. On his own the working man had little chance to effect change in his circumstances. So workers attempted to act together in order to exert power.

Important dates in the development of trade unions

You would not be expected to list these in an examination answer, but you may find it necessary or useful to refer to some of them in the course of an answer.

1799 ⎫
1800 ⎭ Combination Acts made associations of workers illegal.

1824   Combination Acts repealed.

1834   The Tolpuddle Martyrs. Six Dorchester farm labourers were transported to Australia for forming a 'union'.

1868   Trades Union Congress formed.

1876   Trade Union Act legalized unions and picketing.

1900   Taff Vale Judgement: Unions were liable to repay employers for losses suffered from a strike.

1906   Trade Disputes Act reversed this judgement.

1927   General Strike when the Government cut wages of some industrial workers and made general strikes illegal.

1968   Donovan Commission Report. It said that Britain suffered from too many strikes.

1971   Industrial Relations Act passed by the Conservative Government to limit the power of unions.

1974   The miners' strike helped defeat the Conservative Government.

1975   Bullock Committee said there should be more democracy in industry with workers on the Boards of companies.

1981   The Government proposes new legislation to limit union activities: no secondary picketing and no political strikes.

Trade union organization

There are four main types of union.

1 **Craft unions**   Members are generally skilled (having acquired a trade or craft through a period of apprenticeship). The

Amalgamated Society of Locomotive Engineers and Firemen (ASLEF) is an example. Craft unions cover a single trade and include many of the oldest unions.

2 **General unions**   Members are often semi-skilled or unskilled, e.g. the Transport and General Workers' Union (TGWU), who work in many different occupations within different industries. As a result their actions are often very effective because they can disrupt many different industries at once.

3 **Industrial unions**   They are usually found within one particular industry, for example the National Union of Railwaymen (NUR). They may often be in conflict with a craft union in a job demarcation dispute.

4 **White-collar unions**   These usually form round a single profession or occupation, e.g. The National Union of Teachers (NUT). They are generally less militant than the first three types of union.

The structure of trade unions

1 **The national executive**   This provides the leadership.
2 **The area committee**   This controls the local organization.
3 **Local branches**   Members meet to discuss problems.

Unions, like all administrative bodies, have sets of rules and regulations which determine the ways in which they run their affairs. All important issues are discussed at the Annual Conference.

Criticisms of trade unions

1 They cannot always prevent unofficial strikes (which form 95% of all strikes).
2 Those in key industries have exceptional bargaining power.
3 They are often slow to deal with problems because of their bureaucratic structure.

The main functions of unions

1 Act as pressure groups on both employers and government;
2 Help to improve conditions at work;
3 Provide strike pay during official disputes;
4 Provide members with legal advice;
5 Provide further training and education for some members;

6 Advise on health and safety at work;
7 Support the Labour Party financially.

Types of industrial action

1 Official strikes;
2 Unofficial strikes;
3 Token strikes;
4 Overtime ban;
5 Go-slow (or work-to-rule);
6 Sympathetic action;
7 Blacking of goods from companies who have helped break a strike.

The shop stewards

They are elected by the workers on the shopfloor to act as a link with the full-time officials in the union branch office. Shop stewards' main functions are:

1 To act as a spokesman for the workers;
2 To serve on works committees;
3 To give advice to employees on problems with their work;
4 To deal with union matters;
5 To raise funds for the union.

Jackson (*Industrial Relations*) points out that in recent years shop steward activity has become better organized. The Royal Commission (1968) found that two-thirds of the managers interviewed had shop stewards operating in their plants.

Changes in trade union membership

Trade union membership, Great Britain 1900–80

	1900	1910	1920	1930	1940	1950	1960	1970	1980
Trade unions	1323	1269	1384	1121	1004	732	664	532	430
Members (millions)	2.0	2.5	8.3	4.8	6.6	9.3	9.8	11.1	12.0

Source: Social Trends

72 *Outline the main changes which have taken place in the distribution of trade union membership since 1900.*

If the question does not include a table of statistical data then you will certainly require detail such as that shown in the table in order to answer such a question.

1 The table shows that there has been a growth in trade union membership and a decline in the number of trade unions. This is the result of regular amalgamations of unions. (There was legislation which encouraged this in 1917 and 1964.)
2 Union membership can be badly affected in times of economic depression (note the decline between 1920 and 1930; a loss is likely in the 1980s because of the high levels of unemployment).
3 The power and effectiveness of unions can be affected by changes in legislation (note the anti-trade union judgements and laws of 1900, 1927 and 1971). These may discourage membership.
4 The general trend has been towards a smaller number of very large unions. In 1900 the average membership of a union was 2000; in 1920, 6000; in 1975, 25,000.
5 In Britain today the largest unions are those that represent manual workers in industrial occupations. There are 11 unions that have a membership of more than 250,000. Together they account for more than seven million members. The largest unions are:

Transport and General Workers' Union (TGWU)   1.75m
Amalgamated Union of Engineering Workers (AUEW)   1.25m
National Union of General and Municipal Workers (GMWU) 0.75m

6 There has been a major growth in the membership of white-collar trade unions, particularly since 1945.

White-collar trade union membership, Great Britain 1948–70 (thousands)

	1948	1964	1970	% increase 1948–64	% increase 1964–70
White-collar membership	1.9	2.6	3.5	33.6	34.6
Blue-collar membership	7.4	7.44	7.45	0.6	0.2
Total union membership	9.3	10.0	10.9		

On the basis of the facts shown in the table you could be asked:

73 *Explain why there has been such a large increase in white-collar trade unionism since 1945.* (OX)

The following points should be raised in an answer:

1 There has been an increase in the number of white-collar workers in recent years. There has been an expansion in the number of

teachers, civil servants, scientific workers, etc. These have required more protection and control over their specific interests.

2 This increase is also associated with improved opportunities for social mobility. More workers have moved into white-collar jobs from manual occupations. They may be more trade-union minded.

3 Unionization of white-collar workers has occurred particularly in those industries where there are large numbers of people employed in similar kinds of work and where the employees themselves are keen to recognize the value of union protection. In recent years there have been successful strikes and other disruptions by teachers, civil servants, journalists, social workers and air traffic controllers.

4 In the 1970s and 1980s there have been steady attempts by white-collar groups to professionalize their occupations. This has also been encouraged by the trade unions.

5 During the 1960s and 1970s the blue-collar unions were successful in gaining great benefits for their members, and it may be that from this white-collar workers saw the advantages of union membership.

The overall result of these factors is that in the 1980s white-collar workers account for more than one-third of all union members.

74 'The National Association of Head Teachers wants to put teachers on a level with doctors and lawyers, with their own code of professional conduct and a self-disciplining council able to take over from the local authorities and the state the power to deny employment to teachers . . . the National Union of Teachers . . . have no time for a Secretary of State who tries to dictate the curriculum or to test the abilities of the children under her ultimate care. Neither does the NUT look with favour on the Taylor Report which offers parents and local interest groups greater say in the running of schools. Such . . . proposals would undermine the professional status of teachers. It is perhaps a pity that teachers made their bid for professional status so soon after the resolution of an old-fashioned pay dispute in which they used, with considerable disruptive effect, a strictly unprofessional, blue-collar weapon, the work-to-rule. It is hard to claim, in almost the same breath, that you are a professional person with all the moral – indeed professional – standards that such a claim implies and to quote your rule book as you walk off the job at lunchtime leaving the kids to fend for themselves.'

Extract from a leading article in *The Guardian*, 29 March 1978

(a) *To what extent would sociologists agree with this writer's view of the characteristics of a profession?* (5 marks)

(b) *Teaching is sometimes called a 'semi-profession'. What does this*

> mean? Give examples of other occupations which come into this
> category. (5 marks)
>
> (c) To what extent has the distinction between professional
> associations and trade unions disappeared in recent years? (10
> marks) (CAM)

What is meant by a profession?

Greenwood has suggested that professions can be identified by seeing to
what extent they display the following characteristics:

1 Members have high social status. Professions are generally seen to
  be among the most difficult occupations to enter (doctors, lawyers,
  university lecturers, etc.).
2 As a result of their high status they are afforded more social honour,
  power and prestige than those in most other occupations.
3 Members of professions have high academic qualifications as well as
  practical experience. (Doctors and lawyers must study for at least
  seven years before becoming qualified.)
4 Membership of a profession gives specialized knowledge of which
  the layman is ignorant and often legally prevented from obtaining.
  (Only lawyers can draw up specialized legal documents: only
  doctors have access to particular medicines.)
5 Among the special privileges of a professional is that of
  confidentiality between themselves and their clients or patients.
  This is a feature of a relationship which does not occur in many
  non-professional occupations. (Confidentiality is not required of a
  plumber or an electrician.)
6 Members of a profession tend to share a specific culture. This may
  include a particular dress (judges wear wig and gown), a set of
  values about their role and value in society, and a shared set of
  norms about how to behave in particular situations.
7 Professionals are generally controlled in their behaviour by a code
  of ethics which informs them and the public about the kind of
  behaviour required in certain circumstances. The role relationship
  between the professional and other members of the public is
  important.
8 Professionals who embody most of these characteristics are
  generally highly regarded in the community. They are often
  immune from the critical comments of the layman. Their
  competence is thought best judged by their colleagues or the
  professional association or body which supervises their activities.

Professional associations

Well-established professions are supervised and controlled by their own specialized organization. Doctors are subject to the British Medical Council, lawyers to The Law Society. The professional association may have the right:

1 To discipline members (if necessary preventing them from continuing to practise their work);
2 To establish the precise type of education required and to set up appropriate schools for study;
3 To control the standards and numbers being admitted into the profession;
4 To prevent public criticism of particular members and to prevent the public having access to their specialized knowledge;
5 To promote the image of the profession as above reproach and as committed to public service;
6 To negotiate on behalf of members with government over rates of pay, etc.

Some members of professions, for example many teachers and civil servants, join trade unions. Some members of the same profession join their association whilst others join a union. In the case of some long-standing professions, such as doctors and lawyers, they are obliged to join their controlling association. In general, members of a profession who oppose the view that they should ever take militant action over any issue prefer to join an association. It offers them most of the advantages of trade union membership but does not call members out on strike.

An increasing number of occupations are seeking to become professionalized. One way of judging the extent to which they have succeeded is to see how many of the characteristics they have which Greenwood has identified.

Employers' associations

In some industries employers have formed associations in much the same way that workers have formed unions. These serve to draw up policies for advising government departments and to point out the difficulties and problems faced by employers. They also negotiate with unions and meet to discuss issues and possible future difficulties.

In 1965 the CBI (The Confederation of British Industry) was formed. This acts as the employers' equivalent of the TUC (Trades Union Congress). It admits to membership individuals as well as employers' associations. It has become a coordinating body which acts as a spokesman for industry and offers advice to members on industrial matters. More than 13,000 companies are members. There is an annual conference at which all important issues are discussed.

Some of the main activities of employers' associations are:

1 To bargain collectively with unions to determine wage rates, etc.;
2 To establish safety regulations;
3 To organize apprenticeship schemes;
4 To represent the views of members to government and other interested bodies;
5 To send delegates to the CBI conference and to liaise closely with that body.

Key terms and concepts

The following terms and concepts have been used and defined in this chapter. You must be able to use them and explain their meaning for examination purposes:

trade unions; shop steward; national executive; white-collar trade unions; professions; professional associations; employers' associations.

Other terms you may wish to use:

closed shop A worker cannot be employed unless he joins the relevant trade union.
WEA Workers' Educational Association.

11 Strikes

75 *What light does sociological research shed on industrial conflict?*
 (LON)

Strikes are one important measure of the extent of industrial conflict. Also, because they normally gain wide publicity they have become a major area of concern for sociological research. The government publishes official statistics throughout the year indicating:
1 The number of **official** and **unofficial stoppages** that occur;
2 The number of employees involved;
3 The number of **working days** lost. (This means that if 10 men strike for 10 days then 100 working days are lost.)

The statistics relate to stoppages lasting at least one day arising from industrial dispute and which involve at least 10 workers. These statistics illustrate the fluctuating nature of industrial conflict in British industry over the past 70 years.

Number of disputes and days lost, UK 1911–75 (millions)

Year	Disputes (to nearest 50)	Days lost
1911	850	10.1
1912	850	40.8
1919	1350	34.9
1921	750	85.8
1925	600	7.9
1929	450	8.2
1931	400	6.9
1935	550	1.9
1939	950	1.3
1941	1250	1.0
1945	2300	2.8
1949	1450	1.8
1951	1700	1.6
1955	2400	3.7
1959	2000	5.2
1961	2700	3.0
1965	2350	2.9
1969	3100	6.7
1971	2200	13.5
1975	2500	5.9
1979		29.5
1980		12.0

The points to note from statistics such as those in the table are:

1 Industrial conflict was consistently more serious in terms of days lost between 1911 and 1921 than in recent years.
2 There has been an increase in industrial disruption in the 1970s in comparison with the 1950s and 1960s.
3 The number of days lost does not relate directly to the number of disputes and stoppages. It is a reflection of the length of the stoppage. For example, in 1969 there were 3100 stoppages but only 6.7 million working days lost. In 1971 there were fewer stoppages but about twice as many working days lost.

Whittingham and Towers (*Strikes and the Economy*) make these additional points:

1 The typical British strike is still brief (lasting less than three days), unofficial and unconstitutional (that is, only a small minority of strikes have the official backing of the executive of the union, see p. 120).
2 Britain suffers from unofficial strikes to a greater extent than any other western democracy.

Number of official and unofficial stoppages, 1961–71

Year	Stoppages	Official	Unofficial
1961	2686	60	2626
1965	2354	97	2257
1969	3116	98	3018
1971	2228	161	2067

Source: Whittingham and Towers, *Strikes and the Economy*

The point to which the authors are drawing attention is the fact that even in 1971 more than 92% of all strikes were unofficial. This means that they were not authorized by the unions concerned; the strikers did not get paid and most stoppages were not lengthy. Whilst many unions have much industrial power when they use it, it could also be argued that they also seem to lack the power of controlling their membership from undertaking unofficial stoppages.

76 *What is the difference between an official and an unofficial strike?*
Why are such a high proportion of strikes in Britain unofficial? (OX)

To answer such questions you *must* be able to produce a table of statistical data. It would also be useful to elaborate on the possible meanings of an 'unofficial strike'.

Knowles says 'it is one which is not recognized by the executive committee of a union'. (This is the strict definition.) Cameron and Eldridge (*Unofficial Strikes*) provide a wider definition. They say there are five different categories of unofficial strike:

1 A strike may be supported by a union but not declared official because they cannot afford to pay the strikers.
2 A short, unofficial strike may be encouraged by the union as a warning about their strength.
3 A strike may start unofficially and then gain official support later when it is seen to be successful.
4 A strike may have to be unofficial because it is directed against the union itself (for example, directed at its failure to look after the interests of workers made redundant).
5 A strike may remain unofficial because it has the support of some sections or departments of the union but not by the executive as a whole.

There are additional points that help to explain the predominance of unofficial strikes:

1 Often problems arise suddenly in work which require instant action (for example, a machine is considered unsafe, there is inadequate heat, etc.). Men may walk out because it would take too long for the executive to make a decision Also, the problem may be resolved within a few days.
2 Strikes are made official when negotiations have broken down. Unofficial strikes occur before or during negotiations and may highlight a particular problem.

The extent of strike activity in Britain

Research into the distribution and concentration of industrial stoppages in manufacturing industry in Britain for the years 1971–3 (when strikes were running at a high level) was published by the Department of Employment. It revealed the following:

1 The popular impression of the British worker constantly on strike is shown to be a myth. On average 97.8% of manufacturing establishments are free of stoppages in any one year, and 81.1% of employees work in strike-free industries.
2 Over the three-year period 95% of factories were free of strikes.

3 Of the 5% of factories where strikes occurred two-thirds had only one strike.
4 Of 60,000 factories surveyed, strikes occurred only in 150 of them.

The researchers concluded that in manufacturing, Britain does not suffer from a problem of widespread industrial stoppages but from a concentration of stoppages in a relatively small number of factories.

On an average working day in a bad year, only 100 out of 60,000 factories are affected by a strike. In some industries, such as retail distribution and service industries, strikes hardly ever occur.

The researchers also point out that strikes involve about 750,000 workers out of a total workforce of more than 21 million.

77 What are the major causes of industrial disputes? (OX)

To answer this question you could use some of the points made earlier about the effect of the work expectations and work experiences on the worker (see pp. 107–9). You could discuss the significance of:

1 the division of labour;
2 mass production/automation;
3 the concept of alienation.

But you would also need to detail the more precise causes of conflict in work which have been revealed by research (see below).

78 Which industries tend to be most strike prone and why? (OX)

Much the same material can also be used in this question to illustrate why strikes are concentrated in a small number and similar type of industry. Knowles said that of the strikes recorded by the government the causes could be grouped under three headings:

1 **Basic issues** About wages, hours of work, etc.
2 **Frictional issues** About discipline rules and working arrangements.
3 **Solidarity (or topological) issues** About trade union principles, sympathetic action, etc.

He noted that strikes resulting from frictional issues had increased during the period of the survey (1911–47).

Causes of stoppages, 1966–74 (%)

Problems relating to pay	57
Duration and pattern of hours	2
Questions of redundancy	4
Trade union matters	8
Working conditions and discipline	29

Source: Department of Employment (1976)

One conclusion to be reached from the table is that there are many different reasons for stoppages (not just the demand for more pay). Each type of strike may require different remedial action. Analysis of different types of stoppage suggest that the same action may be interpreted differently and have a different meaning to different groups of workers. Hence, the cause of a strike may well depend on how a particular group view a particular incident at a particular time.

The most strike prone industries

Kerr and Seigal made an international comparison of strike records in various types of industry. They found the following pattern shown in the table. Their theory was that industries are more strike prone where workers form a fairly close knit group, in terms of social background, area in which they live, identification with the local community, etc. Thus, miners, dockers, textile workers, all live in communities with their own particular cultural norms and codes of conduct. They come to see themselves as subject to the same problems and accept the need for industrial action at certain times. Such action becomes relatively easy to organize and maintain.

Level of strike action	Type of industry
High	Mining
	Docks and maritime
Medium-high	Textile workers
Medium	Chemical
	Printing
	General manufacturing
	Construction
Medium-low	Clothing
	Gas, water, electricity
	Services, i.e. hotels, restaurants, etc.
Low	Railways
	Agriculture

In Britain strikes are most frequent among workers engaged in un-pleasant, dangerous, repetitive and monotonous work. Stoppages are concentrated in the following industries:

1 Iron castings
2 Vehicle manufacturing
3 Shipbuilding
4 Docks
5 Mining

People are less likely to strike when they have intrinsic levels of satisfaction and enjoyment from the work and where it requires skills, is physically easy, is performed in pleasant surroundings and enables the worker to develop personality and individuality.

This chapter opened by considering the question:

What light does sociological research shed on industrial conflict?

Here are some concluding points which you may be able to include in your answer.

1 Not all strikes are successful in gaining their objectives.
2 Strikers themselves often suffer hardship in the course of a strike (e.g. some benefits are available only in cases of extreme hardship).
3 Samuelson (*Economics*) has said that the number of days lost from work as a result of the common cold is much greater than from disputes in work.
4 Whittingham and Towers agree that in terms of working days lost as a proportion of total work days, strikes are statistically insignificant.
5 These authors argue that if there is a strike problem in Britain it is sectoral rather than national. The problems are centred on particular industries in specific areas.
6 When international comparisons are made, Britain's record is not bad. Those with frequently worse records (per thousand workers) include Australia, Canada, Eire, Denmark and Spain. However, those with consistently better records are generally Britain's main competitors.
7 It is useful to bear in mind the comment of Gouldner (*Wildcat Strike*): 'a strike is a social phenomenon of enormous complexity which, in its totality, is never susceptible to complete description, let alone explanation'.

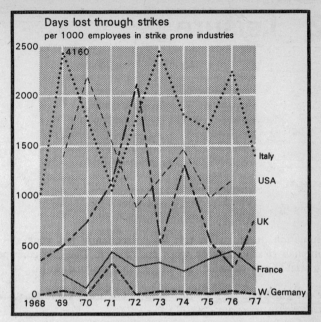

Days lost through strikes per 1000 employees in strike-prone industries

Key terms and concepts

The following terms and concepts have been used and defined in this chapter. You must be able to use them and explain their meaning for examination purposes:

strikes; official and unofficial; trade unions; division of labour; automation; alienation.

Other related terms you may wish to use:

sympathetic action Where one union calls its members out on strike to support the cause of another union.
redundancy Where workers are laid off or dismissed as a result of economic depression or other financial problems affecting the firm or industry.
unconstitutional strikes Where workers come out on strike without consulting the constitution or regulations of their union which describes the correct procedures for dealing with such problems.

12   Leisure

Examination questions on this topic frequently test your ability to distinguish clearly between work and leisure. The two concepts are often related in a question. Sometimes this is stated, as in:

79 *Distinguish between work and leisure and discuss any two ways in which they are related.*   (WEL)

Sometimes it is implied, as in:

80 *Explain, with examples, how the occupation which a person follows affects many areas of his life outside work.*   (AEB)

To do well in a question on this topic, therefore, you must be able to make a distinction between those activities normally considered to be **work** and those which can be more usefully described as **leisure**.

One of the ways by which sociologists make the meanings of a term clear, especially for the purpose of research, is by producing a **typology** (see pp. 29, 93) or an ideal type. This means that the qualities which can be expected to make up the concept can be listed. Then a comparison can be made with patterns of behaviour in the real world to see how far they meet the expected characteristics.

Sociologists point out that the general definition of leisure as 'free time' or 'time when I do what I want' is inadequate. They do not enable the researcher to distinguish clearly whether particular activities fall under the heading of work or leisure. For example, are the activities of a man in prison or during a tea break examples of leisure actions because they are done in time free from the pressure of work? The use of a typology helps to resolve such problems by showing that there are important additional dimensions to the concepts of work and leisure.

Characteristics of work	Characteristics of leisure
1 Contractual obligations specify the precise duties and expectations on the part of the employer and employee. Hence the latter has little sense of free time or freedom of action.	There is no contractual obligation associated with leisure activities. Hence the sense of 'free time'.
2 There are obligations and compulsions in work resulting from the binding contract.	There is little or no obligation or compulsion in leisure. The individual can start or stop the activity when they wish.
3 There is payment on a regular basis.	Payment is not usually associated with leisure activities.
4 There is limited choice in work activities and often only limited enjoyment and satisfaction.	There is wide choice in leisure time and enjoyment and satisfaction are high priorities.
5 Work imposes a specific role on the individual which influences their behaviour towards each other (e.g. doctor–patient).	There is little or no role play associated with leisure activities, e.g. a doctor may play golf with a patient without the role affecting the relationship.
6 There is a strong subjective and psychological element associated with work. People 'know' when they are working.	There is an equally strong subjective and psychological knowledge of what constitutes leisure. People recognize what is their leisure time.

Parker has made the distinctions shown in the table in his typology:

Constraint				Freedom
Work	Work obligations	Physiological needs	Non-work obligations	Leisure
Sold time	Work-related time	Existence time	Semi-leisure time	Free time

1 Work time is that devoted to earning a living.
2 Work-related time is that spent on activities associated with work, including travelling, attending meetings, reading documents, books and articles, etc.
3 Physiological needs include those of eating, sleeping, etc.
4 Non-work obligations are those that the individual feels ought to be undertaken in non-work time, such as visiting, home decorating, etc.

5 Leisure is all that time free from the obligations of contractual work
and free of all obligations connected with semi-leisure.

Parker describes his typology as an analysis of life-space. Its use helps to
throw more light on the nature of work and leisure and to sort out the
real differences and similarities.

81 *Sociologists spend too much time considering the problem of work: far
more important is the problem of leisure.* (OX)

Some of the major problems of work have already been discussed (see
especially pp. 110–17). This question would require only brief mention
of the factors of alienation, division of labour and the causes of industrial
conflict. The major part of the answer should focus on the problems
associated with leisure.

1 **The problem for the sociologist**
   (a) **The problem of definition**
   (b) **How and why have leisure patterns changed?**
       (i) Increases in affluence
      (ii) The mass production of goods
     (iii) The development of the mass media
      (iv) The commercialization of leisure
       (v) Changes in social attitudes about leisure.
           With shorter working weeks and paid holidays and
           increasing emphasis on participation in active leisure
           pursuits, leisure is seen to be a way of helping people relax
           and work more effectively.
      (vi) Educationalists have encouraged more constructive use of
           leisure time.

2 **The problem of leisure for education**
   Many educationalists see leisure as a problem since they argue that
   unless people are able to use their leisure satisfactorily then there
   may be a deterioration in their own personalities and in the culture
   of the society. Repeated research suggests that many problems can
   arise (especially for young people) who fail to find constructive
   ways of using their leisure.
      Downes (*The Delinquent Solution*) found that where some
   working-class youths were unable to find legitimate ways of using
   their leisure time they often turned to delinquent behaviour. They
   looked for excitement and other activities which are often defined
   by the public as 'deviant'; they do not see them as problems of
   leisure.

(c) Factors affecting choice of leisure activities

Social class	Age and sex	Family structure	Occupation
(a) Willmott and Young (*Family and Class*) showed how some clubs and organizations weight their regulations more towards one class than another. This helps preserve their exclusiveness.	(a) Leisure patterns will alter as people pass through different stages of the family cycle, i.e. child, adolescent, parent, grandparent, etc.	(a) Roberts (*Leisure*) points out that the family acts as a normative reference group by giving guidance to members as to what is and is not a suitable activity.	There are frequently specific exam questions on this topic: Parker (*The Future of Work and Leisure*) has produced some important findings. He noted that the response that people make to their work influence their attitudes towards leisure.
(b) People may be deterred or encouraged to join a club or activity by the image that it has, e.g. racing pigeons or playing squash.	(b) Some activities are more suitable to one age group than another or to one sex than the other.	(b) Bell and Healey suggest that where there are 'joint conjugal roles' in a family (see p. 30) husbands and wives share more leisure activities. Where there are segregated roles then the world of husband tends to be 'extra-domestic' (centred more outside the home). They also conclude that family norms are important in shaping leisure activities.	(i) The extension pattern: Some workers said that their leisure was an extension of their work and that it was hard to distinguish between the two, e.g. child care officers.
(c) The socially mobile may seek those activities they associate with the class they wish to join (an example of 'anticipatory socialization').	(c) As adults of both sexes grow older, their leisure activities focus more on the home, so that TV watching becomes the most popular activity.		(ii) The pattern of neutrality. Others said they gained neither fulfilment nor great dissatisfaction in their work. Leisure represented a time to relax, e.g. bank employees.
			(iii) Opposition patterns. Some workers had low levels of satisfaction in work and saw leisure as a time to escape its rigours. It was compensation for the hazards of work, e.g. miners.

Mays (*Growing up in the City*, 1954) studied delinquency in Liverpool and found similar evidence that one of the major causes of deviant behaviour lay in the difficulty that the boys had in using their free time in legitimate and constructive ways. He explains that hooliganism and vandalism are typical spare time 'leisure' activities. (This is a particularly interesting finding in view of the troubles in Liverpool and other cities in 1981.)

The role of education could therefore be particularly relevant in helping to combat such problems. Jones has said that the shorter working week and the increasing problems of unemployment requires a reassessment of the function of education. He concluded that the education system trains people to work well – now it must train people to live well.

3 The problem of leisure for the unemployed

82 *Does unemployment or redundancy provide the individual with more time to enjoy leisure?*

Dumazedier puts forward the view that the values and attitudes associated with a person's leisure will exercise a significant influence on all other spheres of their social life. For example, they will select an occupation that gives them time for their leisure activities since these provide them with a sense of meaning and significance. Work often fails them in this respect.

The roles they adopt in all spheres of life will be shaped by those established in leisure-centred activities. These will define what kind of person they wish to be seen as. Anderson makes a similar point when he says that it is increasingly leisure which gives people satisfaction – whereas for the majority work has become relatively meaningless.

On this argument it might be assumed that unemployment does not present a problem as far as leisure is concerned. But studies by Wilensky suggest that those who have 'enforced' leisure time may actually have more difficulty in gaining value from it. In fact, they cease to have leisure as is normally understood by most people in society ('time from the obligations of paid employment'). Such studies suggest that for such people, far from having more enjoyable leisure time, they become less capable of enjoying leisure. They lose social status, and they may have insufficient economic means to make constructive use of their free time. As outsiders they do not share in the normal rhythm of social life. The effects of long-term unemployment have been shown to have a serious effect on people's lives in that all their normal structures collapse (personal relationships, self-esteem, ambitions and goals). Thus it may be, in an ironical way, that to enjoy leisure in modern society, it is necessary to have a regular job since it is only by understanding the meaning of work that we can make sense of leisure.

83 'There is a growing literature tracing the ways in which the kind of work men do influences their pattern of life. Studies of leisure which have hitherto focused on social class differences are now developing the theme that there are occupational differences within class and status groupings which play a large part in determining the style of leisure, family behaviour, political orientations, as well as more general values.'

S. R. Parker

(a) *Explain this passage in non-technical language.*
(b) *Give some examples of the class differences referred to and illustrate how occupation can affect leisure activities.*

Compare your answer to part (a) with the following suggestion. There is a steady output of research being published which shows how people's lives are influenced by the work they do. Studies of leisure have always focused, until recently, on the class differences which affect people's choice of activity. But now research is showing that even within the same class or status groups there are significant differences in attitudes and behaviour patterns. People may share the same class, but because they follow different occupations they display differences in styles of leisure, behaviour in the family, in political beliefs, as well as in other more general attitudes and values.

To answer part (b) see p. 77 for discussion on class differences and p. 137 for discussion of the significance of occupation on choice of leisure activities.

Key terms and concepts

The following terms have been used and defined in this chapter. You must be able to use them and explain their meaning for the examination.

leisure; work; class; typology; joint conjugal roles; segregated roles.

13 Community studies

Questions on this topic centre on three main areas:

1 A test of your understanding of certain important concepts such as urban, rural, urbanization, neighbourhood, community, etc.;
2 Urban–rural distinctions;
3 The urban way of life; in particular:

    (a) New housing estates;
    (b) New towns;
    (c) The consequences of urban renewal and redevelopment;
    (d) Problems associated with urban life and urban growth.

The concepts

In order to produce a satisfactory answer to most of the questions that you will be asked on this topic you must be able to define key terms or point out the particular problems involved in their use. Sometimes you will be asked a question in which you must produce this information specifically in order to answer the question:

84 *Give examples of, or by any other method show clearly that you understand, the differences between 'an* urban *area' and* 'urbanization'.

In other questions terms will be used that cannot be taken for granted because the answer often hinges on the fact that there are possible confusions in the use of the key term. For example:

85 *Outline and discuss the distinctive sociological features of a* neighbourhood.   (WEL)
86 *Discuss the features which distinguish the culture and social structure of rural* communities *from those in urban society.*   (WEL)

Whilst all the terms emphasized in the questions can be given a general definition (which you can usefully do to show that you have an understanding of their meaning), it is important to remember that sociologists usually find it more useful to develop typologies to describe the distinctions between particular concepts.

Particular qualities that may be expected to be a part of, for example, a rural or an urban way of life may be suggested (see, for example, p. 144).

These are some of the more general points to be made:

Urbanization This term refers to the movement from areas of dispersed population to areas of concentrated population, in particular into large towns and cities. This movement has been encouraged by industrialization.

Urban areas In 1801 7.0% of the population lived in towns of 20,000 or more. In 1981 more than 90% of the population live in areas with more than 50,000. Urban areas also display characteristics in terms of culture, patterns of relationships between people and specific social problems which distinguish them from rural areas.

Rural areas Apart from having smaller dispersed populations associated with country life, they may generally be said to display many of the qualities that are not related to urban life. These distinctions are dealt with more analytically on p. 143.

Community This term is open to two main interpretations. Some writers (e.g. Redfield) have said that it implies the existence of a basic structure or unit that can be objectively defined and located in the real world. This view suggests that a community is found only in rural areas. Other writers (e.g. Pahl) have disagreed, and said that the term is a more imprecise and flexible concept. It is not easily identified or located. This view suggests that a community can exist just as easily in an urban, as in a rural, area since it is a more subjective interpretation of what constitutes 'a community' or 'neighbourhood'.

Neighbourhood

1 Many writers point out that it is a confusing term and means something different to everyone. Lack of a sense of neighbourhood is usually taken to mean 'loneliness', 'insecurity', 'anonymity'.
2 Perry has said that a neighbourhood is the area that embraces all the public facilities and conditions required by the average family for its comforts.
3 Lee has said that there is a strong subjective element in determining what constitutes a 'neighbourhood'. He asked people living in the

same area to draw a map of what they believed constituted 'their neighbourhood'. He found wide discrepancies in the areas delineated.

Distinctions between urban and rural patterns of life

87 *In what ways do social relationships and behaviour tend to differ in urban and rural situations?* (AEB)
88 *Discuss the features which distinguish the culture and social structure of rural communities from those of urban society.* (WEL)

Apart from the factual information you need in order to answer these questions you should notice how there are several key terms in these questions which you must explain in the course of your answer. In particular **social relationships; behaviour; urban; rural; culture; social structure; communities.** You might usefully refer to the advice offered on pp. 9–12 if you are in any doubt as to how you might approach such questions.

These questions are based on the view that there are two extreme or polar types of social organization – described as urban and rural structures. This idea may be traced back to some of the earliest sociologists who were interested to try and answer the question, 'Is it true that where people live influences how they live?' They were particularly concerned with the effects of industrialization on the lives, lifestyles and stability of people in society. They wished to know whether when the old traditional rural patterns of life were disrupted this would have the effect of causing major problems and upheavals in other areas of society.

Tönnies published his book *Gemeinschaft und Gesellschaft* in 1887. He distinguished between 'community' (*gemeinschaft*) which he associated with life in pre-industrial societies (and therefore with rural areas) and loss of community – 'association' – (*gesellschaft*). This was to be found in industrialized urban societies. Tönnies made the distinction outlined in the table opposite.

Tönnies does not suggest that these are rigid categories. He accepts that they pervade different societies to different degrees. He was simply describing the trend from traditional, stable social life in rural communities to that of potential instability as epitomized in urban industrial society.

Durkheim published his book *The Division of Labour in Society* in

In a society based on community	In a society based on association
A person's status is ascribed (given at birth).	A person's status is based on achievement.
Relationships between people are intimate and enduring and based on a clear understanding of each other's place in the society.	Relationships between people are impersonal and transitory. They are frequently contractual relationships, i.e. based on services which they can provide.
A person's status is based more on who they are.	A person's status results more from what they have done.
There are many primary, face-to-face relationships.	There are many secondary, less personal relationships.
There is little geographical or social mobility.	There are high levels of social and geographical mobility.
There is a strong sense of identification with place and locality.	Because people are frequently on the move there is little sense of identification with locality.
There is a strong sense of local culture which is enforced by the Church and the family.	Within urban areas there are often strong sub-cultures sustained by classes and peer groups.

1893. He saw social change as consisting of a movement from **simple (mechanical)** society to **complex (organic)**. He was concerned with a question similar to that of Tönnies: how can social solidarity and stability be maintained where patterns of life are subject to very rapid changes as industrialization has a greater influence on people's lives. His answer was in terms of the social division of labour. This helped to bind each man involved in the production process more closely into his society since it increased each person's dependence on every other.

British and American sociologists examined the validity of some of these ideas in a series of empirical studies.

Redfield *(The Little Community)* Redfield said that there were clear differences between urban and rural life. He confirmed the distinctions that Tönnies suggested. Redfield said that rural communities could be identified by the fact that (i) they were small in size; (ii) they were economically and socially self-sufficient; (iii) inhabitants were socially and culturally similar; and (iv) they tend to be distinctive areas in which there are few tensions, class conflicts or disharmony.

Frankenberg *(Communities in Britain)* Frankenberg reviews several research studies and produces a typology to show some of the major characteristics that have been found in urban and rural societies. His main thesis is that while social life in towns is not necessarily better or worse than in rural villages, it is different. While in his opinion the gains of urban life are greater than the losses, he accepts that the move from rural to urban area can cause loneliness, anomie and alienation. Some of the characteristics of his model are shown in the table.

Urban society	Rural society
Association	Community
Individual has few roles	Individual has many roles
Complex economy	Simple economy
Division of labour (mass production)	Craft economy: little division of labour
Organic, changing society	Mechanical, unchanging society
Achieved status	Ascribed status
Loose-knit social networks	Close-knit social networks
Alienation	Integration

These writers do accept that social relationships in urban areas are qualitatively different from those in rural areas because

1 Urban society is inevitably more anonymous and lonely. People have little sense of identity or community in sprawling urban cities.
2 Urban dwellers inevitably have many more acquaintances than close friends and very few relatives living close by.
3 Relationships with people are based mainly on need – need for particular services.
4 Because city life is hurried and much time is spent travelling to and from work there is limited time for active leisure which will bring people into close contact with each other. There are more passive activities such as watching TV or films.

Such factors allegedly make it difficult for people living in urban centres to develop warm, close personal relationships which are believed to be typical of small villages in pleasant country areas.

However, there are writers who dispute this view. They argue that it is a mistake to assume that such rural areas do provide exactly opposite styles of life and patterns of relationships to those assumed to be typical of urban areas.

1 **Seeley, Sim and Loosley** (*Crestwood Heights*) In their study of a Toronto suburb, they found a strong sense of community spirit and local identity in what was clearly an urban area. Their respondents were found to have a strong commitment to an area from which

they commuted each day and in which they actually spent little time. They say that it exists as a community because of the interpersonal relationships. This is revealed in their concern about the schools their children attend, the activities of the church and community centre and the responsibilities of the family in the area. These institutions are all very significant in the lives of the residents for whom domestic life is of central concern.

2 **Willmott and Young** *(Family and Kinship in East London)*   They demonstrated a strong sense of community in existence in the middle of a great urban centre. Extended families were clearly identified in Bethnal Green; they had roots in the area which stretched back for generations and relationships were not necessarily very different from those described by Redfield in typically rural areas.

3 **Gans** *(The Urban Villagers)*   This study also helped to dispute the view that there is a rural way of life which is strikingly different from an urban setting. His study of a Boston suburb did not find evidence of the anomie, transitory relations or superficial values which a writer like Tönnies would have predicted.

4 **Lewis** *(Life in a Mexican Village)*   Lewis found evidence of class conflict, loneliness and anonymity in a small, rural village in which such patterns of behaviour would not be expected.

Conclusion

It would be useful to point out that the implication in these questions that people's relationships and life-styles are shaped by the area in which they live, may be a mistaken one. The view that rural patterns of life are qualitatively better than urban ones seems to have no significant supporting evidence. It seems to be a rather traditional and romantic view and one which influenced much of the early research. It seems, too, that community can exist wherever interests in an area exist and such interests are not limited by social or geographical boundaries; there is a strong subjective (rather than objective) factor at work in determining what is 'the community'.

Urban ways of life

It is difficult to generalize about urban life because life-styles are influenced by a variety of factors – social class, stage in the family cycle, age and sex, as well as the occupational and industrial structure of the area.

89 *'Soulless deserts'. Is there any justification for the use of this term as a description of new housing estates?* (OX)

90 What are the factors which cause people to move to suburbs and new towns?

In Britain housing estates have been designed in many different ways and according to many different ideas. Some have been based on tower blocks, others on low-level individual units with gardens and clearly defensible space. Some have been a mixture of both. They have been built of every possible medium and followed a wide range of designs.

Some estates are primarily for council tenants; others are available on the open market. Council housing first started in the 1890s. Blocks were built cheaply and simply but had the air of formal institutions, like prisons or hospitals. By the 1930s they had become subject to much architectural interest and many unusual experiments in design were conducted. After 1945 such housing became a major political issue and estates developed more rapidly. In the 1950s and 1960s such housing was built as quickly and cheaply as possible and much of it rapidly fell into disorder. Sometimes this was because it had been built in unsatisfactory ways from prefabricated parts and sometimes because it was badly designed and soon became vandalized or in some cases uninhabitable.

It may be that the image of housing estates as being soulless deserts has arisen from these facts, but this may be an unfair generalization.

The actual quality of the estate, town or suburb depends on

1 When it was designed and built.
2 The way it has developed over time. Some have retained high status, others have fallen into decline.
3 Whether or not it becomes a soulless desert or a fruitful oasis may also depend on the economic climate: whether governments and local authorities are prepared to spend money on resolving problems and meeting the needs of local residents.

In 1967 the South East Economic Planning Council published a report for an area of Britain which houses 17 million people. The report said that the new towns, which will have to absorb some of the expected five million increase in population by the year 2000, should be thriving social communities. It advocated better job opportunities, better facilities for shops, schools, hospitals, colleges, etc. These are important to attract new population. But in 1981, as government spending cuts increased, such developments seem unlikely to be pursued. In some cases some estates and new town developments might well become soulless deserts.

Jennings (*Societies in the Making*) suggests some of the problems that some of her respondents reported in living on new estates.

1 Informal contacts between people were fewer. Neighbours seldom met whilst shopping.
2 Lack of familiar services on the estate took people off to nearby towns where goods were cheaper.
3 People who were unhappy often made journeys back to the area from which they had moved.
4 Because there were fewer churches, libraries, etc., there was a decline in participation in such institutions on the estate.
5 The estate did not always meet the aspirations or desires of the new population.
6 There was an absence of humanizing and personalizing influences on the estates which were normally provided in old established areas by the extended family and neighbours. As a result family units became more independent of the wider community.

A study by Reynolds and Nicholson into living in high rise flats concluded that for most housewives, play problems for children, nervousness and loneliness appeared to be as serious for those living off the ground as it was for those living at ground level. But their findings do support the view that living high off the ground is least satisfactory for families with children, especially under the age of 5. The elderly and those without children said they were happy to live in high rise blocks.

Some reasons why people seek to move to new estates, towns and suburbs

Three factors prompt people to move: (i) opportunity; (ii) choice; (iii) compulsion.

The growing shortage of land in cities as well as its high cost compels the development of new housing in areas beyond the cities. The New Towns Act 1946 and the Town and Country Planning Act 1947 gave the government important new powers in this respect. The new towns and estates provided a different life-style for inhabitants who had previously lived in large traditional urban areas. There was a lower density of population, the provision of gardens, public parks and school playing-fields, and the opportunity of more modern properties.

Opportunity The **opportunity** to make such a move would be taken by those who were socially mobile and who were not tied to an area by strong family and other kinship and cultural ties. Many firms take the opportunity of moving out of city centres where overheads are high into new towns and estates where particular incentives are offered. Employees then take up housing in such areas. Those who do not may have to commute long distances.

Choice Those with young families **choose** to move into homes in new towns and suburbs because the housing standards are generally better than anything they can afford in urban centres. They also obtain more modern facilities in terms of schools, shops, leisure centres, etc. It is easier to obtain a mortgage. Modern properties are designed to high standards.

Compulsion Those living in very old properties in declining areas of inner cities may be **compelled** to move. Local authorities may decide to re-house people so that slum clearance or other redevelopment can take place. Where a firm decides to move from an urban site the employees may be compelled to move in order to retain their jobs.

91 *Examine the suggestion that slum clearance and redevelopment schemes in the major cities have created more problems than they have solved.* (OX)

It is generally acknowledged that Britain was the first country in the world to experience large-scale urbanization following the industrial revolution. The poorest sections of the major cities of Britain may have originally been the homes of the most prosperous businessmen. There large homes have become lodging houses for those with insufficient income or capital to purchase their own property. As the area falls into decay it may become an area for clearance. For many living there, it may be that to be rehoused in new estates is a clear advantage.

Other areas subject to clearance orders may have been the homes of long-established communities of people, such as those in Bethnal Green, where people had a sense of identity and belonging to the area. For them, the move into new estates far away from old friends and the area they knew so well, could create serious problems, since a whole culture may be destroyed.

Other problems associated with urban renewal include:

1 People may be housed in tower blocks which they find unsatisfactory and which become subject to vandalism.
2 Sometimes large numbers of 'problem families' are housed on the same estate thereby exacerbating a series of major social problems.
3 Large numbers of young people grow up together on large housing estates. Often sub-cultures develop which encourage deviant or delinquent behaviour.
4 The clearance of traditional urban areas may also mean the removal of local traders, the corner shop, the local church, the local policeman, and all those informal structures which helped to provide order and control in the neighbourhood. The sense of personal identity and community may disappear when the area is redeveloped. Higher levels of social disorder may result.

On the other hand, there are certain advantages in the clearance of old, decaying areas.

1 Slum dwellings and low-grade property is removed and replaced by that of a much higher standard.
2 Where there may have been conflict over limited housing stock in poor, deprived areas, these problems are remedied when new estates and suburbs are developed in their place. Property is generally distributed according to need at the appropriate rent, or market price.
3 Where there are various social groups housed in the same redeveloped area and the norms of respect for property and pride in the home develop, then social problems are less likely to occur.
4 Some research (e.g. Durant, 1968) suggests that working-class men on new estates often welcome the opportunity to join formal housing associations to help ensure that any problems are dealt with quickly and adequately. They may not have had similar opportunities when living in their previous homes in decaying areas.

Dennis (*People and Planning*) concludes that the choice between the replacement and the retention of existing dwellings is a problem which must be considered very carefully before final decisions are made.

Some questions relate more specifically to the problems associated with an urban way of life:

92 *Describe any three problems of urban growth and discuss any two attempts to cope with such problems during the past 30 years.* (WEL)
93 *How can towns and cities be described as anonymous when they are so frequently crowded.* (AEB)
94 *What insights can sociological research offer in the understanding of common urban problems in Britain today?* (LON)

It must be remembered that it is not necessarily the case that the city has the monopoly of social problems. Both urban and rural areas have their advantages and disadvantages. However, certain generalizations can be made (which could be subject to greater research by sociologists to confirm, reject or explain them). Urban dwellers must face the possible negative consequences of their urban environment in the same way that dwellers in rural areas must accept the limitations of theirs.

Some of the following points have already been touched on. In some cases it could be argued that far from being the source of potential problems, they provide certain advantages for city dwellers.

However, there are some clear disadvantages in living in cities:

1 **Noise and pollution** The Buchanan Report (1963) said that

traffic is causing an increasingly serious nuisance and is destructive of amenities on a wide scale in towns throughout Britain.

2 The **cost of housing** and other accommodation is much higher in urban areas.

3 **Crime rates** are inevitably higher in such areas because the population is greater, the opportunities are increased, and the chances of being caught are greater since there are more policemen available.

4 Large towns and cities have **poor, deprived areas** which continue to house the poorest section of the population. These areas give rise to serious social problems in themselves.

5 Many people who move into urban centres in search of work may feel acutely **lonely**, especially if they are living by themselves in rented accommodation. It is difficult for a sense of neighbourliness to develop in such circumstances.

6 **Suicide rates** are higher in urban areas.

7 Rates of **ill health** are also higher. Apart from the problems of pollution, there are also the stresses, strains and anxieties of life in cities.

8 There is generally a much greater density and **congestion** of population in cities and towns. For example, in the Golbourne district of North London there are more than 230 people living to an acre according to Census details.

Additional factors to consider are outlined on p. 144.

Key terms and concepts

The following terms and concepts have been used and defined in this chapter. You must be able to use them and explain their meaning for examination purposes:

community; urban area; urbanization; rural area; neighbourhood; heterogeneous population; homogeneous population; *gemeinschaft*; *gesellschaft*; social mobility; alienation; division of labour.

Other terms which you may wish to use:

deprived areas Areas that lack the facilities which might be expected as a part of normal social life (shops, parks, transport, etc.).
pollution Excessive noise, smell, etc. which makes social life less pleasant than it otherwise would be.

14 The mass media

The mass media are the various systems of communication by which messages (news, information, ideas, views, etc.) are transmitted to a mass audience. They rely on processes which have been developed since the industrial and technological revolutions; particular use is made of electronic techniques. The mass media include most notably, the press and broadcasting.

Because they have become an indispensible part of daily life sociologists are interested to study the effects of the mass media on their audiences, as well as examining the factors that influence the output, style and content of the various mediums of communication themselves.

The most frequent examination questions ask you to discuss the effects of the mass media on the attitudes, values and patterns of behaviour of their audiences. Some questions specifically concern television:

95 *Should people worry about the effects of television on children?*
96 *What light do sociological studies of the mass media throw on the suggestion that watching television can affect people's behaviour?* (CAM, *adapted*)
97 *Outline and comment upon the part played by television in politics.*

Others are concerned with the significance of the press and television:

98 *The choice of newspapers which a person reads may be a good example of the fact that an individual only sees or hears what he wants to. Discuss this point in relation to mass communications generally.*
99 *Using sociological evidence, assess the influence of the mass media on attitude formation.* (LON)

To answer all of these questions you must be able to explain and discuss:

1 What attitudes are;

2 Problems involved in changing attitudes;
3 Research findings into the effects of the media on attitudes and behaviour patterns.

Attitudes

When we say a person has an attitude about something we mean that they have a fairly fixed and unified set of beliefs which causes them to respond in a particular way to a certain stimulus or event.

An attitude has three components:

1 A **cognitive** or **rational element**: people try to think out reasons for their beliefs.
2 An **emotional element**: people simply 'feel' that what they think is right.
3 There is a **response** by the individual to an event, to what they see or hear. Their behaviour may demonstrate their attitude.

For example, if a person is hostile to trade unions, we may say they have a strong negative attitude. They may have some specific reasons for their views based on their own experiences; they may also hold some beliefs which are not based on any evidence but which they assume to be true. Their behaviour in refusing to join a union also demonstrates the strength of their attitude.

Everyone develops attitudes because we like our world to be organized and consistent. Man in society is forced to deal repeatedly with similar situations and events. Responses to these become organized into a unified and enduring system. Beliefs, feelings and responses are brought into play whenever that stimulus or situation is encountered. As time goes by, a person assimilates more attitudes which become interlinked so that they can interpret almost everything that they observe in the world in terms of their set of attitudes. They help people to make sense of everything that is going on around them.

Those who wish to influence attitudes include reformers, politicians, advertisers and educationalists. Some may wish to intensify an existing attitude; that is, make people feel more strongly about an event than they do already. This is known as a **congruent change**. They may feel more strongly in a positive way or in a negative way. (For example, the person who feels that apartheid is wrong comes to believe and act in ways that show they hold this view more intensely than before. In the same way, a person who believes that hanging should be reintroduced comes to hold that view more strongly.)

Some may wish to change or negate an existing attitude. This is known as an **incongruent change**. This is a move from holding a positive view to holding a negative one or vice versa. For example, the person who feels that apartheid is wrong comes to change their mind and believes that it is a sound policy. The person who believes in capital punishment reverses his or her view.

Much research, especially in social psychology, suggests that attitudes are difficult to change once formed; e.g. it is difficult to obtain an incongruent change. This is because:

1 People become committed to particular views on the world and once they have stated their views on issues it is uncomfortable to change them.
2 People are subject to constant reinforcement effects which help them to maintain their attitudes. There are three important factors at work:
   (a) **Selective exposure**   People tend to be selective in their choice of programme, newspaper, communicator, etc. They tend to select those that present information most likely to conform to their existing views and to avoid those that conflict. A Conservative supporter is more likely to tune into a Conservative party political broadcast and to read the *Daily Telegraph, Mail* or *Express* than a Labour supporter and to spend more time in the company of other like-minded people.
   (b) **Selective perception**   People tend to perceive events that fit into their pre-existing expectations. What doesn't fit is rejected, omitted or reinterpreted until it does make sense. For example, the prejudiced person will notice how black people tend to play inferior roles in films (especially older ones) and in society generally. This helps them confirm their view that they are 'inferior'. If they are exposed to unsympathetic material in which a black person is playing a more important role, this may be either ignored or criticized as bad casting.
   (c) **Selective retention**   People tend to retain information that fits their own pre-existing views and to forget or ignore details that contradict what they believe to be true. The Conservative supporter who watches a Labour party political broadcast may ridicule the speakers and look for fallacies in the arguments used.

The general findings are:

1 It is fairly easy to obtain reinforcement of attitudes, i.e. congruent change.
2 It is possible to obtain some minor changes in attitude. People may be prepared to modify their views a little.

3 It is very difficult to gain a conversion in attitudes, i.e. incongruent change – but not impossible.

However, although there is much evidence to show that changes in attitudes are not easily obtained by what people read or see, there is no doubt that many people (especially parents) remain concerned about the influence of television and the press. This is because people may be susceptible to behavioural changes in certain situations. There are those, such as advertisers, who use specific techniques deliberately to seek changes in attitudes. But these may also operate in informal ways so that some members of an audience may be influenced without being aware of it.

Attitudes may be influenced and changed by the following factors:

The source of the information

A credible communicator whom people know and admire is effective in gaining change. For example, Jimmy Saville was used to persuade people to wear seat belts. People would be less convinced if they were given the information from the Minister of Transport, who would be unknown to many, seen to be politically motivated and 'getting at' people.

The situation in which the information is received

Changes can be gained where people are required to commit themselves publicly to new attitudes (such as at an evangelical meeting); where they are members of an already largely committed audience and being addressed by an eminent speaker; and in a situation in which they do not feel that they are being pressurized.

The form and content of the information

People may agree to make changes in their attitude where they are not being asked to make too extreme a change, e.g. where new information is presented clearly and simply.

---

100 'The reader's taste in political news is affected by his own political opinions, especially if they are strong . . . most readers probably prefer news which confirms their own opinions to news which does not.'

R. Chandler and Bowker (eds.), *Public Opinion: Changing Attitudes on Contemporary Political and Social Issues*, 1972

If the statement above is true of the media generally why then should people worry about the effects of TV on children?

In order to adequately answer the question you would need to refer to some of the following material which contains contradictory evidence about the possible effects of the mass media on their audience.

1969   A government report suggested that a connection between violence on TV and problem behaviour in children did exist.

1970   Himmelweit and Halloran (*Violence on TV*) said the media can never be the sole cause of delinquent behaviour.

1971   Leibert and Baron (USA) found repeated exposure to TV aggression can lead children to accept what they see on TV as a partial guide for their actions.

1972   Katz (BBC report) found viewers do not worry much about too much violence on TV (unless it is very realistic). They were more concerned about bad language and sex on TV.

1975   Noble (*Children in Front of the Small Screen*) said that some types of TV violence are cathartic for some viewers, i.e. aggression purges them of similar feelings.

1977   Reed noted that the government was concerned about the effects of advertising on children.

1978   IBA research (*The Portrayal of Violence on TV*) suggested that violence may reinforce aggressive tendencies among emotionally unstable adolescents.

1978   Belson (*TV Violence and the Adolescent*) concluded that TV violence can lead to real life violence among some with aggressive personalities since it was often glamorized.

1978   Pye Survey showed that 45% of children aged 7–10 watched TV until 9 o'clock; 9% of this group watched until 10 o'clock; 1% watched until 11 o'clock: 79% of families exercised no control whatever over the number of hours their children watched TV.

Conclusions

There are contradictory findings about the effects of TV. The BBC report says the results of their research do not provide the basis for concluding that TV violence is or is not harmful.

In general it seems that the media can never be the single cause of deviant behaviour. But there is a strong suggestion that TV aggression can reinforce such values in those prone to such behaviour (perhaps 10% of the audience).

The mass media and political attitudes

You must bear in mind the points that have been made about the general findings relating to the mass media and attitude formation. But consider also the following:

Jones (*The Political Structure*) states that an efficient system to communicate information and opinions is essential if any form of government is to function effectively. The mass media have an important task in keeping the public informed and for providing opportunities for them to voice dissatisfaction.

1 **The Press**   In Britain the public buys more newspapers per person than in any other country. The government does not own or control any newspaper. The majority of daily newspapers, notably *The Times, Telegraph, Express, Mail* and *Sun*, support the Conservative Party. They have a combined circulation each day of about 11 million copies. The few Labour supporting papers are *The Mirror* and the *Daily Star* whose circulations are about five million. *The Guardian* is a Liberal (and sometimes Labour) supporting newspaper with a circulation of about 350,000. However, research suggests that newspapers are probably read by people for reasons other than their political slant. People are more likely to select a paper that reflects their social status and which meets their taste in general coverage. It is likely that the weekly journals, like *The Economist, Spectator* and *New Statesman*, are more politically influential. They can, however, like TV, help to create images and impressions of particular politicians, which may influence some voters at times of elections.

2 **Broadcasting**   Both radio and TV reach a very high proportion of the public. More than 90% of households have a TV. But people are selective in what they watch and what they recall. Party political broadcasts were begun in 1959, but in recent surveys it has been found that only a small proportion of viewers make use of them to decide on how to cast their vote. Trenaman and McQuail suggest that it is an important medium for providing people with information, for creating an image and impression of certain politicians and of political parties, but programmes about politics do little to change people's voting intentions. They argue that political persuasion needs to be conducted consistently over a long period of time if it is to be successful in influencing attitudes.

Factors affecting the way events are reported

Consider the following questions:

101   On pp. 157–8 are two newspaper articles describing the same events. The first account is from the Mirror, *and the second from the* Guardian.

THE TARTAN SIEGE OF W1

Scores held as Scots go on rampage

By MARGARET HALL and MICHAEL McCARTHY

THOUSANDS of Scottish football fans went on a wild rampage in the West End early today.

The tartan invaders stormed into Piccadilly Circus chanting for the blood of striking train drivers. By early today 42 Scots had been arrested.

When police arrived from nearby patrol vans, the cries of "Train drivers scum" changed to "We shall not be moved."

Several hundred beer-happy Scots were tightly hemmed in by police at the bottom of Regent Street.

Bottles

They waved dozens of banners, one nearly 12 ft. long, proclaiming: "Remember Bannockburn".

Police would let none of them near the statue of Eros in the middle of the Circus, which was surrounded by wooden boards.

As arm-linked policemen tried to clear the area, helmets and bottles hurtled through the air.

Finally police and fans collapsed, one on top of the other.

For a few minutes peace reigned as blue uniformed arms stretched out to help sporran wearers to their feet, and vice versa.

Tartan Terror

Then thousands of fans flooded down the Haymarket and into Trafalgar Square. They chanted anti-English slogans and hammered on the roofs and windows of cars which were unable to pass them.

One car, whose driver sounded his horn, was surrounded by a dozen Scots fans, shouting and swearing, who kicked savagely at the car and tried to get in.

Scots fans in rush to beat Tube ban

By BRENDA HOLTON

THOUSANDS of Scottish soccer fans poured into London yesterday and immediately headed for Wembley to beat the industrial action planned for today by Tube and railway staff.

By lunch time yesterday pubs surrounding the stadium were full of effervescent, early-bird Scots. Many had no tickets for the game against England, and more had no accommodation.

Police said that by 1 a.m. 34 people had been arrested in Central London and two at Wembley. Charges ranged from drunk and disorderly to criminal damage.

But generally, the thousands of Scottish fans who invaded the West End hardly caused a ripple of anxiety amongst the police officers on duty at Trafalgar Square and Piccadilly.

In a variety of tartan scarves, bonnets, trousers and the occasional kilt the fans thronged the street but the majority were on their best behaviour.

Some, with bottles of wine and pint mugs of beer, attempted a Scottish dance but most of them confined themselves to chanting England's downfall.

Noisy but happy

"They were noisy but happy and well-behaved and we are not bothered about how much noise they make," a police officer, stationed close to the boarded up figure of Eros, said.

"There must be a few thousand of them here but I think, because of the trains ban, the greater majority of them must have made their way to Wembley during the day."

(a) *Each of these two newspaper articles gives a different 'picture' of 'what happened'. What methods have the journalists who wrote the articles used to create their different accounts of the same events?* *(4 marks)*

(b) *Why might journalists employed by different newspapers offer such different interpretations of the same situation?* *(4 marks)*

(c) *Using material from these extracts and any other information you think appropriate, discuss the part played by the mass media in creating and perpetuating stereotypes.* *(12 marks)* (CAM, *adapted*)

102 *Never believe what you hear on radio or see on television or read in the newspapers. What has sociology to say about this?* (LON)

The work of a number of contemporary writers has thrown important light on how journalists gather and report news.

1 Hartmann and Husband (*The Mass Media and Racial Conflict*) make use of the concept of 'news values' to explain why the presentation of news varies from one newspaper or news programme to another.

(a) Every editor of every newspaper and news programme knows the kind of people who form the bulk of their audience.

(b) This knowledge shapes the way in which they instruct their journalists to gather and write their news stories. They know what their audience expect and they therefore provide it. These are their 'news values'. As far as the popular press (these are the tabloid papers: *Express, Mail, Star, Mirror* and *Sun*) are concerned, these values centre on sensation, scandal, bizarre incidents and personalities.

(c) Events become newsworthy when they fit into one or more of the news values categories.

(d) The repetition of certain kinds of stories leads the audience to expect similar events to occur in the future. They become sensitized to certain patterns of behaviour. They expect demonstrations to be violent; that there will be outbreaks of football hooliganism; that there will be racial conflict, etc.

(e) These familiar frameworks are established by the use of repeated images and stereotypes. The audience comes to know what football fans are like, how to identify particular members of youth cultures and anticipate how they will behave.

(f) Events become even more newsworthy when they can be reported within the familiar framework which fulfils the expectations of the audience.

Hartmann and Husband conclude that the mass media report events in ways that fulfil the needs and assumptions of their readers and viewers and listeners. This is not to say that they deliberately set out to misinform or mislead the audience. They are simply following their normal procedures and applying their normal 'news values' to their selection and interpretation of events. They give the example of how in 1970 seven of the eight national daily papers carried a story about the increase in the birth-rate to immigrant mothers with great prominence, whereas only four carried the news about the reduction in numbers of immigrants arriving in Britain, and only one of these on the front page. This was because the first story fitted audience expectations whereas the second did not.

The authors suggest that the media should become more concerned with the causes and possible solutions to major issues rather than with sensationalizing trivial items.

2 Trenaman and McQuail (*Towards a Sociology of Mass Communication*) make points similar to those raised by Hartmann and Husband. They describe three factors that influence the way news is reported in the media. They suggest that journalists are 'shaped' or influenced in their approach by the following:

(a) The **institution** in which they work   The media build up over time an image of what constitutes an acceptable form and content of news. This is shared by the journalists who work in that particular medium. News reporting is shaped by this knowledge.

(b) Their knowledge of their **audience**   Research into the type of audience who receive their messages helps the journalist or commentator to decide the form the material will take.

(c) The **personal feedback** received from friends and colleagues   Once the journalist or commentator becomes established within a particular institution they tend to work with unchanging values because they are constantly reinforced in their approach by the comments of colleagues and friends. To some extent they may be shielded from wider critical comment so the ideas and images with which they work go unchallenged.

103 'Belson's *Television Violence and the Adolescent Boy* is based on detailed interviews with 1565 London boys aged between 12 and 17 (and their mothers) conducted in the second half of 1972 and early 1973. The major aim was to establish a causal link between the boys' exposure to television violence and their involvement in violent acts. The study produced a massive array of results, but the central finding and the one that Belson himself sees as "most

noteworthy" is that "high exposure to television violence increases the degree to which boys engage in serious violence".'

G. Murdock and R. McCron,
The Television and Delinquency Debate, 1979

(a) What questions would you expect a sociologist to ask in interviews of this sort? What other methods of research could be used in studying this topic? (10 marks)

(b) What light do other sociological studies of the mass media throw on the suggestion that watching television can affect people's behaviour? (10 marks) (CAM)

To answer part (a) re-read pp. 21–2, 186; to answer part (b) re-read pp. 152–5.

Key terms and concepts

The following terms and concepts have been used and defined in this chapter. You must be able to use them and explain their meaning for examination purposes:

mass media; attitudes; attitude change; selective perception; selective exposure; selective retention; news values; popular press; quality press.

15 The political structure

Patterns of voting behaviour

Politics is about the way in which **power** is distributed in a **society**; with decisions about the way a society should be organized both socially and economically; it is concerned, too, with the ways policies are decided upon and how they are implemented. Political parties are formed by people who hold similar views on these questions and who wish to gain power in order to carry them out.

British politics are simply described in the figure.

Rose (*Influencing Voters*) has said that the study of voting behaviour and the study of the behaviour of the campaigners are both important in understanding politics. This gives rise to such examination questions as:

104 What are the major factors which sociologists use to explain voting patterns? (OX) (See p. 165.)

Although there is some evidence that there may be some changes occurring in voting patterns in the 1980s, voting patterns in Britain traditionally have been fairly fixed. People tend to favour one party or another throughout most of their voting lives. This is because people form their political attitudes early in life (usually as a result of the type of household in which they grow up). Such attitudes are relatively difficult to change. Most elections are won on the decisions of a fairly small number of floating voters.

In order to understand why people come to favour one party rather than another, it is necessary to know what the underlying philosophies of the parties are.

1 **Fascism**   Fascism is associated with Hitler (1933–45) in Germany and Mussolini (1922–43) in Italy. In Britain an example is the National Front Party. It allows no other political parties and advocates rule by dictatorship or elite. Fascism asserts white supremacy.

2 **Conservatism**   The Conservative Party emerged in the nineteenth century. Its main principles were established in 1872 by Disraeli who said the Tory party had three objectives:

(a) To maintain the traditional institutions of the country;
(b) To uphold the Empire;
(c) To elevate the conditions of the people.

These were confirmed by a Committee in 1948.

Today the Party stands for the maintenance of all the traditional structures of society (private enterprise, monarchy, etc.). The main principle is to conserve the best of the past.

3 **Liberalism**   The main period of Liberal power was 1868–1914. Their main principles are:
(a) Reform;
(b) Free Trade;
(c) More regional and less central power.
In 1980 the Social Democratic Party emerged to take up the same central ground.

4 **Socialism**   The Labour Party was founded in 1906 following the steps taken by the TUC to form a party. The TUC still provides much of the financial backing. The main principles were established in 1918:
(a) To secure for producers by hand or by brain the full fruits of their industry.
(b) The equitable distribution of income and wealth on the basis of the common ownership of the means of production.
(c) To obtain the best system of popular administration and control of industry.
Today the Labour Party favours nationalization, extensions of the welfare state and increases in social equality.

5 **Communism**   This is an extreme form of socialism. The philosophy is based on the principles of Marxism. He argued that

only in a classless society could all men become free: this would mean the end of alienation. It would represent an entirely cooperative society in which people would give to others according to their means and take according to their needs.

When people vote for a political party they are voting for an ideology or set of principles about how a society ought to be organized.

Many studies have confirmed that of all the factors in the table social class background and identification remains the most significant in shaping voting behaviour in Britain. Some examination questions therefore focus more precisely on this factor, and you should be able to deal with the topic in more detail.

105 Social class is by far the most important factor in explaining how people vote. Discuss. (OX)

Pulzer (*Political Representation and Elections*) said in 1967 that class is the basis of British party politics: all else is embellishment and detail.
Butler and Stokes (*Political Change in Britain*) said that
(a) Too little attention has been paid to the link between class and party.
(b) There is no doubt that political attitudes are largely related to early family experience.
(c) Only about 25% of the British electorate do not vote in accordance with their objective class membership.
Alford conducted a comparative study into the effects of class on voting behaviour and concluded that it had a more significant effect in Britain than in any of the other countries he studied.
Milne and McKenzie (*Straight Fight*, 1958) found that subjective class identification was particularly significant. For example, people who saw themselves as being middle-class (even though objectively they may have had low-level manual jobs) were more likely to vote Conservative than those who saw themselves as being working class.
What such studies suggest is that the way a person sees their position in the class structure has a stronger influence on the way they cast their vote than how they are personally affected by the economic policies of the party they vote for.
However, in recent years some writers are suggesting that the alignment between class and party is becoming less clearly defined — although the relationship remains comparatively strong.
Some questions ask you to discuss why there are some voters who do not vote on class lines. For example:

106 'In Britain the national figures suggest that around two-thirds of

Factors affecting voting behaviour

Social class	Party image	Age and sex	Religion	Mass media
This helps establish an individual's self-image. Political parties have become associated with class groups. The Labour Party is seen to be the party of the working class and the Conservative Party that of the middle class. Butler and Rose say it is the most important factor. The roots of the Conservative Party are in the wealthy sectors of society.	Each party has a core of voters who identify with the traditional image (or stereotype) it has. This helps them decide how to cast their votes. Images can also be created of politicians and these may influence voting patterns.	There is no firm evidence to show that youth is more radical than an older generation. Most studies show that a first vote is cast in the same way as their parents vote. People tend to get more conservative in their voting as they get older. Women are more likely to vote Conservative than men in all age groups. Abrams and Little found that there were more Labour voters among young semi and unskilled workers.	This is not such a significant factor in Britain (except in certain regions). There is some evidence to show the traditional connection between the Conservative Party and Church of England remains. There remains a tendency for more Catholics to vote Labour. Hornsby Smith and Lee (1978) found 57% of their Catholic sample voted Labour in 1974. Lenski (1966) in the USA found Catholics were less successful in the business world than Protestants.	Where people have fixed views the media are seldom effective in converting them (see pp. 152–4). They may help people to make up their minds which way to vote when they are not well informed. Most research (especially Trenaman and McQuail) suggests that the media tend to reinforce existing views. They may also help to create 'images' about parties and politicians.

manual workers vote for the Labour Party, while around three-quarters of white-collar workers support the Conservative Party. Such figures have remained consistent over most of the general elections since 1945.'

Dunkerly, *Occupations in Society*

What sort of manual workers tend to vote Conservative and why?

There were many studies undertaken in the 1960s to try and answer the question 'who are the working-class Tories?' The question arose largely because the Conservatives had won three consecutive general elections in 1951, 1955 and 1959. Yet they have traditionally represented the middle-class interests in society and only about 30% of the population objectively falls into this category. This meant that a proportion of working-class voters were voting Conservative rather than for the party which has traditionally represented their interests.

1 Butler and Rose explained this in terms of the increasing affluence of many working-class people in the late 1950s. They claimed that the more prosperous and affluent section of the working class were losing their identity as a social stratum and were becoming merged into the middle class. As a result they were voting for the party which they now perceived to represent them best. This is known as the embourgeoisement thesis. It was later tested by Lockwood and Goldthorpe and rejected (see pp. 75–6).

2 Roberts, Cook, Clark and Semeonoff (*The Fragmentary Class Structure*, 1977) retested the thesis. They agree that affluence alone does not cause people to change class. They conclude that embourgeoisement affects only a minority of manual workers who have strong white-collar connections.

3 Nordlinger (*The Working-Class Tories*) concludes that they can be explained by a strong sense of deferrence. They preferred candidates from higher social classes to their own since they were more likely to make good leaders. (Mrs Thatcher's 1979 Cabinet helps to illustrate this idea: of the 22 members, 6 went to Eton, 3 to Winchester, 1 to Harrow, and 1 to Rugby. Only 2 did not attend a public school.)

4 Parkin (*Working-Class Conservatives: A Theory of Political Deviance*) treats working-class Labour voting as deviant and working-class Tory voting as the norm. This is because the central values of British society are essentially conservative. All socialist voting is a symbolic act of deviance. Working-class Labour voters are generally protected by a supportive sub-culture as, for example, on a large housing estate.

Votes cast in Parliamentary Elections 1951–79 (millions)

	1951	1955	1959	1964	1966	1970	Feb 1974	Oct 1974	1979
Labour	13.9	12.4	12.2	12.2	13.1	12.2	11.6	11.4	11.5
Conservative	13.7	13.3	13.7	12.0	11.4	13.1	11.9	10.4	13.7
Liberal	0.7	0.7	1.6	3.1	2.3	2.1	6.0	5.3	4.3
Others	0.2	0.3	0.3	0.3	0.4	0.9	1.8	2.0	1.7
Total	28.5	26.7	27.8	27.6	27.2	28.3	31.3	29.1	31.2

Source: Social Trends No. 10
Note: There are, of course, other smaller parties for whom people vote.

Because there may be some **changes** going on in the **nature** of the **class structure** of modern Britain, you must look carefully to see whether the question raises this point. Consider these questions, for example:

107 *Examine the relationship between social class and voting behaviour in Britain. What, if any, have been the changes in this relationship since 1945?* (OX)
108 The table below summarizes the results of a survey in which a sample of young adult voters was asked
  (i) which party they had supported when they first became voters (this is what is meant by 'earliest party preference' and 'respondent's own first preference' in the table),
  (ii) which parties their parents supported at that time.

Earliest party preference by parents' Conservative or Labour preference (%)

Respondent's own first preference	Both parents Conservative	Parents' partisan-ship Parents divided Con/Lab	Both parents Labour
Conservative	89	48	6
Labour	9	52	92
Liberal	2	—	2
	100	100	100

(Butler and Stokes, *Political Change in Britain*)

(a) *What does 'parent partisanship' mean? What might influence this?*
(b) *How important does parental attitude towards a political party seem to be as far as the voting of their children is concerned?*
(c) *Is there evidence to show that social class influences voting?*
(d) *Is there evidence to show that this is less significant in recent years?*

In each case you are asked, as part of your answer, to explain what changes have been noted in the relationship between class and voting patterns in recent years; also why some people either abstain from voting or vote for one of the minor parties in preference to either of the two major parties.

Abstainers

These are people who fail or refuse to vote in an election. Normally, more than 70% do vote in general elections. It is estimated that at least 10% of the electorate deliberately abstain.

Reasons for abstaining
(a) Forgetfulness;
(b) Apathy;
(c) Hostility to all parties;
(d) To register hostility to a party previously supported.

Who are the abstainers?
(a) The young;
(b) The elderly;
(c) Abstentions are highest among women.

The significance of the abstainers
(a) They can help change an election result. Most voters are committed to one party. Where the seat is marginal (only a few hundred votes separate the parties), failure to vote can be crucial.
(b) They may also be called **floating voters**; they change their votes from one election to the next. They are uncommitted to any party and so may decide to abstain. They become important **target voters** for canvassers during the last minutes of campaigns.

Possible reasons for lack of interest in politics in Britain
(a) People may feel central government is remote.
(b) Political scandals may cause people to become disillusioned.
(c) Saturation coverage by the media may cause a sense of boredom.
(d) People may lack an understanding of political philosophies and fail to see the difference between the parties.

Changes in class support for the parties

1 King (Professor of Politics, Essex University) notes that the Labour Party is losing much traditional working-class support. In 1979 it

gained only 30% of the votes. People may believe that they have failed to control the unions. The British electorate does not favour extremist leaders and it may be that people see more in the Labour rather than in the Conservative party. He concludes that people may be voting less on traditional class lines than previously.

2 Dahrendorf argues that the class structure in Britain has changed; there is now much more social mobility than in the past. As a result, traditional voting patterns may change. He believes that people have been liberated from their class boundaries.

3 Hindess (*The Decline of Working-Class Politics*) locates a circle of decline in political activity in the more working-class areas of large cities; this results in a shift of power towards the more middle-class areas. He argues that as power falls into more middle-class hands this will increase levels of apathy among working-class people. They seem to be losing the belief that political action can achieve change.

4 The work of Roberts *et al.* might suggest that it is the Conservative party which could be in danger of losing voters at future elections because the middle class itself is becoming more fragmented and less cohesive as a class for itself.

Conclusions

1 It may be the failure of Labour's distinctive class appeal to make an impact on a particular segment of the working class which is a key to Conservative support.

2 The working class is becoming more affluent. This may result in more of its members having more contacts with white-collar workers which may influence their perceptions of themselves.

3 The Labour Party may be converging more towards the Conservative position in terms of many policies (especially Northern Ireland, defence and membership of the Common Market).

4 The Labour Party contains fewer people of working-class origin than before. The Party itself may be changing identity.

5 Until the emergence of politicians such as Mr Benn, Mr Heffer, etc. there has been a weakening of Labour identification with distinctive working-class goals. At the same time these politicians are seen to be too extreme to gain wide popularity.

6 The emergence of the Social Democratic Party may be a symptom of the dissatisfaction people feel with the two main parties even though it lacks any coherent philosophical position.

109 **Voting intention by region and class, 1963–66**

Class	Voting behaviour	London and S.E. England (%)	S.W. England (%)	E. Midlands (%)	N.E. England (%)	Wales (%)
Middle Class }	Conservative	74.1	77.4	83.2	72.7	58.0
	Labour	13.0	9.9	8.9	18.6	30.8
Skilled Working Class }	Conservative	33.6	38.2	33.5	26.5	15.2
	Labour	56.0	46.9	59.0	69.2	79.9

Source: adapted from Anthony King, A Sociological Portrait: Politics, *New Society*, 13 January 1972.

Explain clearly what the table tells us about the relation between social class and voting behaviour.

To answer this question follow this plan:
1 Briefly explain what is meant by **social class**.
2 Explain why sociologists are interested in understanding patterns of **voting behaviour**.
3 Suggest why social class is a relevant factor in the analysis.
4 Comment on the data in the table:
  (a) Why do such a high proportion of middle-class people vote Conservative?
  (b) Why is this vote strongest in the E. Midlands and weakest in Wales?
  (c) Why do such a high proportion of working-class people vote Labour?
  (d) Why is the Labour vote strongest in Wales and N.E. England?
  (e) Who are the middle-class Labour voters likely to be?
  (f) Who are the working-class Tory voters likely to be?
  (g) Why are the working-class Conservative votes strongest in S.W. England, E. Midlands and S.E. England and London?
5 Notice that the study dates from 1963 to 1966. Point out some of the changes that may have occurred in class attitudes since.
6 Reach a conclusion about what the table tells us about the relation between social class and voting behaviour in the mid-1960s.

Key terms and concepts

The following terms and concepts have been used and defined in this chapter. You must be able to use them and explain their meanings for examination purposes:

politics; stereotypes; party image; affluence; embourgeoisement; abstainers; floating voters; Conservative; Socialist;

Fascist; Liberal; capitalism; working-class Tory; sub-cultures; institutions; free enterprise; deviant voting; deference.

Other terms which you may wish to use:

party allegiance   The party for which a person votes and supports between elections.

partisanship   The favourable feelings a person has towards a particular group or organization and for which they are likely to vote or provide support.

thesis   A theory that explains the way particular events relate to each other and result in a set of particular consequences.

16   Pressure groups

Questions on pressure groups tend to fall into three main categories:

1 Those which ask for an **explanation** of what pressure groups are and for some **examples** of how they operate.
2 Those which ask for a **discussion** of their **functions** and how they may **influence** governments.
3 Those for which you need to know some of the **distinctions** between **political parties** and **pressure groups**.

Consider the following questions:

110 (a) *Describe, with examples, the different types of pressure groups with which you are familiar.* (8)
   (b) *What methods do pressure groups use and why are such groups important in modern Britain?* (12)   (AEB)
111 'Most people are vaguely familiar with the formal institutions of government – Parliament, local councils, political parties, the civil service, the courts and the police – and they recognize them for what they are. But few people would perhaps label such groups as . . . Shelter, or the National Union of Teachers as political.'

Richard Tames, *People, Power and Politics*, 1978

   (a) *What sociological term is used to describe such groups?* (2 marks)
   (b) *How do such groups operate in our political system?* (8 marks)
   (c) *Why are they important?* (10 marks)   (AEB)

Pressure groups are formed when a number of people who hold one or more interests in common join together in order to put pressure on those who hold power.

Some pressure groups work to influence central government (or a government department); others may work to influence a local authority or a body that is likely to behave in ways of which they disapprove. Other interest groups may seek to promote a new idea that they wish the same bodies to adopt. For example, a government may be encouraged by one pressure group to remain in the Common Market and listen to the demands of another to leave; a local authority may be asked by one pressure group to build a by-pass and discouraged by another from doing so; a television authority may be criticized by one interest group for showing too much violence and defended by another for resisting censorship.

Pressure groups are important because they enable people to have some direct effect on the policies and decisions of those who have the power to shape the kind of society in which people live.

Types of pressure group

Defensive or protective groups	Promotional groups
These are groups formed mainly to protect the interests of their members. They include such groups as: a. Trade unions b. Motoring organizations (AA and RAC) c. The British Medical Association	These groups are formed to promote or champion a particular cause. They include: a. Campaign for Comprehensive Schools b. Campaign for Nuclear Disarmament c. Child Poverty Action Group d. Local Radio Association

Some groups both defend and promote causes; those that set out to achieve a particular end generally disappear once that aim is achieved. For example, a group may form to prevent an airport being built in a particular area. Once the government has agreed to their demands the pressure group disbands. It may quickly reform, of course, if the issue arises again at a later date.

Example of pressure groups at work

(a) Defensive

A group of workers may feel that their health is adversely affected by their conditions of work. Their trade union is asked to conduct an investigation on their behalf. The union, through a shop steward or other representative, presents the case of the workers. If the company rejects the complaint the union may then decide to open negotiations with them. If these negotiations are unsuccessful, then the workers may eventually be called out on strike in order to put more pressure on the management. This may ultimately result in the workers gaining the changes they requested.

(b) Promotional

The Local Radio Association was established in 1964. It arose when a public relations adviser was asked by a proposed company (Radio Yorkshire) how he might help establish 'commercial radio'. Very quickly the LRA gained the backing of many media celebrities, businessmen and equipment manufacturers. The fans of what were then 'pirate radio stations' also gave support. The LRA was successful in putting its case to the Conservative Party (which was then in Opposition) so that it became a part of their agreed programme when they next gained power. The main opponents were the Labour Party and the Musicians Union, as well as the GPO which was concerned about the limited availability of wave lengths.

However, the organizers of the pressure group conducted studies showing all the possibilities of commercial radio. The findings were circulated to all MPs, Members of the House of Lords and journalists for use in the media.

The Conservatives came to power in 1970. Commercial radio was legalized in 1972 and the first station was on the air in 1973.

The second area on which questions arise is concerned with the function and influence of pressure groups. Consider the following questions:

112 *Do pressure groups play an important part in enabling people to influence government decisions in modern Britain?* (AEB)
113 *What is a pressure group? Discuss with examples the role of pressure groups in the British political system.* (OX)

Commenting on the significance of pressure groups for government departments, Jones (*The Political Structure*) says that the complexity of modern government has exaggerated its remoteness from the electorate. This has encouraged the growth of pressure group activities in an attempt to exert direct influence on politicians and to cut through the routine and slow procedures. Their influence is always diverse and varied.

Blondel (*Voters, Parties and Leaders*) makes the point that in a democratic society it is crucial to have both political parties and pressure groups. The parties are responsible for organizing the policies and for implementing them. Pressure groups are important because they provide a form of representation outside the political parties. They help to channel the ideas, views and demands of the people in society who are subject to the decisions of the politicians. Membership of a pressure group is therefore a way of exerting pressure on them to abandon, modify or implement some new policy which they otherwise would not have done. Whether or not they are successful depends on the following:

1 Their organization (aims and procedures);
2 Their prestige or standing in the community;
3 Their level of support (size of membership);
4 Their wealth;
5 The dedication of the membership (for how long are members prepared to wait for success?);
6 Their ability to get at the source of power.
   (Ecstein in *Pressure Group Politics* says they must have a clear understanding of the structure of the decision-making processes of the body they are trying to influence.)

Some examples of pressure groups which have been successful in influencing government policies include:

1 LRS (see p. 174).
2 CND. In 1980 the Labour Party under Michael Foot agreed that it would abandon nuclear weapons if it regained power at the next election.
3 Women's Liberation Movement. Long-standing pressure from this group helped to ensure the package of legislation passed in 1975 (see pp. 44–7).
4 Local pressure groups were organized in the 1970s and 1980s to oppose the government's intention to build a third London airport. They successfully opposed the siting of this in Maplin, Stansted and Wing.
5 The TUC was successful in gaining the repeal of the Industrial Relations Act (1972) as a result of constant pressure on the Government.

The third area on which questions are asked is based on the differences and similarities between political parties and pressure groups.
   Consider the following questions:

114 *Give examples or by any other methods show clearly that you understand the differences between a political party and a pressure group.* (AEB, *adapted*)
115 *Outline and comment upon the part played by the following in British politics: (a) pressure groups; (b) political parties.* (AEB, *adapted*)
116 *Describe, with examples, different types of pressure groups.*

McKenzie says that the basic function of parties is to select, organize and sustain teams of Parliamentarians, among whom the electorate can choose at times of elections. This means that the electorate can cast their votes for competing teams of potential rulers. Each team has an underlying philosophy with which all members agree (see p. 163).

Blondel has said that parties are not just collections of elected members of Parliament. They are social groups (they encompass people from a wide range of social backgrounds) and they have a corporate life. There is a strong hierarchy of power and influence in a political party.

Rose (*Politics in England*) points out, however, that it is difficult to draw an exact line between parties and pressure groups because there is much mutual inter-penetration between them. This is most apparent in the Labour Party and pressure groups such as trade unions and co-operative societies between which there are very close connections. The Labour Party has been described as a coalition of diverse class, trade union and other pressure groups. The interrelationship between party and interest group also exists between the Conservatives and the business world. Aims of Industry, the Confederation of British Industry and the Institute of Directors do much work to campaign for free enterprise and therefore enjoy a special relationship with the Conservative Party.

The comments of these writers indicate that there are many comparisons to be made between parties and pressure groups – but there are also some major differences which exist between them.

The similarities

1 They bring together many people with similar aims, interests and goals and a set of theories about how to achieve their ends.
2 They are hierarchical in structure. There is a small group who direct policies and a mass of more general supporters.
3 The members of political parties in Opposition seek to influence the government in relation to most of their policies. Some members of the Government may seek to modify or change a few aspects of the policies of their own Cabinet. Members of pressure groups (who are usually drawn from a cross-section of the public) generally seek to influence the government or the opposition party in one particular area of policy only.
4 A trade union, as a pressure group, may sponsor candidates to become MPs. A political party also recommends candidates as potential members.
5 It is possible for membership of both a party and a pressure group to overlap. A politician may join a pressure group and so give it additional status. Members of pressure groups may join political parties in order to gain closer access to decision-makers.

6 They are both important in keeping the Government and the party in opposition informed about changing attitudes, new demands, etc., and responsive to current trends.

The differences

1 Pressure groups do not compete in elections.
2 They do not have wide-ranging policies. They are generally concerned only with one issue.
3 They do not seek to form a Government.
4 Whereas any MP can join a pressure group, a pressure group member can only become an MP as a result of winning an election.
5 Elected MPs are paid a salary. Membership of a pressure group is voluntary and may require a subscription.
6 Pressure groups have no official representation in Parliament, although their interests may be voiced by MPs who support them.

Key terms and concepts

The following terms and concepts have been used and defined in this chapter. You must be able to use them and explain their meanings for examination purposes:

pressure groups; defensive pressure groups; promotional groups; TUC; political parties; the electorate; power; hierarchical.

Other terms you may wish to use:

democratic society   A government freely chosen by members of the society in frequent elections. It is then responsible to the governed and can be replaced by an opposition party.

dictatorship (totalitarian society)   Government by a single person, class or group whose authority is total and allows no organized opposition. It is not therefore open to pressure from groups seeking change.

17 Crime and deviance

Questions on this topic tend to relate to the following areas:

1 Distinguishing between crime and deviance;
2 Stating and interpreting relevant statistics;
3 Discussing who are the offenders;
4 Stating explanatory theories and commenting on them.

Distinguishing between crime and deviance

*117 Give three examples of different kinds of deviant behaviour, and
explain why they are or are not socially acceptable.* (AEB)
*118 The law tells us what constitutes crime in modern Britain but
opinions on what is deviant may vary. Explain why this is
so.* (AEB)
*119 One of the problems in sociology is to achieve a definition of
deviance. Explain why this is so. Use examples to illustrate your
answer.*

Mays (*Crime and the Social Structure*) defines a crime as 'an offence
against society'. He says that it consists in the commission of acts which
have been legally proscribed. A criminal is a person who has trans-
gressed the legal norms of the society in which he or she lives. More
precisely, there are two types of crime.

(a) **Indictable offences**   These are serious offences punishable by
the law of the state which must be brought to court by the police
and, if proven, punished by the prescribed penalties, usually
imprisonment or fine. Indictable offences include murder, larceny,
forgery, etc.
(b) **Non-indictable offences**   These are less serious crimes which
are tried in lower courts. They are also subject to prescribed
penalties, usually a fine. They include motoring offences, assault,
damage to property, etc. Most offences are of this type.

There are some offences known as **torts** which are not technically crimes (even though there is a breach of law). They are civil offences, such as slander, trespass, nuisance, etc. They are brought by one individual against another. It is possible to settle such actions before judgement by payment of damages.

It is clear, therefore, that the term 'crime' is a specific legal term with a technical meaning. Sometimes confusion arises in its use because it is forgotten that not all crimes are serious offences. When people speak of criminals or a crime wave they may fail to take into account that offences are non-indictable and mainly traffic offences.

To overcome this problem of usage many sociologists prefer to use the concept of **deviance** since it can be used to cover all infractions of rules and laws (in both a legal and non-legal sense) and both of a serious and non-serious type.

Deviance is understood by sociologists to mean behaviour which somehow deviates from what a group or society as a whole expects to be done or from what is considered by observers of the action to be the desirable way of doing things. The person who acts in a particular way may not see their action as deviant, but it is seen to be by those whom it offends.

Becker has said that deviance is the infraction of some agreed upon rule. He adds that deviance is created by society. By this he means that social groups create deviance by labelling offenders as 'deviants' because they have offended social rules. In his view deviance is not simply a quality present in some kinds of behaviour and absent in others: it is the product of a process which involves responses of others to the behaviour.

Deviance itself could be divided into two types:

(a) Illegal (criminal) acts which carry legal sanctions;
(b) Legal but non-normative types of behaviour. These may offend the group and carry certain group sanctions (social pressure to conform or leave the group – or risk being disliked).

Deviant behaviour of an illegal type that is committed by young people between the ages of 10 and 17 is termed **delinquent** behaviour. When committed by others it is **criminal** behaviour.

In its non-legal sense deviant behaviour refers to non-conformist actions, that is acts that do not conform to the accepted norms of the group to which the individual belongs: for example, the non-smoker in a group of smokers; the working-class Tory in a group of Labour supporters; the teenager who prefers classical music to pop; the child in the classroom who hands in homework before the teacher asks for it, etc.

Willmott and Young (*Social Grading by Manual Workers*) showed that judgements about the social class of selected occupations tended to become more variable further down the occupational scale. They had a small group of 'deviant' respondents who rated the status of certain occupations according to the social contribution made by the occupations. They rated many manual occupations higher than some professional and white-collar jobs.

It is important to remember that deviance is a relative term because the same act may be said to be deviant when committed by one person and 'stupidity' or 'a joke' when committed by someone else. An act may become deviant according to who is committing it and who is observing it. For students throwing bags of flour on a rag-day their behaviour is described as 'high spirits'. Other youths throwing bags of flour on another occasion may be described as hooligans.

Crime is a more absolute concept: an act that breaks the law is criminal, regardless of who commits it or who sees it being committed.

The statistics and their interpretation

120 (a) Do increases in criminal statistics always mean increased social disorder?
(b) Why has the crime rate in Britain increased since 1951? What have been the main changes in the pattern of criminal behaviour during this period?

To answer questions like these you must have a general knowledge of the statistics for the period covered. You need not know the figures precisely but you must show a reasonable accuracy. Remember that you cannot hope to answer a question that asks you to explain the change in rate of an event (whether it is crime, divorce, marriage, etc.) without producing some statistics. For the purpose of learning them you can always round them up or down to a convenient number. You may then begin to see a pattern running through them which will help your memory.

Number of indictable offences known to the police (thousands)

England and Wales	1951	1961	1966	1971	1972	1973	1976	1977
Total number of known offences	525	807	1200	1646	1362	1358	2136	2463
Crimes of violence	7	17	26	46	52	61	68	82
No. proceeded against of total	144	193	250	351	373	366	457	474
No. found guilty	133	182	233	322	340	338	359	429

Source: Social Trends No. 9 (adapted)

The details in the first table show how the number of persons proceeded against is always a small fraction of the total, although the number found guilty is always high. The number of violent offences is comparatively small when compared with the total number of indictable offences that are recorded by the police.

Number of persons proceeded against for non-indictable offences and number found guilty (thousands)

England and Wales	1951	1961	1966	1971	1972	1973	1976	1977
No. proceeded against	626	1014	1269	1445	1569	1674	1753	1661
No. of motoring offences	291	655	898	988	1089	1192	1211	1130
No. found guilty of all offences	584	970	1213	1366	1486	1591	1657	1550

Source: Social Trends (adapted)

In the second table notice how the number of motoring offences is about half of the total number of the non-indictable offences that were prosecuted.

Problems in interpreting the statistics

1 When people talk of 'an increase in crime' they seldom distinguish between indictable and non-indictable offences. A high proportion of criminals commit minor traffic offences. Only a tiny proportion commit crimes of violence.
2 Wiles (*Criminal Statistics and Sociological Explanations of Crime*) points out that there is a 'dark figure' in crime: i.e. acts prohibited by law but not reported to the police and therefore not appearing in criminal statistics.
3 Where the statistics do show an increase this may result from
   (a) Increased public concern with a particular offence. The public may become more sensitized to a certain kind of offence because of coverage by the media. The sudden concern with mugging after 1972 is an example.
   (b) The statistics being compiled by the police. They may have devoted more time to policing some areas more heavily than others and as a result made more arrests. These will appear later in the statistics giving the impression that certain kinds of offences are on the increase.
4 Changes in legislation can affect the statistics. For example, a change in the definition of burglary as a result of the 1968 Theft Act meant that the statistics before and after that date cannot be directly compared.
5 Many criminal acts may have been unintentional (especially those relating to minor traffic offences), and it would be wrong to see

increases as evidence that people are becoming more criminally minded.

6 More general explanations for increases in criminal behaviour are sometimes put forward. Policemen may blame weak politicians for failing to support them; others blame weak judges and the influence of liberal reformers for failing to impose strong deterrents on offenders. Some point to the weakening of the family as an institution, the increase in divorce and lack of parental guidance. Other commentators point to violence in the media and the strains resulting from unemployment and urban living. These points generally rest on the value judgements of the commentators and would require further research and careful analysis.

7 The authors of *Social Trends No. 3* point out that methods of recording crimes used by police forces throughout the country have varied considerably over the years. Consequently, statistics of offences known to the police have to be treated cautiously.

8 More laws have been passed – especially traffic laws – and so there are more laws to break. Also the police have become more efficient in clearing up certain kinds of offence, although the average clear-up rate remains at about 45% p.a.

Some changes in the patterns of criminal behaviour

1 There has been an increase in the number of theft offences. These now comprise about 95% of all serious crime.

2 There has been an increase in the number of violent offences. These have increased from about 1% of the total offences to 4% between 1951 and 1977.

3 There has been an increase in the percentage of traffic offences from about 50% in 1951 to 60% in 1977.

4 Most offences recorded are indictable, but the majority of people prosecuted and found guilty have committed non-indictable offences.

5 There has been a slight increase in the number of women committing serious offences. Numbers rose from 31,000 in 1965 to 60,300 in 1975. But the proportion of women offenders remains very small compared with the number of male offenders.

6 There has been an increase in **mugging** since 1972. This term was not used before this date and was previously generally described as robbery in the open from a person. After much publicity based on cases in the USA the term gained currency in Britain and an increasing number of offences were reported.

7 There has been an increase in the number of offences committed by young people. In 1969 62% of offenders were under 25 and 45%

were under 21. In 1975 about 50% of serious offences were committed by those under 21.

Some examination questions focus more precisely on criminal activity among the young. For example:

121 What sociological explanations have been put forward to account for the increase in juvenile delinquency in Britain? (OX)
122 Why is the crime rate of male adolescents higher than that of any other age group? (OX)

Once again, to answer such questions you require some statistical details as shown in the first table. The second table illustrates another way of expressing similar data.

Crime statistics: males found guilty of indictable offences, England and Wales, 1972–6 (rate per thousand of the population)

	1972	1973	1974	1975	1976
Ages 10–13	12.3	12.5	14.1	12.9	12.1
14–16	46.0	47.4	54.2	52.3	51.4
17–20	54.8	55.2	59.5	64.3	63.4
21–29	24.3	23.5	25.1	27.1	27.8
30 and over	5.7	5.4	5.9	6.4	6.9
All	14.8	14.6	16.0	16.9	17.3

Source: Social Trends, 1977

Number of males guilty of indictable offences, 1970–76 (thousands)

	1970	1972	1974	1976
Under 17	66.6	69.1	83.9	80.8
17–21	69.6	75.0	82.4	91.6
Over 21	144.0	149.3	155.3	177.8

Source: Social Trends

Juvenile delinquents are young people aged between 10 and 17 who are taken to court and found guilty of breaking the law. Examine the questions and then the statistics carefully.

1 It is not necessarily correct to say that there is an increase in juvenile delinquency each year. The amount of recorded juvenile crime fell in 1976. On the other hand the proportion of crime committed by the adult population has increased over the period shown.
2 Although there are fluctuations in the number of offences committed by juveniles an increasing number have been recorded in

comparison with 1970. However, this is not unique to Britain, it is true for all advanced industrial societies.

3 Some writers have associated this with the increase in levels of unemployment among the young in such societies.

4 There are also increasing numbers in the age group at risk. Some adolescent youth may find that deviant and delinquent behaviour offers excitement, bravado and a chance to gain status in the eyes of their peers.

5 The nature of modern urban life offers more opportunities to commit delinquent actions either deliberately or by chance.

6 The police may have come to see youth as the source of many potential problems and so they may spend more time observing and checking them. As a result more become offenders and so appear in the statistics.

7 Some commentators (e.g. Sir Eric St Johnston in 1969 report) suggest that declining religious values and the strength of the family as a socializing institution may have their effect on the attitudes and values of contemporary youth.

Who are the offenders?

123 How would you explain social class differences in rates of juvenile delinquency? (OX)

Much repeated research has shown a close correlation between the number of young offenders who appear in court and their social class background. The great majority are from classes 4 and 5.

McDonald (*Social Class and Delinquency*) found that most delinquents in terms of their own admission and their known offences come from households in the unskilled manual worker group. This leads to the conclusion that the typical offender in our society is a working-class male juvenile of school age living in an urban centre.

There are examples of these findings in the work of Mays 1951–61. His findings in Liverpool are shown in the first table.

Liverpool police records

Social class	% of detected offenders	
	1951	1961
1 and 2	0	0
3 (non-manual)	18	14
3 (manual)	21	27
4	20	21
5	41	38

Croydon police records

Social class	% of probation and approved school cases
1 and 2	0
3	1 case per 3003 families
4	1 case per 380 families
5	1 case per 187 families

Source: Morris, *Delinquency and the Culture of the Criminal Area*, 1957

Douglas, Ross and Hammond (*Delinquency and Social Class*, 1966) analysed data from the National Survey of Health and Development based on a sample of 12,468 births in 1946. They found the lowest incidence of delinquency in classes 1 and 2; class 3 had three times the incidence of 1 and 2, and class 5 had seven times the incidence. These gaps were found to be even wider when only indictable offences were considered. They found no children from classes 1 and 2 appeared before the courts more than once in their study.

The implication that black youth are particularly prone to delinquency is a more recent phenomenon. Hall argues that this has arisen since 1972 with the panic associated with mugging. Street crime in the USA was largely a black phenomenon. The idea was then imported into Britain when the press began to prophesy that similar troubles could be expected. There were also widely reported speeches by politicians, such as Enoch Powell, making similar claims. This had the effect of sensitizing the public to the issue. They then began to 'know' what the typical mugger was like: young, male and black. However, there is no firm evidence that there are a disproportionate number of black offenders among the known delinquents.

There are many writers who are moving away from theories which emphasize the fact that the majority of offenders are necessarily of working-class origin.

Sutherland (*White-Collar Crime*) suggests that middle-class children do commit offences quite frequently, but either they are seldom caught or they do not come to court to face trial because they are dealt with by parents, teachers or other agencies.

Willmott (*Adolescent Boys of East London*) comes to similar conclusions. He suggests that working-class boys are more likely to be perceived as trouble-makers. Delinquent behaviour may also be a feature of the lives of many middle-class children but it tends to go unrecorded.

Vaz (*Middle-Class Delinquency*) also argues that middle-class delinquency among youth is on the increase. He points out that in the USA certain offences, including motoring, use of drugs, gambling and drinking, may be higher among boys from white-collar backgrounds than from manual classes.

There are some studies, known as 'self-reporting studies', in which people are asked what offences they have committed, which indicate that offenders come from all social backgrounds. For example, Belson (*Juvenile Theft: Causal Factors*) interviewed a cross-section of 1425 boys aged 13–16. He found the following:

88% said they had stolen from school;
70% said they had stolen from a shop;
33% said they had stolen from a stall;
25% said they had stolen from a vehicle;
18% said they had stolen from a telephone box;
11% said they had stolen from a meter.

He concluded that by the time the average boy left school in London he could have committed as many as 100 petty thefts.

Conclusions

1 Crime is committed by all social classes but a much higher proportion of working-class children appear in court.
2 Most offenders live in urban centres; rates are highest in the poor deprived areas.
3 For some youth crime, deviance and trouble are a *part* of life – though not necessarily a *way* of life.
4 Sex differences in delinquency rates have remained fairly steady for many decades, although there has been a slight increase in the number of female offenders in recent years. Females are generally more resistant to the forces that push the individual into deviant behaviour. Nye argues that girls are less frequently delinquent because they are kept under better control by their families. The indictable offences for which a girl is likely to be prosecuted are usually simple forms of stealing, especially from shops. Other offences are forms of sexual misbehaviour of a kind that call for her care and protection rather than punishment. Delinquency in the male at an equivalent age is much more varied, dangerous and dramatic.

How would you answer the following questions?

124 'In an attempt to check the accuracy of (official) *Criminal Statistics*, so-called "self-report studies" have been conducted. The approach is simple – it involves asking people what crimes they have committed! However, it is done in such a way that their answers are anonymous and they feel confident that no one will check up on them. These studies are not without their own problems of reliability, but they have shown some interesting results. Above all, they suggest a vast under-recording of crime. But self-report studies generally confirm the characteristics of offenders as shown in the *Criminal Statistics* – with one important exception. The marked social class difference does not show up in self-report studies. Many of these studies show that crime is fairly equally distributed between the different social class groups. This is a very important finding, since it challenges many theories that have been put forward to explain criminal behaviour.'

R. Roshier, *Crime and Punishment*, 1976

(a) *What is the 'marked social class difference' shown by the official* Criminal Statistics? *(5 marks)*

(b) *Why do you think this marked difference does not show up in self-report studies? Which theories of criminal behaviour does this finding challenge? (15 marks)* (CAM)

125 'Many forms of vandalism never become defined as problematic, simply because they are invisible: they might occur within the confines of an institution such as a factory, hospital or school. Other forms are, similarly, in Edwin Lemert's term "normalized"; they occur with a certain regularity and individually are quite trivial. An example would be the defacement of walls of public toilets with various forms of graffiti (one would be extremely surprised to find bare walls in the toilets of a pub, park or railway station). These forms of vandalism only get defined as problematic when somebody says "Look, it's getting beyond a joke" or "Things are going too far".'

S. Cohen, Who are the vandals?, *Society Today*, 25 February 1977

(a) *Explain in your own words what is meant by the claim that certain forms of vandalism have become 'normalized'. (3 marks)*

(b) *What other forms of crime, besides petty vandalism, are often considered to have become 'normalized' in our society? Suggest reasons in each case. (7 marks)*

(c) *Outline, with the help of examples, the ways in which the mass media can influence the extent to which a particular form of behaviour comes to be defined as a 'problem'. (10 marks)* (CAM)

Theories of criminal behaviour

126 *Comment on any three possible explanations of crime.* (WEL)

127 'The idea that delinquency is the result of *gang* activity is a

common one. Some criminologists argue that the main factor
causing delinquent gangs is the "status problem" faced by
working-class boys. They realize that the opportunities for
"getting on" are all but closed to them; that they are condemned
to lives of insignificance and, by society's evaluation, low status.
Some, of course, are happy to accept this situation. But others
experience "status frustration" and as a result become involved in
delinquent gangs. They do so, it is argued, because it is a way of
gaining status denied to them elsewhere. It is a way of rejecting
"respectable" society and the values it represents.'

I. Wortley, *Soccer Violence*, 1975

(a) *How far does the behaviour of juvenile gangs support the view
    that their members are rejecting 'respectable' society and the
    values it represents? (8 marks)*
(b) *Does the idea of 'status frustration' help us to understand the
    many forms that juvenile delinquency takes? What other
    explanations have criminologists offered? (12 marks)* (CAM)

Closely associated with a class theory that has already been discussed
is a sub-cultural explanation of crime. One form this takes is to
emphasize the status frustration which some people, especially in the
lower social class groups, feel in the course of their everyday lives. The
influence of a person's peer group attachments and the values of the
community in which the individual lives are stressed.

Theorists who use such explanations include:

1 **Merton,** who argues that deviance is generated by the structure and
  culture of the environment in which the individual lives. He says
  that societies establish goals of success and provide a means for
  achieving them. Those who cannot do so by legitimate means turn
  to illegitimate methods.
2 **A. Cohen,** who says that low socio-economic status explains high
  levels of status frustration. This is resolved by deliberately rejecting
  middle-class success goals and conforming to a delinquent sub-
  culture. High status is placed on delinquent acts among members of
  the peer group.
3 **Cloward and Ohlin,** who make use of the idea of both Merton
  and Cohen. They suggest that whether or not a young person enters
  a criminal sub-culture varies according to the opportunity they have
  for entering such an environment. These sub-cultures emerge in
  areas where there is an established pattern of organized crime
  among adults. Where they do not have such opportunities, the
  young person may join a conflict sub-culture, which results in 'gang

warfare' or acts of vandalism; or they may join a 'retreatist sub-culture'. This usually involves the use of drugs, alcohol, etc.

4 **Miller,** who argues that much of the delinquency associated with working-class youth does not arise because they have entered a delinquent sub-culture, but because the working-class culture to which they are attached emphasizes such values as toughness, aggression, excitement, and qualities of masculinity. In practice this can lead them into conflict with the law. He says that much delinquency results from the acting out of such values at inappropriate times.

Ecological theories

Park helped to found this school of analysis in Chicago in the 1920s. He and his colleagues wished to measure the incidence of particular patterns of behaviour, including delinquency, within specified areas of cities. They wished to discover the connection between patterns of social life and values and the physical characteristics of the area.

1 **Shaw and McKay** *(Juvenile Delinquency and the Urban Area)* They looked at delinquency in terms of the changing character of an area. They noted that the highest rates were in areas closest to the city centre, especially in those with declining population and physical deterioration. They concluded that delinquency factors became inherent in the community and imprinted themselves on each new wave of inhabitants in the area.

Critics argue that the theory does not explain patterns of deviance in British cities so well since they have developed in different ways from those of America.

2 **Sainsbury** *(Delinquency and the Ecology of London)* He says that it can be shown that suicide rates in London boroughs differ from one another and these differences correlate with certain social characteristics – especially the mobility of the population and anonymity among its inhabitants. He found that suicide rates were highest in areas where there was a high turnover in population, large numbers were living in boarding houses, few facilities existed for leisure or entertainment, and unemployment rates were high. He found certain areas of the city displayed more of these characteristics than others.

Key terms and concepts

The following terms and concepts have been used and defined in this chapter. You must be able to use them and explain their meaning for examination purposes:

crime; deviance; indictable offence; non-indictable offence; mugging; juvenile delinquent; delinquency; white-collar crime; status frustration; ecological theory; class; pressure to conform; norms; 'dark-figure' of crime; adolescence.

Other terms you may wish to use:

peer group Others of a similar age and social background with whom a person mixes in a social context. Peer groups have a strong influence on the behaviour of their members.

sanctions Penalties aimed at preventing or discouraging certain types of behaviour. Legal sanctions are a formal type; public opinion can be an informal sanction.

18 Population

Questions on this topic are frequently based on information in tables and graphs that illustrates changes in population trends over time. You are likely to be questioned on:

1 The **definition** of important terms, especially **birth or fertility rate, death or mortality rate** (including **infant mortality rate**), **migration,** and their relevance for understanding the trends;
2 The **causes** and **consequences** of the changes;
3 The problems of population control, world population, the age structure of the population of Britain, or the relationship between social class and fertility patterns.

Do not be put off answering a question because the material is in tabular form. The question will often be broken down into a series of short sections, some of which may require only brief answers. (You can be guided by the number of marks awarded for each part.)

However, you may be faced with a question in which no data is provided and you are asked to discuss the changing trends. In this case you *must* be able to provide the necessary details. You cannot answer the question adequately without presenting this information. But make sure it is relevant to the dates mentioned in the question. For example:

128 Describe and account for the major changes in birth rate in Britain since 1900. (OX)

The important terms

Here are some typical questions that illustrate the need for clear definitions:

129

**Vital statistics, United Kingdom
(per thousand population)**

	1902	1932	1967
Birth rate	28.6	16.3	17.5
Death rate	17.3	12.2	11.2

Source: Registrar General UK

(a) *Define birth rate and death rate.*
(b) *Why was birth rate low in 1932 and higher in 1967?*
(c) *Why might you expect birth rate to have fallen since 1967?*
(d) *Why was death rate higher in 1902 than in 1967?*
(e) *How can population increase whilst birth rate falls?*

130

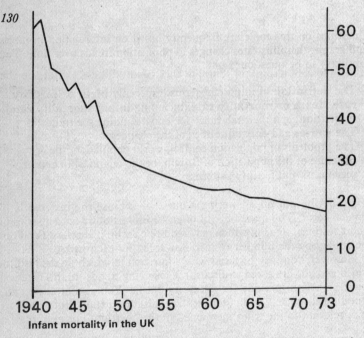

Infant mortality in the UK

(a) *Describe the trend shown in the graph.*
(b) *Why were rates high between 1940–45?*
(c) *Why have rates fallen in the last twenty years?*
(d) *Explain the meaning of 'mortality rate' and 'fertility rate'.*

1 **Birth rate (fertility rate)** The ratio of total number of live births
to the total population. This is usually expressed as 'births per
thousand of the total population'. It is sometimes termed **crude**

birth rate because it is an approximate measure of fertility. It could be obtained more accurately if only the numbers of women of child-bearing age were considered.

2 **Death rate (mortality rate)**   The ratio of the total number of deaths to the total population. It is usually expressed as 'deaths per thousand of the total population'.

3 **Migration**   This refers to numbers **immigrating** and **emigrating** from the country. This factor has little effect on the population size of Britain since the numbers involved are small and in recent years more people have left than have entered the country.

4 **Infant mortality**   This is the death rate of children who are born alive but who die before the age of 1 year. It is normally expressed per thousand live births. The rate is higher for boys than for girls (in 1974 the rate was: boys, 18.8, girls, 14.2).

These are the factors that influence **population growth**. Where the birth rate is higher than the death rate, then the population will increase in size (even though birth rate may be falling). For many centuries in Britain both rates were high and so population increased slowly in size. In the eighteenth and nineteenth centuries the death rate dropped rapidly whilst the birth rate remained high. The result was a faster growth in population size.

Death rates (including those for infants) fell as a result of:

1 Improvements in standards of living as people became more affluent;

2 Improved housing and conditions of life;

3 Changes and improvements in diet;

4 Improved conditions of sanitation and hygiene;

5 Great advances in the training of doctors and nurses as well as in the whole field of medical science;

6 Improved features of social and economic life which helped overcome some of the problems of poverty and deprivation: families became smaller in size but healthier.

The causes and consequences of changes in the population

This area provides the most usual and frequent questions on population. But you may be asked to consider these factors during particular time periods.

131 *'Population growth is affected by the birth rate, death rate and net migration.' How and why have birth rates and death rates varied in Britain over the last 120 years?*

132

Family size distributions after 10 years of marriage, England and Wales (%)

| Number of liveborn children: | Year of marriage | | | | | |
	1951	1956	1961	1963	1964	1965
0	14	11	8	9	9	10
1	27	22	18	17	17	18
2	35	38	44	46	48	49
3	16	19	22	21	19	18
4 or more	8	11	9	8	6	5
Total	100	100	100	100	100	100

Source: adapted from *Office of Population Censuses and Surveys*

(a) *What is the most popular number of children per family over the years shown in the table?*

(b) *What trends can be identified in childless families and families with four or more children?*

(c) *What explanations have sociologists offered for the trend towards smaller families since 1900?* (AEB)

133

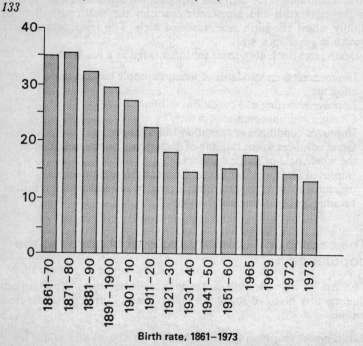

Birth rate, 1861–1973

Source: J. B. Meredith Davis, *Community Health, Preventive Medicine and Social Services*, 1975

(a) *What, according to the table, was the average annual birth rate between 1951 and 1960?* *(1 mark)*
(b) *What is meant by the term 'birth rate'?* *(3 marks)*
(c) *Identify* two *trends in birth rate changes over the period shown in the diagram.* *(4 marks)*
(d) *Account for the changes in the birth rate during the period covered by the table.* *(12 marks)* (AEB)

134

Birth rate, UK, 1951–75
(per thousand)

1951	15.8
1961	17.9
1966	18.0
1971	16.2
1972	14.9
1973	13.2
1974	13.2
1975	12.4

Source: Adapted from *Social Trends*, 1977

(a) *What trends does the table show before and after 1966?* *(2 marks)*
(b) *What other factors have to be considered when accounting for the change in size of a population?* *(4 marks)*
(c) *What explanations may be offered for the changes in the table?* *(14 marks)* (AEB)

Notice how for all of these questions you need:

1 Knowledge of the changes that have occurred in birth rate, death rate and population size;
2 Reasons why particular changes have occurred in particular time periods.

Comparison of birth and death rates, Great Britain, 1700–1977

	est. 1700	1801	1871	1901	1911	1921	1931	1951
Birth rate	36	36	35	29.6	24.6	23.1	16.3	15.8
Death rate	35	30	20	17.1	14.8	12.4	12.5	12.6

	1961	1971	1972	1973	1974	1975	1976	1977
Birth rate	17.9	16.2	14.9	13.2	13.2	12.4	11.9	11.6
Death rate	12.0	11.6	12.0	12.0	11.9	11.8	12.1	12.0

Source: Social Trends (adapted)

Reliable evidence about the growth and composition of the population has existed since 1801 when the first Census was taken. There has been a Census every ten years since then, with the exception of 1941. Information is collected by the Office of the Registrar General who is responsible for the eventual publication of the data.

Population growth, England and Wales, 1570–2001 (millions)

1570 (est.)	4
1670 (est.)	5
1701 (est.)	7
1801	9
1851	18
1881	29
1901	32
1911	36
1921	37
1931	39
1951	43
1961	49
1971	52
2001 (est.)	62

Average family size

1861–69	6.1
1900–09	3.3
1920–24	2.2
1930–34	2.1
1940–44	2.0
1950–54	2.3
1960–64	2.2
1970–74	2.0
1974–79	1.9

Source: Social Trends

For the purposes of analysis it is convenient to break the population trends into various stages:

1 **1570–1801** This was a long period of relative stability of population. Both birth rate and death rate were high. There was much disease, unreliable food supplies and low standards of medical care. Hence population grew only slowly.

2 **1801–71** This was a period of rapid population growth. There was a high birth rate and falling death rate. There was a large

average family size; it was still necessary to have a large family to ensure the survival of a few. Also there was no reliable method of family planning. The Queen and other members of the aristocracy established a trend for larger families which was imitated by those in lower social class groups.

3 **1871–1914** The birth rate continued to fall. Average family size also decreased markedly.

(a) Following the Education Acts (1870, 1880, 1902) which made education compulsory and of increasingly longer duration and following a series of Factory Acts which limited the age of working children and the type of work they could do, children became more of an economic liability rather than an asset.

(b) Economic depressions of the 1870s and 1880s increased fears of poverty and unemployment.

(c) In the 1870s Charles Bradlaugh (MP) and Annie Bessant published a book advocating family planning methods. They were prosecuted for doing so, and this gave their cause increased publicity.

(d) Improved medical standards meant that smaller families had higher survival rates and larger ones were less necessary.

(e) The Education Act 1902 established Teachers' Training Colleges on a wider base. This provided more career opportunities for women. Large families were less feasible for those starting a career.

(f) The emancipation of women was encouraged by the suffragette movement in the early years of the century.

4 **1914–51** The decline in birth rate and death rate continued as a general trend.

(a) An increasing number of women were employed in industry during the two world wars. The trend continued at their end.

(b) During the economic depression 1925–39 more than five million people were unemployed.

(c) Smaller families became more fashionable in contrast to the Victorian norm.

(d) The number of marriages in the 1920s and 1940s fell as a result of the high number of wartime deaths of males.

(e) Family life was disrupted by these social and economic upheavals.

5 **1951–64** The trend of a falling birth rate and family size was reversed in this period to a slight increase in both on average.

(a) The introduction of the welfare state in 1948 meant that standards of health improved. Also there was the introduction of child benefits, family allowances, free medicine and schooling.

(b) It was a time of optimism following the war. Families were reunited.

(c) It was a period of economic boom and increased affluence. Mr Macmillan (PM) told the electorate in 1958, 'You have never had it so good.'

(d) There were low rates of unemployment, good housing opportunities and good prospects for the future.

(e) The Queen had four children and this may have helped to establish a new trend towards larger families.

6 **1964–78** In this period there was a rapid decline in the birth rate. Average family size fell to the lowest since 1941.

(a) The new contraceptive 'pill' was introduced in 1964.

(b) The Abortion Act was passed in 1967 together with the Family Planning Act, both of which helped families limit their family size.

(c) There were an increasing number of women in the labour force (more than nine million in 1974).

(d) As people became more aware of the problems of increasing population, it became fashionable to have smaller families.

(e) The expansion of higher education facilities gave more people more opportunity for such education. This caused more of them to postpone marriage and family until they were older.

(f) People began to put more emphasis on the need for more material goods (larger home, second car, etc.) rather than on expanding their family.

(g) The 1970s and 1980s were periods of economic decline with increasingly high levels of unemployment.

The changing age structure of the population

From time to time government demographers publish their projections of likely future population trends; that is, they make estimates based on existing knowledge. These estimates are used in the preparation of future policies.

Some projections, made in the 1960s before the fall in birth rate became evident, predicted a population of between 65 and 70 million by the year 2001. Others, in the early 1970s when the decline was established, lowered the prediction to between 60 and 65 million by the end of the century. Predictions may change as new information is gathered from the Census and other sources on which future trends can be based.

Consider the following question. The data here present a more optimistic picture in which there is a much slower rate of growth. There are even slight falls in numbers in some age groups between 1976 and 2001.

135 **Population projections, Great Britain, 1976-based principal projection (millions)**

	1976	1977	1981	1991	2001
Persons aged 0–15	13.3	13.0	11.8	11.7	12.9
Age 16–64/59*	31.8	32.0	32.7	33.7	33.7
Age 65/60* and over	9.4	9.4	9.6	9.8	9.3

*Age group for men/women
Source: Social Trends, 1977

(a) *What changes in the structure of the population are, according to these figures, likely to take place in the 1980s and 1990s? (4 marks)*

(b) *These figures are based upon the Government's 'Principal Projection'. What does this mean and why is it necessary to make a number of alternative projections? (7 marks)*

(c) *If this projection is correct, what consequences are the changes likely to have for Government policy and, in particular, for patterns of public expenditure? (9 marks)* (CAM)

This question raises more specific issues:

136 What consequences would you expect from a rise in the proportion of elderly people in the population? (OX)

1 In 1976 there were more than 15% of the population aged over 60; 6% were over 75. The number aged over 85 is likely to increase from the estimated 450,000 in 1976 to 635,000 by the end of the century.

2 Although the most recent projections do not suggest that these proportions will change very much, any increase must be considered by the government policy-makers. It may be that a Minister for the Elderly would be required.

3 The elderly are always a group likely to fall into poverty (see p. 250). Hence special provision must be allowed for increasing pensions and other benefits.

4 If the population as a whole remains fairly static and there is an increase in the number of elderly people, then there will be fewer economically active people supporting more retired people. This will have a significant effect on the way the economy is structured.

5 There will be a need for more flexible retirement policies. It may be necessary for people to go on working beyond normal retirement age; or if unemployment was a problem, earlier retirement may be necessary.

6 Townsend has said that it should not be necessary for people to disengage from society on retirement. Therefore opportunities must

be provided to ensure that they can continue to play an active part
in the life of the community.

7 Because 80% of the population already live to the age of 60 and
more than 30% live beyond the age of 80, government policy-
makers must consider the increasingly relevant position of the elderly
in society.

Problems associated with world population

It is estimated that on a single day the human race increases by more than
100,000 − the size of a large football crowd. Over the last 100 years the
rate of increase has been sufficient to double the population every 50
years.

The following estimates of world population have been made:

1650	500,000,000
1850	1,200,000,000
1970	3,000,000,000
2000	6,000,000,000
2050	24,000,000,000

Consider the following questions:

137 Study the following data carefully and then answer the questions.

Country	Population	Birth rate	Death rate	Infant mortality	Expectation of life Male	Female
UK	55 millions	18.4	11.5	19.0	68	74
USA	200 millions	19.4	9.4	24.7	67	74
India	500 millions	38.4	12.9	139.0	42	41
Brazil	80 millions	43.0	11.1	170.0	39	46

(a) *Explain briefly the meaning of:*
   (i) *birth rate;*
   (ii) *infant mortality.*
(b) *In which country is the population likely to be increasing most
   rapidly? Explain how you arrive at your answer.*
(c) *State any two possible consequences for an under-developed
   country with a high birth rate.*
(d) *Suggest a reason for the birth rates and infant mortality rates
   being so much higher in India and Brazil than in the UK and
   the USA.* (WEL)

138 'There are over 4000m people in the world today, and UN
experts predict that the world population could exceed 7000m by
the end of this century. The rate of increase reached 76m a year
by the end of the 1960s, although it has shown signs of a slight
decrease since then. . . . Population is growing more quickly in
some parts of the world than others. . . . For many developing
countries the shortage of food is the most pressing problem
created by the rapid increase in population. More mouths have to
be fed every year, and yet a high proportion of the existing
population is not getting enough food of the right kind. . . . Food
production has been increasing, but has only just been keeping
pace with the population increase. . . . More and more of the
babies born in developing countries have been surviving infancy.
. . . This means that the adults at work have had to carry an ever-
increasing burden, to provide for the basic needs of the children,
who cannot contribute to production in the community until they
are older.'

Facts about Development 1, CWDE, 1977

(a) *Identify more precisely those parts of the world in which the
problem described in this passage has reached 'crisis' proportions.
(3 marks)*
(b) *What are the major causes of the continuing increase in world
population? (5 marks)*
(c) *What difficulties have been encountered in attempts to reduce the
birth rate as an alternative to increasing food supplies? Illustrate
your answer by reference to at least two specific examples. (12
marks)* (CAM)

The areas of the world facing greatest problems

1 Population will increase most rapidly in those areas where the birth
rate is very high and death rate is falling. This will be less of a
problem in thinly populated industrialized societies (such as
Australia or the USA) than in densely populated, under-developed
societies which cannot easily accommodate increases.
2 In such areas, where there are also falling infant mortality rates
there may be lack of adequate food supplies. These would include
areas of Africa, South America, India and other parts of Asia, which
are sometimes termed the third world.
3 In these places there is often much malnutrition (food is lacking
quality and nutrients are missing from the diet) as well as under-
nutrition (food lacking in quantity). The result is deficiency diseases
which lower resistance. About 15% of the world's population suffer
from serious hunger.

4 Generally the economies of these societies are weak in that there are low levels of employment and inadequate funds available for the governments to provide welfare benefits for citizens in need.

The causes of increases in population in poor areas

1 Lack of family planning advice and methods for limiting families;
2 Birth rate remaining much higher than death rate;
3 Steady decline in infant mortality rates;
4 Decline in killing diseases;
5 Having a large family may be a cultural norm and a sign of status. It is very hard to break or change cultural traditions.

Some possible solutions

1 Where a government is able to intervene they can offer incentives to encourage people to limit family size.
2 The ability to act may be influenced by the existing economic and political structure, the religious and cultural norms of the society and the levels of educational development. They must be able to explain the problems and persuade people to change their attitudes.
3 There could be increased aid from the rich developed countries to help deal with the problem of food and housing shortages.
4 There needs to be an increase in the number of medical advisers as well as much technological innovation to help increase food supplies, etc.
5 Powerful governments may reorganize the social and economic structure of the society to prevent social breakdown. (For example, China, with the world's largest population, introduced a new social order in 1948, based on the principles of communism, in order to remove basic economic hardships.)

Problems of population control in Britain

1 Kingsley Davis says that families must remain small to prevent social disorder in the future. Couples must be made to realize that it is socially irresponsible to have large families.
2 If the problem became serious he advocates legislation to increase the legal age of marriage. Also to increase substantially the fees for marriage licences, tax benefits for the single and to withdraw family allowances.
3 Improved family planning programmes and more liberal attitudes towards abortion and sex education in schools.

4 There would have to be changes in attitudes so that childlessness or one-child families became more of the norm.
5 It is generally argued that to maintain a stable population level the average family size must remain at about two children. People must be persuaded not to have any more children that they may want.
6 In 1976 deaths in England and Wales exceeded the number of births for the first time since records started in 1837. There were 13,000 more deaths than births. This meant that the population fell for the first time through natural causes. The population also fell as a result of net migration: more people left the country than arrived in it. This suggests that apart from artificial methods of control there are also authentic systems at work.

Social class and fertility rates

139 How would you explain social class differences in fertility during the last 100 years? (OX)

1 You must discuss the concepts of social class and explain how repeated research shows its significance on patterns of social life.
2 Wrong has reviewed the trends and patterns of class differences in fertility for each of three broad periods:
   (a) **1870–1910** Fertility tended to be inversely correlated with social class, i.e. the higher the class, the lower the birth rate. This was particularly marked for those in groups at the upper and lower ends of the social scale. After 1870 the decline in the birth rate was led by groups of highest economic status.
   (b) **1910–40** Patterns of class fertility differentials were not so uniform. Intermediate groups (mainly white-collar workers) led the decline in fertility. This was a trend taken up by low status, non-manual workers. The inverse pattern continued but was less marked. The major exceptions were upper working-class groups who began to have smaller families. The trend was that family size decreased as income increased. Wrong says that this represents a stage in the process of transition from the inverse pattern.
   (c) **1940–64** The decline in the birth rate was reversed. There was a reduction in the number of women remaining childless and there was an increase in the size of completed families. The higher status groups increased their fertility (i.e. they had larger families). The inverse pattern was increasingly replaced by a direct relationship between class position and family size. He predicted that the future trend would result in a correlation between family size and level of income.
   (d) **Post-1964** In fact, the trend has become a reversal to the

inverse trend. People of higher social class positions have tended to have smaller families. People have spent their increased incomes on material goods rather than on increasing family size.

Social class and infant mortality rates

Morris and Heady analysed 80,000 **stillbirths** (death in first week of life), **neonatal deaths** (death in first four weeks of life) and **post-natal deaths** (death in first year of life) in England and Wales 1949–50 and compared the results with known data for 1911. They wished to discover whether inequalities between different class groups had narrowed during the period.

They found that although there had been a reduction in infant mortality the class differences remained much the same. There were increases in the rates of mortality in each category from 1 to 5.

In 1911 the post-natal deaths rate of miners' children was four times as high as for children of professional workers. The figure was almost the same in 1949. The authors concluded that the gap was more disturbing in 1949 because so little progress in health care had been made.

Kelsall said that the rates for infants born into families of unskilled labourers lags some 40 years behind those with fathers in the professional groups.

Douglas studied confinements in the first week of March 1946 to find which mothers were most likely to give birth to premature babies. He found 4% in class 1, 6.5% in class 3 and 7.2% in class 5. Those in the lowest class groups showed greatest risk of death from bronchitis and pneumonia.

Davie, Butler and Goldstein found similar results in their 1972 study.

Spicer and Lipworth examined infant mortality rates and said that it appeared that children born to mothers in class 3 had higher mortality rates than those in classes 1 and 2. Mothers in classes 4 and 5 were wo se off still.

Whilst there was some reduction in mortality rates in the highest social class groups between 1949 and 1964 this was far greater than the reduction in the lowest groups (41% in classes 1 and 2 compared with 23% in classes 4 and 5).

The general conclusion is that class remains a significant factor in the life chances of children in contemporary society.

Key terms and concepts

The following terms and concepts have been used and defined in this chapter. You must be able to use them and explain their meaning for examination purposes:

birth rate; fertility rate; death rate; mortality rate; migration; immigration and emigration; infant mortality rate; social class.

Other terms which you may wish to use:

demography   The specialized study of population.
social stability   Change occurs slowly and through accepted means (e.g. by passing new laws) so that society remains in a state of order. Social instability could occur if the population increased at too rapid a rate so that there were insufficient food supplies.

19 Education

The questions on this topic fall into three main areas:

1 The causes and consequences of changes in the educational
  structure in England and Wales;
2 The functions of the educational system;
3 The factors affecting educational achievement.

The changing structure of education

140 *The tripartite system and the comprehensive reorganization were
    successive attempts to bring about equality of educational
    opportunity. What changes did these attempts bring about and what
    problems still remain?* (AEB)
141 *Has the shift towards comprehensive education provided an increase
    in equality of educational opportunity and achievement?*
142 *Explain the meaning of tripartite and comprehensive secondary
    education and outline the arguments advocating comprehensive
    secondary schools.* (WEL)

Education: problems of definition

There is no general agreement about **definition**. There is no absolute
agreement about the **aims** of education. In general it could be said to
include all those processes of learning (both formal and informal) in
which skills, knowledge, sense of morality, individuality, etc. are incul-
cated in people. The aims of education vary from one time period to
another. What is important in contemporary society to form the
'educated person' may not be so in 500 years.

Nevertheless, it may be said that the processes of education should
enable a person to be able to organize their environment so that they can
act more effectively.

The **informal** agencies of education include the family, friendship groups, the mass media and other organizations to which people may belong on a voluntary basis.

The **formal** agencies include schools, colleges and other institutions that are designed to provide detailed and specific knowledge in order to enable a person to take an effective part in the life of their society.

All societies require a means of transmitting their values and ideologies so that the traditions and customs are perpetuated. In simple societies these are achieved when the young pass through phases of initiation into the cultural ways of the society. In complex industrial societies the formal educational system is designed for similar purposes.

The formal structure of education

In Britain the educational system is shaped by Acts of Parliament and controlled by local education authorities (LEAs) which are responsible to the Minister of Education. Parliament provides broad guide lines as to the structure of the educational system without specifically stating what shall be taught or what methods shall be used in teaching.

Key dates

1870   **Forster's Education Act**   Education was established for the first time on a national basis.

1880   **Mundella's Education Act**   Education was made compulsory. The leaving age was put at 10.

1902   **Balfour's Education Act**   Local Education Authorities were established and empowered to provide some secondary education. The leaving age was 13–14.

1918   **Fisher's Education Act**   Older and more able pupils to be given training in advanced practical work. Leaving age was now 14.

These Acts established and implemented the system of elementary education in which all children attended the same school from the age of 5 until 14. Those who showed particular ability could take a scholarship examination to gain a place in a local grammar school (some of which had been in existence since AD 1000). Others attended grammar schools or made use of private education if their parents could afford the fees. The major change to this system of elementary education came in 1944.

1944   **The Butler Education Act**   146 LEAs were to produce a system of education suited to the age, aptitude and ability of every child. There were to be three stages of free education: primary, secondary and further. The only compulsory feature of the curriculum was a period of religious education. The Act advocated 'parity of esteem' between children and it established the **tripartite system** of education, that is grammar schools, secondary modern schools and technical schools. At the age of 11 all children in the state system had the opportunity of being selected for a particular type of secondary education on the basis of the result of an intelligence test. This was known as the '11-plus'.

The outcome was that between 1944 and 1964 (when the system began to change) about 25% of school children attended grammar schools (the figure varied from one part of the country to another), about 60% attended secondary modern schools, and the remainder were in private education and in technical schools.

The aims of the grammar school

1 Children were selected according to their IQ level. The belief was that only a small elite of children would benefit from a high-level academic education.
2 The system ensured that the top jobs were filled by those who had received specialized education.
3 The small number of universities were also largely filled by those from grammar schools and public schools which, it was argued, maintained high standards.

The aims of the secondary modern and technical schools

1 The children who attended them had not gained high enough marks in the IQ test; therefore they were not thought to be suited to academic education. The schools they attended were designed to provide skills more suited to manual workers.
2 They provided the majority of workers for the manual occupations in industry.
3 The curriculum did not emphasize academic qualifications, and there was little or no provision for them.

Criticisms of the tripartite system

1 The IQ test on which the system was based was criticized for being unreliable.
 (a) It was argued that they measured only a capacity to conform to the attitudes of the tester: a question that asks for the odd one out – house, igloo, office, hut – could have several 'correct' answers other than the one demanded by the exam.

(b) It did not measure a true range of ability.
(c) It was not necessarily a 'fixed' factor; some studies showed scores could be improved with practice.
(d) It was felt that it was unfair to base a child's future on the outcome of a test.

2 Critics argued that the system perpetuated social class divisions. The school population was divided into an elite and a non-elite.

3 Those who achieved top occupational positions as a result of their educational background also gained additional social prestige and status.

4 Much talent was lost because children in secondary modern schools could not take any examinations until 1964, when the CSE was introduced. Until that time more than 60% were leaving school without any paper qualifications.

5 The Crowther Report (1959) and the Robbins Report (1963) expressed the fear that the aim to expand higher education was handicapped by limitations imposed by the tripartite system; too few children would have the opportunity of gaining access to higher education.

6 Much research suggested that assignment to a low status school or stream affected the individual's self-image. Many saw themselves as 'failures' because they had not gained access to grammar schools and so lowered their expectations. The work of Elder and Pidgeon illustrated this.

7 Secondary modern schools were only occasionally provided with facilities and buildings comparable to those of the grammar schools.

The comprehensive system

In 1946 the Labour Government advocated the introduction of the comprehensive system to replace the tripartite structure. It was defined as 'the secondary education of all children in a given area without organization on three sides'. The first comprehensive schools were in London, Essex and parts of Wales. In 1964 when Labour was returned to power they introduced the system on a national basis.

It operates on the basis that all the children leave junior school together and enter a comprehensive school without selection.

The aims of the comprehensive system

1 To abolish the 11-plus and the stigma of 'failure';
2 To develop greater social intermixing;
3 To provide greater opportunity for all pupils to find their particular levels of ability and to obtain suitable qualifications;

4 To overcome the traditional methods of streaming which were generally employed in secondary modern schools;
5 To provide a wider range of facilities and a staff who could offer a wider range of subjects to meet the needs of all pupils;
6 To increase the opportunities of all children so that more could obtain access to higher education.

Criticisms of the comprehensive system

1 The schools are generally very large with more than 1000 pupils.
2 They may limit parental choice because there is generally only one large comprehensive school in an area.
3 Some critics say that able pupils may be handicapped when educated with the less able.
4 It is seen by some to be an experimental system whereas grammar schools have been in operation for hundreds of years.

The results of some studies

Neave (1973) showed that the comprehensive school was providing the best means of increasing the number of working-class children reaching university. The proportion had remained fairly constant between 1928 and 1968 at about 28%. He suggests it has increased since then to about 38%, and the newer comprehensives are doing better in this respect than the older ones.

Research of the National Children's Bureau (1974) indicated that the top ability children made as much progress between 11 and 16 in reading and maths whether they went to grammar or comprehensive schools. Children of lower ability did slightly better at comprehensive schools rather than at secondary moderns.

Stevens (1980) says that broader comprehensive education may mean that the cleverest children are no longer reaching the same level of detailed disciplined academic work at the same age as they did under the tripartite system. She concludes that there has been neither a dramatic collapse nor an increase of academic attainment at the top level.

In *Class and the Comprehensive School* Forde states that she favoured the comprehensive school at the outset of her research. However, having investigated a number of features of schools (of all types) she concludes that she could find little evidence to show that the comprehensive school was achieving the aims its proponents claimed for it.

The debate has continued through the 1970s and into the 1980s. The authors of the Black Papers on education (Cox and Pollard) remain critical on the grounds that it is a great unresearched leap into the dark.

Other writers, such as Townsend and Clegg, claim that they have evidence to show that the comprehensive school is more successful than the tripartite system, in that it is justifiable on educational, egalitarian and social grounds.

However, the debate is almost always clouded by the problems of political ideologies which tend to influence the views of writers on this topic.

The functions of education

143 'During the nineteenth century . . . public concern with elementary education was . . . the need to ensure discipline, and to obtain respect for private property and the social order, and that kind of instruction which was indispensable in an expanding industrial and commercial nation.'

> D. Glass, *Education and Social Change in Modern England*
> *What are the functions of education in the United Kingdom today?*
> *How do schools socialize and control children?*

144 *The main purpose of education is to pass on certain values to a new generation. Do you agree?* (LON)

145 *Comment on any three ways in which curricula of British schools may be related to the wider society.* (WEL)

The functionalist perspective

The **functionalist** sees society as a machine or biological organism. Each part (or social institution) is connected to another so that the development or change in one part will affect another. For example, if the heart fails then life ceases. The sociological functionalist is interested in the question, 'how is order and stability maintained in society?' He seeks the answer by looking for the functions of the different institutions that he observes in society. The analysis of the educational system in terms of its functions helps to provide some answers to questions about social order. The main functions are generally considered to be to act as agencies of:

1 **Socialization and social control** The formal educational system should develop important social skills in people. They should be able to understand what constitutes acceptable and unacceptable behaviour. They should develop an understanding of particular rules and regulations, of the importance of the interdependence of one person upon another in society. Such values can be promoted through the ways in which the school is structured and organized.

2 **Cultural transmission** It passes on to its members the accepted values of society. Where concepts such as 'individuality', 'independence', 'democracy', etc. are held to be important, then these will be developed within the school. For example, religious principles are promoted so that a common identity and common source of social values are accepted. All the common values, traditions and customs of the society can be taught to pupils in schools and their significance understood and shared.

3 **Selection and recruitment** Pupils are provided with the relevant skills required for life in a particular type of social and economic structure. It provides ways of identifying those who are considered to be most suitable for particular occupations. People come to accept that such processes of selection are valid because they are constantly subject to them in school.

In a developed technological society industry is the source of wealth and high living standards. It is argued by many educationalists that if schools fail in their function of training people for work in a competitive society, then the economy will ultimately suffer.

Conclusion

The functionalists argue that the formal school education serves to transmit dominant values and ideologies of society to its younger members. In doing so it helps promote order and stability. People learn their appropriate roles (which also helps to build stability into the social system). In absorbing the cultural values people are given a greater sense of identity.

The more complex and specialized a social system becomes, the more important is the role of the educational system in fitting its members to their place in it.

The factors affecting educational achievement

Some questions are of a general type:

146 *What are the major social factors affecting educational opportunity and achievement?* (OX)

147 *Describe in detail three ways in which social factors may influence people's educational achievement.* (WEL)

Others may ask you to discuss the particular significance of the school.

148 'The boys [at Lumley Secondary Modern School] are not distributed throughout the streams in a random way; rather, from

our knowledge of a particular boy's stream we can within limits
predict some of the main values he will tend to hold . . . the
higher the stream of a boy, the greater the tendency for him to be
committed to the school's values. . . . He likes school and the
teachers, to whose expectations he conforms, whose values he
supports and whose approval he seeks. This trend is particularly
true of 4A boys, and as we move from the highest streams to the
lowest, this trend tends to reverse itself, and the values held by
low stream pupils are the opposite of those held by their peers in
4A.'

D. Hargreaves, *Social Relations in a Secondary School*, 1967

(a) *What are the values typically held by low-stream pupils in
secondary schools like the one studied by Hargreaves?* (6 marks)
(b) *To what extent may the actions of teachers contribute to the
development of 'delinquescent' or 'anti-school' sub-cultures
amongst their pupils?* (14 marks) (CAM)

These questions focus on the relevance of the school and suggest that
for some children the way the school itself is organized and structured
can have a significant effect on the response of those children to the
processes of learning.

There is then a *third* type of question which focuses on the significance of social class background on levels of educational achievement.

149 *Why are the children of middle-class parents more successful at school
than the children of working-class parents?* (OX)

150   **Percentage of children under 5 receiving pre-school provision
in Great Britain**

	A*	B*	C*	D*	E*	F*	G*	All
Day nursery/ playgroup	30	24	24	22	18	12	4	19
Nursery school or class/primary school	7	9	13	7	10	12	12	10

*Indicates parental social group as follows:
A: Professional
B: Employers and Managers
C: Intermediate Non-manual
D: Junior Non-manual
E: Skilled Manual
F: Semi-skilled Manual
G: Unskilled Manual
Source: General Household Survey, 1974

(a) *Explain in your own words what these figures show about the pre-school experience of children from different social groups.* **(3 marks)**

(b) *Would it be correct to argue that differences in school achievement can be explained by the amount of pre-school education which children receive? Give reasons for your answer.* **(7 marks)**

(c) *To what extent is the concept of 'cultural deprivation' a useful one in explaining why children from some social backgrounds tend to be unsuccessful in school?* **(10 marks)** (CAM)

151   **Intentions of 16-year-old school children, England and Wales, 1975**

	Father's occupation	
	Non-manual total	Manual total
Percentage of students who have certain levels of attainment		
5+ GCE 'O' levels or CSE 1	34	11
1–4 GCE 'O' levels or CSE 1	34	32
No GCE or CSE 1	32	57
Percentage of students who wish to stay on in full-time education		
5+ GCE 'O' levels or CSE 1	88	75
1–4 GCE 'O' levels or CSE 1	59	45
No GCE or CSE 1	30	17
All students	60	32

Source: Adapted from *Social Trends*, 1976

(a) *Explain the relevance of 'father's occupation' on educational attainment.*

(b) *Why might children from 'white-collar backgrounds' be at an educational advantage?*

152 'The chances of the child of an unskilled worker being a poor reader at seven are six times greater than in the case of an upper middle-class child, who arrives at school tuned into educational demands. . . .'

Jilly Cooper, *Class*, 1979

(a) *Why are children from the homes of unskilled workers at an educational disadvantage?*

(b) *How might such children become successful in later years, whereas others remain with low qualifications?*

153 'Many children are already failures by the age of 5 – and some are simply born failures. . . . For even at that tender age a large percentage of our children have already failed in the accepted sense of the word. Many of our children are born to fail.'

A primary school headmistress, the *Sun*, 7 June 1977

(a) What evidence is there that some children are 'born to fail'?

(b) Why are some children 'failures' by the age of five?

To answer these questions it is helpful to consider the figure.

Social class background

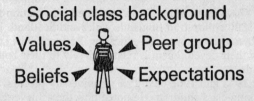

Values ▲ ▲ Peer group

Beliefs ▼ ▼ Expectations

The external cultural & environmental factors

These are some factors that influence the child once he/she attends school. They relate to the way the institution of the school is organised and structured

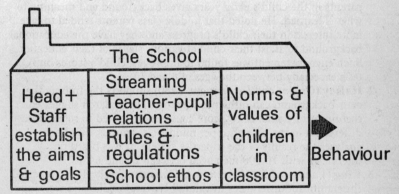

	The School		
Head + Staff establish the aims & goals	Streaming	Norms & values of children in classroom	Behaviour
	Teacher-pupil relations		
	Rules & regulations		
	School ethos		

Institutional factors

These are some factors that influence the behaviour of the child before going to school. They continue to have a significant influence on the child thereafter

Social class

When selecting and answering a question you should therefore either emphasize the cultural influences which are external to the school itself, or the institutional factors which relate to its internal organization. In some cases (questions numbered 145–151) you need to discuss both.

The significance of the external cultural factors

1 **Douglas** *(The Home and the School)* collected information from a sample of 5000 children in England, Wales and Scotland. He followed them throughout their educational careers. The study shows how their development is related closely to their home backgrounds.

Between 1938 and 1968 only 25% of university places were taken up by working-class children. He noted how the achievements of working-class children fall steadily behind middle-class children who were in the same ability groups when they were admitted to school. Nearly eight times the proportion of sons of professional fathers went on to further education in comparison with the sons of the unskilled.

He places particular emphasis on the parent's attitude towards education. The lack of interest or failure to encourage is a significant factor in poor performance.

Douglas also says that the care of sympathetic and perceptive parents in the child's early years gives background and meaning to what is learned. He noted that middle-class parents tended to take more interest in their child's progress and they have the educational background to assist their child at various stages of their education. Such encouragement was found to improve a child's scores on IQ tests especially between the ages of 8 and 11.

2 **Halsey** *(Origins and Destinations*, 1980) supports the finding that class background can influence IQ score. His research suggested that up to 11 points of IQ score could be attributed to social class differences in the case of upper middle-class pupils. His book analyses the results of the tripartite system. It was based on interviews with 10,000 men aged between 20 and 64.

3 **King** *(Values and Involvement in a Grammar School*, 1970) revealed the significant differences in values between middle- and working-class children. Values held to be important among middle-class candidates for grammar school were to have a knowledge of what is good and valuable, to develop traditional Christian values, to take pride in one's work, to make constructive use of leisure and to develop character. Among the early leavers who were mainly working-class children, these had low ratings.

King *(Education)* also points out that every survey done in the

UK into educational attainments shows that middle-class children have a longer educational life than working-class pupils.

4 **Clegg** *(The Challenge of Change)* says that a group of resentful, largely working-class children, who see themselves as the rejects of a qualification conscious society will become more conspicuous. He argues that violence and resentment may grow if unemployment and dull jobs are all that is offered to them.

5 **Lacey** and **Pidgeon** (in separate studies) both emphasize the significance of parental interest and educational attainment on the performance of their children. Middle-class parents are more likely to visit school and discuss matters with the teachers than are the parents of working-class pupils. The middle-class child was also much less prone to get into serious trouble in or out of school. They also had better levels of health and so were less frequently absent from school.

6 **Banks** makes the point that during their years of schooling the child's experience of the world around them continues to be moulded by peer contacts, local community values and the media – all of which are outside the control of the school.

7 **Davie, Butler and Goldstein** *(From Birth to Seven)* studied a group of children born in the first week of March 1958. They have followed them through at seven-year intervals ever since. They found that the chances of an unskilled manual worker's child being a poor reader at 7 are six times greater than those of a professional worker's child. The chances of a child from class 5 being a non-reader at this age are fifteen times greater than those of a class 1 child. They argue that one of the major reasons is because the middle-class children arrive in school tuned in to the educational demands of the school. More working-class children (even by the age of 7) are showing hostility towards the teacher, withdrawal, depression and a 'writing-off' of adult standards.

The significance of the internal institutional factors

1 The study *(15,000 Hours)* was carried out by **Rutter** et al. over six years and found that a child's performance in school was strongly affected by the types of teachers he or she encountered. Those who created satisfactory norms of endeavour encouraged the children, marked their work carefully and took an interest in them, all had a motivating effect. Also the authors say that the ethos of the school was important. The successful school had consistent norms, values and rules. Also it was found to be important to have a consistent spread of ability coming into the school. Success was not particularly associated with small size of school nor with level of

resources available. They conclude, however, that the way the school is organized and structured can have a direct effect on levels of ability and success.

2 **Elder**'s research suggests that streaming is a dangerous feature of a school since it effectively labels a child as a 'D' stream type or 'failure'. This can result in the child developing a strong negative self-image. Children often then perform in accordance with their self-assessment. Also teachers may come to see the children in a particular way and assume that those in the lowest streams are limited in their abilities. In both cases 'self-fulfilling prophecies' may result (see p. 240).

3 **Medlicott** (*Streaming and the Comprehensive School*) suggests that the move towards mixed ability teaching in the comprehensive school has not yet been subject to enough research to assess its value. He argues that it may depend on the ability of the teachers. There is no firm evidence that the brighter children suffer from being educated with the less able – but the system does require dedicated and able teachers.

4 **Hargreaves** (*Deviance in Classrooms*) is interested in how the deviant in a classroom is identified by a teacher and how he or she is then treated. He asks to what extent the deviant is a victim of the school structure. He is an **interactionist theorist**. This approach draws attention away from the act that is described as deviant and points more at the person who does the defining and the relationship they have with those they define.

Hargreaves examines the way in which pupils develop particular cultures (see pp. 96, 99, 101–2) by which they can deal with the problems which face them in the classroom. He analyses different forms of impudence on the part of pupils and shows how they are recognized by the teacher. His work is important because it shows how labels are developed and become attached to particular pupils over time. In this way he shows the importance of some of the institutional factors in affecting the behaviour and attainment levels of some pupils.

5 **Shipman** (*The Sociology of the School*) points out that it would be surprising to find any organization in which there was no clash of interests. In a school, staff will exercise their power to ensure that they get their way. This may mean overcoming the resistance of the children. The children themselves may find going to school is a restriction on their liberty; they may find the routines, regulations and rituals also restraining influences. With poor teacher–pupil ratios the 'dull' and 'slow' children are likely to be sacrificed in the quest for academic success. Efforts may be concentrated on the few who can cope well. The teachers and pupils share certain norms which establish expectations and rules of conduct. Where the norms

of the pupils do not coincide with those of the school, then conflict is likely to result.

6 **Bernstein** *(Class Codes and Control)* makes use of the analysis of language use to explain why some children achieve more in school than others.

Middle-class parents were found to use a more complex language structure which was acquired by their children. He describes this as an elaborated code. Sentences are longer; vocabulary is more complex; ideas are more abstract. The emphasis, too, is on the ability to express ideas orally.

The working-class language code is described as 'restricted'. Sentences are shorter, vocabulary is simple and ideas more concrete. There is no particular stress on the ability to speak clearly and well.

As far as school is concerned, Bernstein points out that the teacher, although not necessarily middle-class, has acquired a middle-class language structure as a result of lengthy education and the need to pass examinations. As a result they will tend to use an elaborated code in the classroom.

The middle-class child can make use of both codes: the restricted one in the playground and the elaborated code in the home and in the classroom. This means that there is greater communication between the middle-class child and the teacher: more questions are asked and more questions are directed to them. The working-class child has less ability to manipulate words and ideas, is therefore less curious and less able to raise or answer questions in the classroom. For Bernstein, this is a crucial part in the explanation of why working-class children are less successful in school and why so few go on to further and higher education.

Key terms and concepts

The following terms and concepts have been used and defined in this chapter. You must be able to use them and explain their meaning for examination purposes:

education; formal education; informal education; primary education; secondary education; the structure of education; academic education; tripartite system; comprehensive system; streaming; language codes; elaborated code; restricted code; socialization; social class; cultural values; selection; functionalist perspective.

Other terms which you may wish to use:

IQ Intelligence quotient. First devised by the French psychologist, Binet, in 1905. He devised the concept of 'mental age'. Terman later introduced the concept of an index of mental development:

$$IQ = \frac{Mental\ age}{Chronological\ age} \times 100$$

agency of social control Every society requires formal and informal methods of gaining the conformity of its members to a set of basic social values. Those who deviate from these norms may be punished formally (through the law) or informally through force of public opinion. The educational structure is such an agency and it operates in both ways. Children who misbehave may be punished or they may risk being disliked by their peers.

20   Religion

154 *Why are sociologists interested in religion?*

Religion in society

1 Some sociologists are interested in the significance of religion as an agency of **social control**. Sociologists have always been interested in the question, 'what are the sources of social order and stability in a society?' Some have said that this is achieved when people share particular beliefs, values and ideals in common. Some writers (for example, Durkheim) have concluded that where there is a dominant religion with which people identify, then a sense of unity and social cohesion results.

2 They may wish to know more precisely what is meant by 'religion'. It is difficult to define precisely and when asked religious people themselves may have some confusion as to its meaning. Tillich has said, 'it is that which concerns us ultimately'; Yinger has said, 'it is a system of beliefs by which people struggle with the ultimate problems of life'. But critics may ask 'what are the ultimate problems?', and different people may develop different means of dealing with such problems. In general it may be helpful to say that there are a number of features that help to identify more orthodox religious beliefs: They normally involve acceptance of a divine force at work in the universe, a spiritual leader or teacher, rituals and ceremonies normally conducted in a sacred place by specialist practitioners, meetings of believers, a specific moral code and sacred book which informs the adherents about what is required of them to obtain salvation.

3 Some studies have been made of **religious substitutes**; that is, the ways in which some people may turn away from and reject orthodox religious values and beliefs and substitute an alternative system. They may become devoted to a political party, to a belief in science or some other organized system. This fulfils the functions of religion in the lives of orthodox believers. For example, a Marxist may see Marx as the Messiah: his writings are the sacred books, his

teachings provide the moral code by which the heaven on earth will ultimately be obtained.

4 Some sociologists have been interested in the emergence of religion in a society.

Durkheim (*Elementary Forms of Religious Life*) said that in simple societies religion is more a form of magic or superstition. The aim is to try and influence events in the short term, in order to help crops grow or to gain protection from enemies in battle. Almost every aspect of society is closely associated with religious/magical prescriptions, since life is precarious and knowledge very limited.

In more complex, technological societies, religion becomes more sophisticated; the underlying philosophical ideas on which religions rest are elaborated.

Marx and Engels believed that the roots of religion were in primitive times when man struggled with forces of nature which he did not understand. They said that in modern societies religious ideals were imposed on the oppressed workers by the ruling class to persuade them that their sufferings on earth would be rewarded in heaven. Hence religion became 'the opiate of the people', a drug to hide reality from them and to ensure that they would never seek to change the social structure.

5 Weber saw the main task of sociology being to help understand patterns of human behaviour. He saw the study of religion as being concerned with the effect that belief in the supernatural has on such behaviour. He argued that religion could be seen as the source of social change (as opposed to the Marxian view that it was a source of social stagnation. He said that a study of history showed that all the major breaks with tradition came from the teachings of religious prophets. In the west the emergence of reform movements were almost always associated with Christian or Jewish leaders. He also made the point that capitalism emerged in the west as a result of the teachings of the Protestant theologians Luther and Calvin. They taught that hard work and the accumulation of wealth was a pathway to salvation. Catholicism does not have the same emphasis nor do the religions of the east.

6 Some sociologists are interested in establishing what are the functions of religion. This may also give rise to such specific questions as:

155 *What are the social functions of religion?* (AEB)
156 *Describe what is meant by religious beliefs and discuss any two social functions of religion.* (WEL)

The social functions of religion may usefully be divided into two groups:

those that fulfil certain needs of individuals and those that are valuable for society as a whole.

(a) For the individual

   (i) Religion helps to provide answers for people about the uncertainties and difficulties of life. Those with religious beliefs may have a better sense of their purpose in the universe.

  (ii) The moral codes (e.g. the Ten Commandments) which all religions have may help to provide a useful code of conduct for people.

 (iii) Involvement in a religion may help to satisfy a person's emotional needs and sense of well-being. Through confession and other ceremonies the individual may feel better able to cope with his or her day-to-day life.

 (iv) Involvement in ceremonies, rituals and meetings may increase the individual's sense of commitment to a group and a community of like-minded people.

  (v) As the individual passes through different phases of life these are often marked by different religious rituals (such as baptism, confirmation, marriage, etc.). They may help to provide a new status or role which gains social acceptance.

(b) For society

   (i) Religion can be an important source of social stability and order in a society. Particular codes of conduct are established and those which are considered to be anti-social are invested with the notion of 'sin'. Supernatural sanctions may support the norms and mores of the society and so provide more stability and cohesion. For example, religious ceremonies add depth to the meaning of marriage in western society.

  (ii) The major social events in a society are often associated with religious ceremonies. For example, the Coronation, the marriage of royalty, the launching of ships, etc. This may help constantly to re-establish the underlying religious values of a society. The often very large audience may then feel a greater sense of identity and involvement in their society.

 (iii) Religion in a society may affect economic behaviour. As Weber suggested, the Protestant Ethic may have given rise to the spirit of capitalism in the west. Also the element of social criticism in Christianity may have given rise to the socialist movement and other organizations for social reform.

(iv) For Marxists religion is a means by which the ruling
class maintain their control.

7 Some sociologists are particularly interested in the changing trends
in religion. There are also, sometimes, specific questions on this
aspect. For example:

157 *Britain is now a secular society. Explain and comment on this
statement.* (WEL)

There is much debate among sociologists about how important religion
is in the lives of people in contemporary society. Some argue that
evidence from statistics shows that people make much less use of
religious rituals and ceremonies in their lives (baptism, christenings,
church marriage, etc. in addition to frequent attendance at church
services); others argue that this is a mistaken view because people retain
a deep sense of religion even though they may not show it in their
outward activities. A high proportion of people who do not go to church
nevertheless still believe in most of the important aspects of
Christianity.

Among the sociologists who put forward the argument that religion is
in decline in contemporary Britain is Bryan Wilson (*Religion in a
Secular Society*). This view is sometimes termed the 'secularization'
argument.

Secularization is a difficult term to define but is generally taken to
mean the decline in the significance of religion in people's lives. Wilson
says it is the tendency for people to discount the possible significance of
the supernatural in their daily lives, so that such interpretations become
less and less relevant. Consequently, the institutionalized church
becomes increasingly redundant for most people.

1 He points out that church attendance is falling. A Census in 1851
showed there was an average weekly attendance of about 40% of the
population at church services. It is currently estimated that between
10 and 15% of the population attend regularly.
2 There has been an overall decline in the numbers being confirmed
in the Church of England. Between 1964 and 1974 there was a fall
of 30%. In the same period there was a fall of 20,000 in the number
of Roman Catholic confirmations, and a fall of 34,000 in Methodist
membership.
3 In 1979 there were more civil marriage ceremonies than religious
ones for the first time since registry offices were established in
1837.
4 Wilson says that the clergy have lost status in the community. A

report by Paul in 1964 and again in 1974 showed that there were too few clergy looking after too many people. They were poorly paid and often out of touch with contemporary problems. In 1971 the Church of England had 10,071 parish clergymen. Only 27 were under 30; 51 were aged between 80 and 92. The average age was 53.

5 He argues that whilst the established churches continue to have 'an institutional presence' they lack a solid base among the general public. He thinks that the changes which occur from time to time in doctrine and structure (changing the language of prayer books, introducing new patterns of worship, etc.) are largely irrelevant and confusing to most people. What is crucial is the central message of Christianity and this is of no real interest to most people today.

6 He sees the ecumenical movement as a sign of weakness. It represents the declining churches uniting to prevent complete decay.

7 He argues that the churches fail to give a moral lead to people. They change their doctrines to suit the moral climate. They follow rather than lead in social attitudes.

8 He concludes that whilst there will always be some 'religious' people, religion will ultimately become little more than a 'leisure activity' for most people. He sees the future of orthodox churches in terms of a reversion to small sects which will accommodate the minority which continue to practise their religion.

Wilson argues that this process of decline has resulted from a series of weakening influences:

1 The growth of scientific rationalism, i.e. the search for explanations of events which can be shown to be scientifically valid;

2 The impact of new books and writers who attack traditional religious values and who have a wide following;

3 The possible weakening of stable family relationships and the strength of peer group influence on the behaviour of the young.

Among the sociologists who put the counter argument is the British sociologist, David Martin.

1 He accepts some of the points put by Wilson. He agrees that there has been a steady and fairly continuous fall in membership and attendance figures for most Christian churches and organizations. However, he argues that such statistics can be subject to other interpretations. For example, although attendance figures are low, repeated studies show a high proportion of the population identify

with a religious group. As many as two-thirds of the population describe themselves as 'Church of England'. About two in ten identify with the Roman Catholic Church. About one in ten identify with the free churches. Also a high proportion of people admit to extensive 'personal devotion' (prayer, reading religious books and papers, visiting churches, etc.).

2 The statistics may not be as bleak as Wilson says. For example, whilst only a small proportion of the population may attend church regularly every Sunday, fairly high proportions attend more infrequently:

25% attend every other Sunday;
30% attend every month;
40% attend every three months;
45% attend once a year.

3 He believes that the majority of people have a strong sense of and need for religion. This is evidenced by the high proportion of people who are superstitious and who have beliefs in 'subterranean theologies' (the stars, luck, the supernatural, etc.).

4 Religion is still the basis of the moral code of most people. It is still linked with important national festivities and continues to legitimate many social institutions (e.g. marriage, coronation, etc.).

5 He sees the ecumenical movement as a sign of strength in the churches, since they are able to appeal to more people on a wider basis.

6 There are an increasing number of new sects which have appeal for many young people in particular. These are growing in membership (e.g. Bahai, Rastafarianism, Pentecostalism, etc.).

7 He concludes that there are many potential weakening influences as far as orthodox religious movements are concerned (reforms may have helped to destroy many of the important myths and symbols to which people need to relate). Nevertheless, all that is happening is that people are turning from orthodox forms of religion into more unorthodox forms. But people are no less 'religious' for that. It is just that they prefer to express their religious needs in new and different ways. It could even be argued that after the churches shed their half-hearted, peripheral members they will be the stronger for it.

Consider how you would answer this question:

158 *How does religion contribute to social control in a modern industrial society? Does it remain an important influence in people's lives?*

NB: see also p. 35.

Key terms and concepts

The following terms and concepts have been used and defined in this chapter. You must be able to use them and explain their meaning for examination purposes:

religion; rituals; Protestant Ethic; religious substitutes; functionalist perspective; views of Marx; views of Weber; views of Durkheim; secularization; sects.

Other terms you may wish to use:

ecumenical movement Attempts to find common ground between all the major churches so that it would be possible for members of one church (e.g. Church of England) to worship in another (e.g. Methodist). This would require each one to change its doctrine and rituals to some extent.

rituals Customs and patterns of behaviour having symbolic significance and which often signal important events.

magic The ability to manipulate forces over which there is normally no human power, by use of spells, potions, etc. Magic seeks to compel the powers of nature to obey man.

superstition The ability to control the powers of nature and the social world in the short term by the use of rituals, charms, mascots, etc. There is a belief in the existence of malevolent, but controllable, forces at work.

21 Race relations

159 Is there a race problem in Britain? (OX)

In order to decide whether there are problems between races in Britain it is necessary to decide first what is meant by the word **race**.

Many attempts have been made to clarify the term. In general it is used to denote the sharing of common social and physical traits. Races are usually distinguished from each other by the relative frequency within them of certain characteristics.

The idea of a pure race in which all the elements of other groups are eliminated is not possible. Even the Nazis could not adequately define or identify all the characteristics of the Jewish members of their society.

One general classification of racial types is Negroid, Mongolian and Caucasian. There has been a great amount of intermixing between these groups over millions of years and certainly no predictions can be made about racial types in terms of character, personality or intelligence.

By noting the problems of defining the characteristics of 'a racial type' or 'racial group' it becomes clear how dangerous it is to try and classify people in a simple way by a label which may be inaccurate or misleading.

It is more helpful to talk of **ethnic groups** rather than racial groups. This means people who have a particular social and cultural background which is different from that of the society in which they live. They form a sub-culture or sub-group within the host society. Race implies shared physical characteristics.

There are problems from time to time which involve people from different backgrounds. But these are usually problems arising from a failure to understand each other's cultural values rather than as a result of the fact that people are opposed to each other on racial grounds.

Ethnic minorities tend to live in areas apart from the host society and often in poorer (or economically different) circumstances. They maintain their cultural traditions, their language, their food and their dress. Also people like their understanding of the world to be consistent and clear. The use of labels and classifications into 'types' is one of the ways that people achieve this. The problem is that they are often unaware of the dangers associated with oversimplifying events.

In answering this question it would also be necessary to go on to discuss the kinds of problems that are sometimes said to have a racial (or ethnic) origin. These are also sometimes the basis of other questions:

160 *The major problem faced by immigrants to Britain is not prejudice or discrimination, but poor housing.* (OX)
161· *Why do most immigrants to Britain live in the inner city areas of the major conurbations? Examine the main characteristics and problems of these areas.* (OX)

What is meant by 'social problems'?

A **social problem** is some feature that is generally judged by some group or organization to be undesirable. They may then decide to try and remedy the situation by pressing those who are in a position to take action to do so.

Not everyone may necessarily perceive a particular issue to be 'a problem'. However, there is widespread agreement that race relations do raise certain difficulties both for the minority groups and sometimes for members of the host society. But the form the problems take depend to some extent on the political and social values of those who raise the issue and those who are directly involved in it.

What is meant by 'immigrants'?

Britain has had a small number of coloured citizens for many centuries. In the nineteenth century thousands of freed slaves were absorbed into the population without friction.

Many sociologists points out the dangers of using the term **immigrant**. It carries with it connotations which do not help race relations. In 1976 the Under Secretary of State at the Department of Employment said that to speak of black British-born children with regional accents as 'immigrants' is ludicrous. The assumption is that any black person has recently arrived in Britain. There is no easy definition of the term but it is generally taken to mean a person who has recently moved into a new society from one in which they have habitually lived.

But birth place is not an entirely satisfactory criterion since people born abroad whose parents are British could be classified as 'immigrants' when they return. **Citizenship** is not satisfactory as a definition either, since the majority of coloured citizens normally termed immigrants are British passport holders and British citizens as a result of agreements made at the time of independence when colonies formerly controlled by Britain became self-governing.

Many writers, therefore, object to the term because they argue it serves only as a label which perpetuates stereotyped images.

What is meant by prejudice and discrimination?

Prejudice means to pre judge. A racially prejudiced person is one who has decided that he or she does not like a person of another race regardless of who they are or what they have done. (It is most frequently used in this negative way, although it would be possible to use it in a positive sense.)

Discrimination is the act of prejudice; that is, to treat a person in accordance with one's prejudices. Failure to give a person a job or a home because they are black would constitute an act of discrimination based on prejudice. (It would also be possible to have an act of **positive discrimination**, in which the job was given to the person because they were black.)

The main problems faced by immigrants to Britain

1 If they are considered to be 'a problem' they may be treated as such. There may then be a failure to get at the root of the difficulty which is often bad housing and poor job prospects.
2 When members of minority groups are designated 'immigrants' this acts as a label or stereotype which causes people to perceive them in a negative way and to treat them accordingly.
3 Members of minority groups tend to suffer from a major lack of housing and job opportunities.
4 They suffer extensively from daily prejudice and discrimination.

162 Are bad housing and poor job opportunities more serious problems than prejudice and discrimination?

Sociologists would argue that it is almost impossible to say which is the major problem since the various factors are interwoven. Each is a major problem in its own right. They all have a serious effect on the extent to which minorities can enjoy life in contemporary Britain.

It is frequently prejudice and discrimination which cause members of ethnic minorities (especially those from the New Commonwealth) to live in the poorest areas and to face greatest difficulties obtaining jobs and the prospects of the highest rates of unemployment.

In answering these questions you must make use of data from

research studies. These details will also form the basis of other questions such as:

163 Is there less hostility to racial minorities today? What sociological evidence is there that racial prejudice and racial discrimination exist in Britain?
164 The following extract is taken from Thomas Mann's novel Dr Faustus. In the novel the author describes a small German town and some of its inhabitants. The town (which is of course fictitious), is called Kaiseraschern.

'Many eccentrics and harmlessly half-mad folk live within the town's walls. The children, the "young 'uns", pursue these poor creatures, mock them, and then in a superstitious panic run away. A certain sort of old woman used always without more ado to be suspected of witchcraft, simply because she looked "queer". Her appearance may well have been, in the first place, nothing but the result of suspicion against her, which then gradually justified itself till it resembled the popular fancy: small, grey, bent, with a spiteful face, rheumy eyes, hooked nose, thin lips, a threatening crook. Probably she owned cats, an owl, a talking bird. In Kaiseraschern there was more than one such specimen; the most teased and most feared was Cellar-Lise, so-called because she lived in a basement in Little Brassfounder's Alley – an old woman whose figure had so moulded itself to popular prejudice that even the most unprejudiced could feel a shudder at meeting her, especially when the children were after her and she was putting them to flight by spitting curses. Of course, quite definitely there was nothing wrong with her at all.'

(a) Explain how the notions of 'stereotyping' and of 'the self-fulfilling prophecy' are relevant to the events discussed in this passage. (8 marks)
(b) Using this passage and any other examples you consider appropriate, write a short essay on 'social attitudes to outsiders'. (12 marks) (CAM)

Housing

Rex and Moore's Race, Community and Conflict is based on research commissioned by the Survey of Race Relations in Britain. It is a study of a decaying area of Birmingham which has attracted a great number of 'immigrants' and ethnic minorities.

The area examined was Sparkbrook. The houses were built less than 100 years ago. They were abandoned by the merchant class which originally owned them. They were taken over by landlords who split them into separate dwellings. They then began to fall into decay. But because of the relative soundness of the housing fabric they were not condemned. Such areas are sometimes termed 'twilight zones'. They generally have poor standards of housing, multi-occupation and high levels of immigrant settlement.

There are three main areas in Sparkbrook.

1 The big houses east of the Stratford Road. Once the middle-class area but now the homes of the poorest residents.
2 The area west of the Stratford Road. This was found to be the area of the 'respectable working class'.
3 The Ex-Barber Trust Housing. This area housed the 'better-off' working class.

Rex and Moore concluded that the coloured community were largely forced into the poorest sectors of this area of Birmingham (as they are in almost every large urban area into which they move) because:

1 They cannot easily get mortgages to buy their own property.
2 There are usually members of their own ethnic groups already there which attracts more into the area.
3 Where there are large numbers in the family it is convenient to take on a large property such as those available in the poorest areas.
4 As a result of prejudice and discrimination they are discouraged from trying to gain access to the traditionally white residential areas.

Daniel (*Political and Economic Planning Report*, 1966) studied the problems faced by immigrants in housing and employment. The researchers interviewed a sample of coloured respondents to see whether they believed that they had been discriminated against: 72% believed they had been. In order to find out more about the nature of prejudice and discrimination that the immigrants suffered, the researchers asked three subjects to apply for jobs, houses, other forms of accommodation, mortgages and insurance.

Each subject, an Englishman, a West Indian and a Hungarian, was given similar status and qualifications.

The results showed that a high proportion of the coloured applicants were turned away by someone comparatively low down in the administrative hierarchy. Most of the English applicants were not. In theory all should have had equal opportunity of obtaining the post advertised or the mortgage required.

Each applicant applied for various types of accommodation. The results were:

Occasions on which discrimination occurred   60

Occasions on which all were given the same or similar
  information   45

An analysis was made of the types of discrimination that occurred. Of
the 45 refusals the West Indian was told that the accommodation was
taken on 38 occasions when both the others were told that it was still
vacant.

The West Indian was asked for a higher rent than the other two four
times. The West Indian and the Hungarian were both told that the
accommodation was taken when the Englishman was told it was still
vacant on two occasions.

Smith and Whalley (*Racial Minorities and Public Housing*) conducted
ten detailed case studies into the way local authorities distributed housing. They suggest that where discrimination occurs it may be largely
unintentional. Immigrants who have recently arrived are at the bottom
of waiting lists and seldom fulfil residential qualifications. They tend to
get the poorest housing as a result. They conclude that public housing
has often reinforced disadvantages, rather than compensated for them,
as far as this sector of the community is concerned.

Employment

Daniel (1966) asked each of his three subjects to apply for the same jobs,
having given them all the same qualifications. He found that of the 40
jobs for which they applied:

The Englishman was accepted for 30.
The Hungarian was accepted for 17.
The West Indian was accepted for 3.

It was found that even when the West Indian was best qualified he still
came out lowest in the order of acceptance.

PEP Report 1974 (Racial Disadvantage in Employment) found a series
of major difficulties faced black workers:

1 More than half of the factories investigated practised some form of
  discrimination.
2 Only 8% of factories in the study took active steps to prevent it.
3 A black worker had to make twice as many applications as a white
  worker before finding a job.
4 Black workers were heavily concentrated in non-skilled manual jobs
  and were more than twice as likely as their white counterparts to be
  working permanent night shift.
5 Few factories had any workers from minority groups as supervisory
  staff.

6 Resistance from white workers to such moves was not common but was often effective.
7 Trade unions were sometimes found guilty of failing even to attempt to counter discriminatory practices.

Deakin has examined the pattern of employment among immigrants. He says that although they originally arrived at the beginning of the century to escape persecution, in more recent years they have come for economic reasons. They usually seek to escape the poverty of their own country. They have been encouraged to come by successive British Governments in the 1950s and 1960s at times of labour shortage. He says there is no real evidence to show that black workers take the jobs of whites, since in general they tend to undertake those jobs that white workers least want. But when there is high unemployment they often suffer the most difficulty since they are among the first to be laid-off and last to be re-employed.

The Home Office Report (Ethnic Minorities, 1981) confirms that coloured people continue to suffer major problems in everyday life as a result of their minority status. In the privately rented sector discrimination is still substantial. The effect of the recession on minority workers has been more severe than on white workers. There did seem to be less discrimination among local housing authorities than in earlier studies. But they do tend to have to pay more for the same housing than whites. Because they tend to have lower incomes and operate on tighter margins this has a disproportionate effect on them. They experienced a greater degree of poverty than white households in 1981. The Report concludes that despite the attempts of the various Race Relations Acts, there is continued discrimination on a large scale against those perceived as coloured immigrants.

National Opinion Poll (1975) found that young white people are more tolerant of immigrants than are older white people. But young blacks feel that there is more discrimination than older blacks. They felt that this was true as far as pubs and clubs were concerned. Also one-third of the West Indians questioned said they thought that the police discriminated against them. The Report also discovered the extent of the ignorance about the numbers coming into the country. In 1974 the total was 25,500. Three-quarters of those questioned had no idea at all; the majority over-estimated. Among the whites questioned they found that on balance opinion was in favour of steps being taken to promote good race relations.

Abrams (1967) attempted to discover what proportion of the population was prejudiced. He devised a scale to measure replies to a questionnaire. These ranged from hostile to favourable. He found a 10% hardcore of prejudice, the bulk of whom were strong authoritarian personalities. He defined these as people who show an exaggerated need to respond to authority and who express strong fear of groups with whom they do not identify. They tended to project their hostilities onto such groups. He found women were generally more tolerant than men.

165 How effective have changes in the law been in reducing racial discrimination?

To answer a question like this, you must know some of the causes of opposition to black people in Britain. You must then be able to outline some of the important pieces of legislation and comment on their effectiveness in combating the factors you have previously mentioned.

Some causes of hostility towards coloured people

Psychological factors

Psychologists have shown how frustration can lead to aggression (known as **displaced hostility**). When people feel angry or deprived they often place the blame on others. This is sometimes termed **scape-goating**. Immigrants are often blamed for a whole series of social problems (such as lack of jobs or homes) when in fact they suffer from the same difficulties but to an even greater extent.

Prejudice and discrimination is also associated with particular personality types, especially those known as **authoritarian personalities**.

Sociological factors

If prejudice and discrimination have become a norm among a group, then the open expression of hostility by group members is likely to integrate them more strongly into the group. Governments often produce a potential threat to stability ('strikers', 'agitators', etc.) in order to increase a sense of hostility against a certain section of society. They can then gain more power by acting strongly against the source of the danger.

Hostility to members of minority groups is often based on the **stereotypes** which exist about those groups; that is, there is an assumption that all members of the group share the same characteristics which are normally of a negative and unfavourable kind.

The cultural roots of prejudice and discrimination arise from fear, misunderstanding or misconceptions about the cultural values of immigrants. Their behaviour is seen to be different and less acceptable because it is related to a different culture from that of the host society.

A class theory of prejudice and discrimination emphasizes that economic differences between members of a society give rise to alienation and antagonism. Because immigrants are likely to take up the lowest social positions in the society they migrate to, they are subjected to most hostility from those they threaten most. This threatened group will be the class immediately above them in the social hierarchy.

Those who are most prejudiced tend to be most ignorant of the facts relating to the numbers of coloured people in Britain and have little understanding or sympathy for the cultural values which they uphold.

Some of the important race relations legislation

The Commonwealth Immigration Act 1962

This reduced the annual intake who were coming to work to a ceiling of 7500. Those who applied for entry could do so within two categories **(voucher holders)**:

1 Those who had obtained employment in manufacturing industries; had work said to be of economic or social value; or had been recruited through special schemes.
2 Those qualified as doctors, dentists, teachers or nurses; graduates in technology; or with a firm offer of a job or with two years' experience since obtaining their qualifications.

There were also stricter limitations on the number of dependants that those qualified for vouchers could bring into the country. One of the consequences was that demand for entry increased before the Act was passed and became law.

The Race Relations Act 1965

This stated that it is unlawful to discriminate on the grounds of colour, race, ethnic or national origin, in providing goods, facilities or services to the public, in employment, housing or other areas of social life. These include professional and business services and those of local and public authorities, banking, insurance and education. It also penalizes incitement to racial hatred and established the Race Relations Board, the members of which were appointed by the Home Secretary. The duties of the Board were to investigate complaints and assist complainants.

The Race Relations Act 1976

The main provisions are

1 The definition of discrimination is extended to include discrimination on grounds of nationality.

2 The Act covers discrimination in private clubs with more than 25 members.
3 The Race Relations Board is replaced by new procedures. Complainants can now initiate proceedings in courts or industrial tribunals themselves.
4 A Commission for Racial Equality is established which replaces the Race Relations Board. Its major role is the elimination of discriminatory practices in firms and institutions.
5 Employers are liable for the unlawful actions of their employees unless they can prove that they took such steps as were reasonably practicable to prevent their employees from discriminating. Then, the employee alone is responsible.

The Nationality Bill 1981

It proposes to create three new categories of citizenship:

1 British citizenship for those born in the UK to a British citizen or person settled here;
2 Citizenship of the British Dependent Territories (e.g. Hong Kong) which provides no right of abode in the UK;
3 British Overseas Citizenship – which also does not provide a right of abode in the UK.

To what extent does the legislation overcome discrimination?

It is unlikely that legislation will easily overcome the psychological factors that cause some people to be hostile to immigrants. However, it may be possible for legislation to defeat some of the cruder forms of discrimination. It is illegal to display anti-coloured notices or make reference to racial background as a reason for failing to offer a job or accommodation or other services. In time this may help to change attitudes. If people grow up in a society where such behaviour is socially unacceptable, then they are less likely to think in such terms.

Nevertheless, recent research does indicate that hostile attitudes do remain in evidence in many areas of social life. There seems to be a continuing process which ensures that coloured citizens fall mainly into the lowest occupational categories, which helps to support the stereotype and which causes the development of self-fulfilling prophecies.

Prejudice seems to increase at times of economic crisis when many of the problems facing a society are projected into the minority group and explained by their presence.

Much evidence points to the fact that although younger people are becoming more tolerant, in general British society has not progressed much beyond the stage of a minimum acceptance of coloured people.

The passing of Race Relations Acts is an attempt to manipulate the structures of society in order to increase the opportunities of immigrant groups and ethnic minorities so that they can become more socially mobile and lead more contented lives.

However, such legislation can be counterproductive if it breeds a sense of discontent among some sections of the host society.

The problem of racial harmony is an urgent one and sociologists' research continues to have an important role in making the facts clear and in providing explanations for the causes and consequences of disharmony.

166 *Outline the possible causes and consequences of immigration into a country.* (WEL)
167 *Outline the major changes which have taken place in the pattern of migration into and out of Britain since 1900.*

The causes of immigration

1 **Persecution**   Where a group are suffering persecution in their own society they may decide to escape to a new country. For example, Jews escaped from Hitler's Germany after 1933; the Ugandan Asians escaped from General Amin's attacks on them in 1972.
2 **Encouragement**   For example Enoch Powell recruited immigrant doctors and nurses to come to Britain in the 1950s to assist with the health service. Other campaigns were undertaken to assist with the transport services.
3 **Entitlement**   When British colonies became independent people had the right to become British citizens and passport holders, and to come to Britain if they wished.
4 **To escape economic hardship**   For example, if there is a low standard of living in their own society, they may decide to leave. Pakistanis, Indians, West Indians, etc. may decide to seek higher standards of life in Britain. Many Irish went to the USA following famine in Ireland in the 1840s.
5 **To join relatives**   In Britain voucher holders (see p. 236) may be entitled to bring wives and dependent children into the country when they have become established in a job.

Changes in patterns of migration into and out of Britain

There has been a long history of migration into Britain. In the sixteenth century it has been estimated that about one-third of all tax-payers were 'aliens'. This first became seen as 'a problem' in the nineteenth century. The following general pattern has occurred:

1870–1914   Mainly Jewish immigrants from Eastern Europe. Some Irish escaping economic deprivation. Garrard (*The English and Immigration*) describes the causes and consequences of the influx of Jewish immigrants after 1870. They suffered the same difficulties as coloured immigrants today. They were also perceived in the same negative stereotypes. This gave rise to much anti-immigrant feeling.

1904   260,000 people emigrated.
82,000 immigrated from Europe.
There was an inflow of about 5000 Jewish immigrants every year until 1914. They were escaping persecution. At this time a Royal Commission reported that less than 1% of the population were immigrants.

1914–39   Small numbers of immigrants entered Britain from various countries throughout the world. Because numbers were small few controls were required.

1931–51   There were more people entering the country than leaving. There was a net gain of about 450,000. Small numbers of coloured people (mainly West Indian) came to Britain during the war as servicemen. Many Jewish immigrants arrived to escape the persecution of Hitler.

1951–61   There was a net gain of about 10,000 people in this period. It is estimated that there were about 200,000 coloured people in Britain, whose origins were in the Caribbean, Africa, Asia and the Middle East. They settled mainly in London, Liverpool and Cardiff (dock areas). A high proportion of these came as a result of recruiting campaigns when there was a shortage of labour. There was also some immigration from displaced Europeans, especially Poles and Hungarians.

1961–6   There was a net gain of 75,000 people in this period. Immigration rates tend to increase when legislation is about to be passed. People wish to enter the country before the door is closed. The Commonwealth Immigration Act reduced the numbers who could enter to work to a ceiling of 7500. However, they were entitled to bring in dependent relatives. As more of the British colonies gained independence, so more British citizens were created who had rights of entry.

1967–75   There was a net loss of about 45,000 in this period; that is, more people emigrated than came into Britain. Large numbers emigrated to Australia, Canada, New Zealand and the USA (especially highly qualified professional workers and those with technical skills). Britain's economy began to decline which encouraged emigration and it discouraged immigration.

1977–80   There was a net loss of about 40,000 people. Those countries that previously encouraged immigration began to make it more difficult to gain entry. Britain's declining economy further discouraged immigration.
In 1977 it was estimated that there were 1,771,000 coloured people (including those of mixed descent) in Britain. This represented about 3.3% of the population.

1986   It is estimated that the coloured population will reach about 2.6 million (about 4.7% of the total population).

Social Trends gives the following annual totals of immigrants admitted since statistics started in 1962.

1963	59,806	1967	64,968	1971	48,838	1975	53,165
1964	55,900	1968	64,318	1972	72,508	1976	55,025
1965	57,352	1969	48,084	1973	59,677		
1966	52,318	1970	42,390	1974	42,078		

Key terms and concepts

The following terms and concepts have been used and defined in this chapter. You must be able to use them and explain their meaning for examination purposes:

race; ethnic minorities; immigrants; prejudice; discrimination; PEP Report; social problem; stereotypes; sub-cultures; authoritarian personality.

Other terms which you may wish to use:

self-fulfilling prophecy   A prediction is made that an event will occur because it has already done so elsewhere (e.g. mugging in the USA) or as a result of a label that has been attached to an individual or a group (e.g. 'D' stream children will never do well). Prophecies are also made on the basis of stereotypes ('immigrants are prone to violence'). When, later, an individual or member of the labelled group behaves in accordance with the expectation, this is taken as proof that the original prophecy was correct. Behaviour which does not conform to the expectation is ignored.

New Commonwealth immigrants Those born in the West Indies, India or Pakistan who have come (as is their right) to live in Britain.

22 The distribution of income and wealth

168 Explain why the distribution of personal wealth in modern Britain is more unequal than the distribution of income. (CAM)

It is important that you can make a clear distinction between wealth and income.

Wealth The stock of accumulated assets measured in pounds sterling. This stock of assets includes anything that can be turned into cash for the benefit of the owner.

How wealth is held in Britain, 1971 (%)

Land and buildings	32
Company shares	17
Mortgages; building society deposits	15
Life assurance policies	15
Cash in the bank	9
Household goods, furniture, etc.	3
Other types of wealth	9

Source: Social Trends No. 15

In order to explain why the distribution of wealth is unequal it is necessary to show first that this is the case (see table).

Distribution of wealth, Great Britain 1911–74

Year	% of wealth owned by top 1%	% of wealth owned by top 10%
1911–13	69	92
1936–38	56	88
1966	32	72
1974	24	65

Source: Report of the Royal Commission on Wealth and Income, 1975

Some writers (e.g. the authors of *Social Trends No. 9*) suggest that these statistics show that the gap between the rich and poor is diminishing.

Others (e.g. Atkinson, *Unequal Shares*) argue that the main redistribution has been between the very rich and the rich. His view is that wealth remains more unequally distributed than income mainly because of the significance of inherited wealth in the pattern of wealth holding. A high proportion of the wealth held by the rich in society derives from unearned income. About two-thirds of those with more than £100,000 inherited more than £25,000 of it.

Reasons why the distribution of wealth is unequal

In general, the very rich are those who are

1 Old land-owning families. (The Duke of Westminster inherited more than £500,000,000 on the death of his father in 1979.)
2 Inheritors of industrial empires. (The Pilkington family has control of a glass manufacturing industry which may be worth more than £150,000,000.)
3 Major shareholders and participants in family trusts.

There is another category of 'the rich' who have not relied on inherited wealth; they are the builders of business and industrial empires who started from scratch and became millionaires in their own lifetimes (e.g. Sir Charles Clore, Sir Jack Cohen, etc.) But such self-made men are comparatively few.

Halsey (Reith Lectures, 1978) commenting on the distribution of wealth in Britain noted that the richest 1% of the population got about the same amount as the poorest 20%. This, he said, showed spectacular inequalities at the centre of British society.

Income   There are three types of income:

1 **Earned income**   This takes the form of wages and salaries from some form of employment.
2 **Unearned income**   This consists of receipts from investments, rents, interests and dividends.
3 **Social income**   This derives from social welfare benefits, pensions, etc.

The distribution of income in Britain

The question you have been asked to consider implies that the distribution of income is more equal than that of wealth. In answering the question it is necessary to consider the following points:

1 *Department of Employment Gazette* (1971) stated that there had been a reduction in differentials between high and low wage-earners throughout the 1960s.

2 A comparison between the wages earned by those at the top and bottom of the income scales between 1975 and 1978 showed that the gap between the average weekly earnings of non-manual and manual male workers widened from £13.70 to £21.50.

3 In 1978 the highest paid workers (gross incomes) included electricity power engineers (£136.10), marketing sales managers (£131.40), and teachers in higher education (£121.30). Those at the bottom of the income scale included retail food workers (£42.20), bespoke tailors (£43.00), and catering workers (£57.00).

4 *Economic Trends* (1978) found that those in the top 5% of incomes actually had a larger share of total income than those in the bottom 30%.

Conclusions

Holman (*Poverty*) says that both income and wealth remain unevenly distributed. A minority holds resources far out of proportion to its numbers. There is a concentration of earned and unearned income in a minority of hands.

However, although there are some workers who earn very high incomes, in 1978 the majority were within a band between £70 and £140 per week (gross). This suggests some equality in distribution of income. On the other hand, wealth includes unearned income, and although this is taxed (like earned income), it is an obvious advantage to receive such income in addition to occupational income.

169 **Trends in the distribution of personal incomes (after income tax has been deducted), United Kingdom, 1938–73**

	Percentage shares of income received by given groups of the population at the dates shown			
	1938/39	*1949/50*	*1964/65*	*1972/73*
Richest 1% received	11.7	5.8	5.0	4.0
Richest 5% received	25.3	16.7	14.8	12.9
Poorest 30% received	15.4	15.9	14.5	15.9

Source: Adapted from the Royal Commission on the Distribution of Income and Wealth, *Initial Report on the Distribution of Income and Wealth*, HMSO

(a) *In the light of the information presented in the table, comment on the claim that 'income differentials in Britain have narrowed steadily since before the Second World War'.* (3 marks)

(b) *The information in the table does not give an accurate impression of the differences in* real incomes *between different sections of the population.*

(i) *What other kinds of rewards besides occupational earnings could be included when calculating a person's real income? (5 marks)*

(ii) *Why is the gap between the* real incomes *of the richest and poorest groups of earners significantly greater than the gap between their occupational incomes? (4 marks)*

(c) *Explain why the distribution of personal* wealth *in modern Britain is more unequal than the distribution of income. (8 marks)* (CAM)

Key terms and concepts

The following terms and concepts have been defined and used in this chapter. You must be able to use them and explain their meaning for examination purposes:

wealth; income; the rich; the poor; poverty.

Other terms you may wish to use:

real income   The goods and services which can be bought with money earned: that is the actual purchasing power of the money.

money income or earned income   This measures the household's income in terms of a monetary unit, i.e. so many pounds sterling.

23 Poverty

The questions on this topic are generally straightforward. They centre on the problem of defining the central term **poverty**, explaining why poverty exists, stating which categories of people are likely to constitute **the poor**, and discussing how poverty might be overcome.

You may be asked to explain:

170 *What is meant by poverty? Outline three reasons for the existence of poverty.* (WEL)

Or to discuss a statement such as:

171 *'The poor are no longer with us.' Do you agree?* (LON, *adapted*)

Apart from gaining the information necessary to answer these questions it is useful to have a brief historical knowledge of the development of research into poverty. Occasionally, an exam question may ask you to:

172 *Examine the contribution of Booth and Rowntree to the study of poverty.* (OX)

You should find that if you can answer these questions you should also be able to answer almost any other which is raised on this topic.

The work of Booth and Rowntree

The earliest scientific studies into the extent of poverty in Britain were carried out at the end of the nineteenth century by Booth in London and Rowntree in York.

1 Charles Booth was a businessman and statistician. His work was first published in 1899, entitled *Life and Labour of the People*. He found that 35% of the population of East London could be classed as poor and more than 12% were very poor.

2 Seebohm Rowntree was greatly influenced by the work of Booth

and decided to investigate the extent of poverty in York. He distinguished between primary and secondary poverty.

Primary poverty Families whose total earnings were insufficient to obtain the minimum necessary for the maintenance of physical efficiency were in this category.

Secondary poverty This described families whose total earnings would have been sufficient for physical efficiency if it were not that some portion was used wastefully.

He established a minimal nutritional requirement necessary to sustain a person in everyday life. It was a line of physical survival which he assumed was universal and unchanging. Anyone, anywhere would always require the same minimum dietary standard in order to survive. He calculated that in 1901 about 15% of people in York were in primary poverty. His last study in 1950 suggested it had fallen to about 1.5%.

Absolute poverty Both researchers made use of the idea that an absolutely clear line could be fixed between those who were and those who were not in poverty. It was assumed that people's basic requirements for survival were the same in any age and in any society.

Relative poverty This concept describes the poor as those whose incomes and life-styles are considered to have fallen too far below those of the normal standards of the society in which they live. The poor are identified in relation to other people. Although they may be able to survive economically, they are considered to be living at an unacceptably low level. This standard is a relative one because it constantly changes according to the changing standards of society as a whole.

When answering a question on poverty it is important to make the distinction between the two types of interpretation of the concept. The important things to remember about relative poverty are:

1 It involves a comparison with others in the same society.
2 It compares standards in a society at a particular time.
3 It contrasts to the view that poverty is a matter of absolute fact which is unchanging over time and place.

Bearing these points in mind, consider how you would answer the following question:

173 Poverty as Relative Deprivation
        'Poverty is not an absolute state. It is relative deprivation.
    Society itself is continuously changing and thrusting new
    obligations on its members. They, in turn, develop new needs.
    They are rich or poor according to their share of the resources

that are available to all. This is true as much of nutritional as monetary or even educational resources.

Our general theory, then, should be that individuals and families whose resources, over time, fall seriously short of the resources commanded by the average individual or family in the community in which they live, whether that community is a local, national or international one, are in poverty.'

Peter Townsend, *The British Journal of Sociology*, September 1962

   (a) *How does the above extract help us to understand changing standards of poverty over a period of time and in different places?*

   (b) *How can we say that we are experiencing a higher standard of poverty in Britain today than 50 years ago?* (AEB)

If you were asked to

174 Discuss some of the difficulties in defining poverty. (CAM)

it would be useful to point out also that there are difficulties in using a relative definition of poverty. For example, it is difficult to decide what is 'an acceptable standard of living'. Is the failure to own a television set a measure of poverty because the majority of people in a society own one? One answer could be that owning a TV set remains a luxury rather than a necessity in modern Britain and so lack of a set would not be a good measure. But if it could be shown that the same person also could not afford many of the other items that we take for granted in our daily lives (a radio, vacuum cleaner, washing machine, etc.), then it may be that we could assess this person as being in relative poverty.

Townsend has said that studies of poverty based on income levels are generally unsatisfactory because income levels are not satisfactory measures. For example, two nuclear families of the same size and social class may have the same income. But one may be living in an area with better access to a wide range of important resources: good housing, schools, doctors and hospitals, etc. He says that it is really necessary to establish 'acceptable styles of living' in order to decide who is and who is not in poverty.

The poverty line in modern Britain

In contemporary Britain there is more emphasis by Government departments on a relative definition of poverty than on absolute poverty. That is, the line moves up and down according to the needs of individual families. The circumstances of each family in need is assessed by the Supplementary Benefits Commission.

Supplementary benefits are administered by the Ministry of Social Security. They provide pensions and other allowances to people who are not in full-time work and whose incomes from pensions, etc. are not enough to meet their needs for the basic necessities of life. It is paid as of right and does not depend on having paid contributions into the scheme. The Supplementary Benefits Commission makes allowances for married and single people, for each child and for rent. The total becomes the poverty line for the family concerned. It represents the level below which the state believes its income should not fall.

175   **Percentage of households of different types classified as being 'in poverty' (i.e. households with an income of less than 140% of supplementary benefit level in 1975**

All households	29
All elderly people	64
Elderly people who are working	28
Elderly people who are *not* working	69
Elderly people not working and *with* an occupational pension	53
Elderly people not working and *without* an occupational pension	79
All couples (excluding elderly people)	14
Couples where the man is disabled	50
Couples where the man is *not* disabled	13
Couples (not disabled) with 2 or fewer children	10
Couples (not disabled) with 3 or more children	34
Couples with 3 or more children *with* wife working	19
Couples with 3 or more children *without* wife working	48
All single-parent families	58
Single-parent families where the parent is employed	37
Single-parent families where the parent is not employed	87
All single people	18
Single men	14
Single women	25

Source: Adapted from *The Causes of Poverty*, Background Paper No. 5, Royal Commission on the Distribution of Income and Wealth, HMSO, 1978

(a) *What is supplementary benefit?* *(2 marks)*
(b) *Why do British sociologists usually define poverty in relation to the level of supplementary benefit rather than in terms of absolute poverty?* *(6 marks)*

(c) Using the information in the table, outline the main causes of poverty in modern Britain. (12 marks) (CAM)

Who are the poor?

According to the absolute definition of poverty it is rapidly being eliminated because diet and nutritional standards have improved so much. The incomes of people have also increased so that everyone is more able to obtain the basic requirements of physical survival.

According to the relative definition of poverty the poor exist so long as one group of people have living standards far below those of the majority of people in society. This is a matter of **relative deprivation**. People compare themselves to others in their own society – not with people in other societies where standards may be very different.

On this definition the poor are most likely to be included in one or more of the following five categories:

1 **The unemployed** In the last ten years the amount of unemployment has increased by almost two million. Piachaud (1975) found that where the husband was often unemployed then the family was more than twice as likely to be in poverty.

Unemployment (thousands)

	1971	1973	1975	1977	1979	1981
Men	660	515	777	1069	2000	2500
Women	126	103	200	414	450	500

Source: Social Trends

2 **The low-paid** The Low Pay Unit (which monitors the pay of the lowest paid groups in Britain) points out that the relative pay of the poorest 10% of manual workers has hardly changed since records began in 1886.

Low pay is a relative matter; but in 1981 – when the national average wage was about £100 per week – low pay would be regarded as an income of below £60 per week on which a family had to be supported.

Abel-Smith and Townsend suggest that low pay is one of the most important causes of poverty especially where there are children in the family.

In 1981 it was found that registered child-minders, for example, were earning on average £16 a week for a 42-hour week looking after three children.

3 **The elderly** There are an increasing number of elderly people in the community. Studies show that most elderly households depend

on social security. Their other problems are those of loneliness and ill-health.

Number of men aged over 65 and women aged over 60 in the population, 1951–81 (thousands)

1951	1961	1971	1981
6600	7500	8800	9600

Source: Social Trends

4 **One-parent families** Piachaud (1975) found that 58% of one-parent families were households that were in poverty. In 1981 it is estimated that there are more than 700,000 parents bringing up children single-handed. This is a particular problem for women in a broken home since their earning capacity may be limited by the problem of looking after young children.

5 **The sick and the disabled** In 1981 it is estimated that there are about 3.5 million physically handicapped people in Britain. Many of them require state benefits in order to survive economically and because many have limited earning opportunities they are likely to fall into poverty.

Brief details from studies into the extent of poverty in Britain

1 **1965. Abel-Smith and Townsend** They made the following calculations:
   (a) The unemployed   7%
   (b) The low-paid   40%
   (c) The elderly   33%
   (d) One-parent families   10%
   (e) The sick and disabled 10%
2 **1966. Circumstances of Families** This study showed that about 500,000 families (including one million children) were living below supplementary benefit levels.
3 **1968. Department of Health and Social Security Survey** This found that 75,000 men in full-time work were living below the poverty line.
4 **1973. Bosanquet** He used a broad definition of poverty based on the numbers of people requiring benefits or likely to require them. He estimated that as many as 10.6 million people were living just above, on, or below the poverty line.
5 **1976. The Supplementary Benefits Commission** This stated that about five million men, women and children were dependent wholly or partly on supplementary benefits.

Why do the poor remain poor?

Various explanations have been put forward by sociologists and other observers. They include the following:

1 Coates and Silburn (*Poverty: The Forgotten Englishmen*) describe a cycle of deprivation (or a vicious circle of poverty). This view suggests that the poor suffer a series of problems which reinforce each other. These prevent them from gaining access to the scarce resources of society. They live in a cycle of poverty which is hard to break. They tend to live in poor areas; they have a poor education; they have poor job opportunities; they marry early and produce a large family – whose members remain deprived.
2 Harrington (*The Other America*) discusses the culture of poverty. This view says that the poor form a sub-culture which is separate from the main culture of society. The poor feel helpless and inferior; they have a strong sense of fatalism and resignation to their fate. These negative views tied into their patterns of life form a culture (a view of the world and their place in it) which is passed on from one generation to the next.
3 Townsend (*Poverty*) suggests that the poor remain poor because they lack power; as a result they are unable to change their situations effectively. They seldom belong to powerful pressure groups (trade unions, for example), they have no influence with political parties, and they do not participate in local decision-making groups (housing associations, etc.). They rely on the goodwill of other caring members of society to act on their behalf.
4 Gans (*More Equality*) argues that poverty continues to exist because it serves certain functions in society.
  (a) All the worst, unpleasant and most menial jobs are filled by those on or below the poverty line.
  (b) Poverty helps to create jobs: without a large pool of poor and deprived people there would be fewer social workers, policemen, doctors, etc.
  (c) He says that poverty helps to guarantee the status of those who are not poor.
5 There is a widespread belief that if people are poor, then it is their own fault. Therefore, little is done about it by governments (since poverty programmes do not win votes). It is also felt by many of the general public that the welfare state provides sufficient benefits to keep people out of severe poverty.
6 There is some evidence from research studies that many people who are in or close to poverty do not claim all the benefits to which they are entitled and which might help to lift them out of severe states of deprivation. This may be especially true among the elderly.

Can poverty be defeated?

1 Abel-Smith says that governments must recognize the existence of poverty and introduce policies to assist those at the lowest end of the social scale. This would include decent housing for low wage families, improved educational opportunities and improved benefits for the needy.
2 Piachaud also says that the main weapon against poverty should be improved social security payments.
3 Trade unions advocate the introduction of a national minimum wage to try and eliminate low wage-earners from potential poverty.
4 Townsend says that Britain needs a central department of social planning so that scarce resources, such as housing, educational and health facilities, etc., are distributed more fairly in the community.
5 Some economists suggest that changes could be made in the taxation system to increase the burden on the rich and reduce it on the poor.
6 Social attitudes will have to change so that poverty is widely seen as 'a problem' and one that can and should be defeated. Holman argues that unless people can become more concerned about the needs of others, poverty will remain with us.

You are advised to re-read the detail presented on pp. 250–52; make some summary notes and then with reference to these (and not the text) answer the following question:

176 'Some people think of poverty as a condition in which families go hungry or starve and others as a condition relative to the standards enjoyed on average or by most people in society. . . .'

P. Townsend, *Poverty in the UK*, 1979

(a) *Which groups in society tend most frequently to find themselves in poverty in modern Britain?*   (5 marks)
(b) *Why do the poor always tend to remain poor?*   (15 marks)
(AEB)

Key terms and concepts

The following terms and concepts have been used and defined in this chapter. You must be able to use them and explain their meaning for examination purposes:

poverty; primary and secondary poverty; relative and absolute poverty; the poverty line; supplementary benefit.

Bibliography

CHAPTER 2

A. Oakley, *The Sociology of Housework*
J. W. B. Douglas *et al.*, *All Our Future* (Panther)
— —, *The Home and the School*
R. Davie, N. Butler, Goldstein, *From Birth to Seven* (Longmans)
G. Kleck, Study reported in *American Journal of Sociology*, Vol. 84, No. 4
P. Fisherman, Report in *Social Problems*, Vol. 25, No. 4
P. Marsh, E. Rosser, R. Harré, *Rules of Disorder*

CHAPTER 3

R. Fletcher, *The Family and Marriage* (Penguin)
M. Farmer, *The Family* (Longmans)
M. Anderson, *The Sociology of the Family* (Penguin)
T. Parsons, R. Bales, *Family, Socialisation and Interaction Process* (RKP)
E. Leach, *A Runaway World* (BBC Publications)
D. Cooper, *Death of the Family* (Penguin)
P. Laslett, *The World We Have Lost*
P. Willmott, M. Young, *Family and Kinship in East London* (Penguin)
M. Sussman, L. Burchinall, 'Marriage and Family Living' in Anderson
R. Rosser, C. Harris, *The Family and Social Change* (RKP)
E. Bott, *Family and Social Network* (Tavistock Press)

CHAPTER 4

C. Turnbull, *Wayward Servants*
A. Oakley, *Sex, Gender and Society*
A. Coote, 'The Role of Women', *Observer*, 1974
T. Blackstone, 'Why Are There So Few Women Scientists and Engineers?' *New Society*, 21 Feb. 1980
Equal Opportunities Commission Report, July 1980, for recent information on legal changes in respect of women at work
Low Pay Unit Research Project, *Minimum Wages for Women*, Sept. 1980
E. A. Johns, *The Social Structure of Modern Britain* (Pergamon)
A. Oakley, 'Mothers and Children in Society', *Nursing*, 1981
R. & R. Rapaport, *Dual Career Families*, 1971
— —, *Families in Britain* (RKP), 1982
Foggarty *et al.*, *Women in Top Jobs*
A. Heath, 'Women Who Get On In The World', *New Society*, 12 Feb. 1981
A. Oakley, 'The Failure of the Women's Movement', *New Society*, Sept. 1979

CHAPTER 5

Report of Royal Commission on Marriage and Divorce, 1956, Command 9678
J. Dominion, *Marital Breakdown* (Penguin)
Yudkin, Holmes, *Working Mothers and Their Children* (Sphere)
M. Kellmer-Pringle, *The Needs of Children*
Chester, *Divorce*
Wallerstein, Kelly, *Surviving the Breakup*
C. Gibson, 'Social Trends in Divorce', *New Society*, 5 July 1973

CHAPTER 6

S. Parker *et al.*, *The Sociology of Industry* (Allen & Unwin)
K. Roberts *et al.*, *The Fragmentary Class Structure* (Heinemann)
D. Butler, R. Rose, *The British General Election of 1959* (Cass)
D. Lockwood, J. Goldthorpe, *The Affluent Worker in the Class Structure* (Cambridge University Press)
J. Westergaard, H. Resler, *Class in a Capitalist Society* (Penguin)
A. Halsey, *Origins and Destinations* (Oxford University Press)
J. Goldthorpe, *Social Mobility and the Class Structure in Modern Britain* (Oxford University Press)
A. King, 'The People's Flag is Deepest Blue', *Observer*, May 1979
R. Dahrendorf, *Class and Class Conflict in an Industrial Society* (RKP)
P. Townsend, 'Inequality in the Workplace', *New Society*, Oct. 1979
R. Cobb, Sennet, *The Hidden Injuries of Class*

CHAPTER 7

G. Neave, *How They Fared* (RKP)
J. Forde, *Class and the Comprehensive School*
D. Glass, *Social Mobility in Britain* (RKP)
Glennester, Pryke, *Power in Britain*, ed. J. Urry and J. Wakeford (Heinemann)
A. Giddens, 'An Anatomy of the British Ruling Class', *New Society*, 4 Oct. 1979
D. Boyd, *Elites and their Education* (NFER)
Carter, *Into Work* (Penguin)
H. Himmelweit, Vince, *Television and the Child*
D. Downes, 'Peer Groups' in *Sociology of Modern Britain*, ed. Butterworth, Weir
R. Merton, *Social Theory and Social Structure* (Free Press)

CHAPTER 8

P. Berger, *Sociology: Biographical Approach* (Penguin)
F. Milson, *Youth in a Changing Society*
J. Hemmings, *Adolescence*
B. Sugarman, *Social Class, Values and Behaviour*
B. Wilson, *Youth Culture and the Universities*
J. Jupp, 'The Discontents of Youth', *Guardian*, 1971
T. Roszak, *The Making of a Counter Culture* (Faber)
S. Cohen, *Folk Devils and Moral Panics* (MacGibbon & Kee)
G. Murdock, R. McCron, 'Scoobies, Skins and Contemporary Pop', *New Society*, 29 March 1973
D. Hargreaves *et al.*, *Deviance in Classrooms* (RKP)
K. Leech, *Youthquake* (Sheldon)

S. Frith, 'Punk Bohemians', *New Society*, 1979
D. Hargreaves, *Social Relations in a Secondary School* (RKP)
H. Becker, *Outsiders* (Free Press)

CHAPTER 9

S. Parker, *The Future of Work and Leisure*
J. Brown, *The Social Psychology of Industry* (Penguin)
F. Hertzberg, *The Motivation to Work*
A. Fox, *A Sociology of Work in Industry*
W. Daniel, 'What Do Workers Really Want?', *New Society*
T. Lupton, *On the Shop Floor* (Pergamon)
H. Benyon, *Perceptions of Work* (Cambridge University Press)
Ogburn, *Social Change* (RKP)
W. Daniel, 'Automation', *New Society*, 1969
R. Blauner, *Alienation and Freedom* (Chicago University Press)

CHAPTER 10

Williamson, *Trade Unions*
M. Jackson, *Industrial Relations* (Croom Helm)
R. Hyam, *Strikes* (Fontana)
E. Greenwood, in *Attributes of a Profession from Man, Work and Society*, ed. Noscow, Form (Basic Books)
T. Burns, *Industrial Man* (Penguin)
J. Eldridge, *Sociology and Industrial Life* (Nelson)

CHAPTER 11

Whittingham, Towers, *Strikes and the Economy*
Cameron, Eldridge, 'Unofficial Strikes', in *Industrial Disputes*, ed. J. Eldridge
C. Kerr, A. Seigal, 'The Interindustry Propensity to Strike', in ed. Kornhauser, Dubin, Ross
Gouldner, *Wildcat Strike* (RKP)
Samuelson, *Economics*

CHAPTER 12

P. Willmott, M. Young, *Family and Class in a London Suburb* (RKP)
K. Roberts, *Leisure* (Longmans)
D. Downes, *The Delinquent Solution* (RKP)
J. Mays, *Growing Up in the City*
J. Dumazedier, *Towards a Society of Leisure* (Collier-Macmillan)

CHAPTER 13

Redfield, *The Little Community*
R. Pahl, *Readings in Urban Sociology* (Pergamon)
E. Durkheim, *Division of Labour in Society* (Free Press)
Tönnies, *Gemeinschaft und Gesellschaft* (Harper)
R. Frankenberg, *Communities in Britain* (Penguin)
Seeley, Sim, Loosley, *Crestwood Heights*

H. Gans, *The Urban Villagers*
O. Lewis, *The Children of Sanchez* (Random House)
Jennings, *Societies in the Making*
Dennis, *People and Planning*
The Buchanan Report, 1963

CHAPTER 14

R. Chandler, Bowker, *Public Opinion*
Halloran, *The Effects of Television*
G. Noble, *Children in Front of the Small Screen*
IBA Research, *The Portrayal of Violence on TV*
W. Belson, *TV Violence and the Adolescent Boy*
G. Jones, *The Political Structure* (Longmans)
D. McQuail, *Towards a Sociology of Mass Communications*
C. Husband, P. Hartmann, *The Mass Media and Racial Conflict*
G. Murdock, R. McCron, *The Television and Delinquency Debate*

CHAPTER 15

R. Rose, *Studies in British Politics*
G. Lenski, *The Religious Factor* (Anchor Books)
Milne, R. McKenzie, *Straight Fight*
E. Nordlinger, *The Working-Class Tories* (MacGibbon & Kee)
F. Parkin, 'A Theory of Political Deviance', *British Journal of Sociology*, 1967
B. Hindess, *The Decline of Working-Class Politics*

CHAPTER 16

R. Tames, *People, Power and Politics* (Nelson)
J. Blondel, *Voters, Parties and Leaders* (Penguin)
Ecstein, *Pressure Group Politics*
R. Rose, *Politics in England*

CHAPTER 17

J. Mays, *Crime and the Social Structure*
P. Willmott, M. Young, 'Social Grading by Manual Workers', *British Journal of Sociology*, 1956
P. Wiles, 'Criminal Statistics and Sociological Explanations of Crime', in *Crime and Delinquency in Britain*, ed. Carsons, Wiles
L. MacDonald, 'Social Class and Delinquency', in *Crime and Its Treatment*, ed. J. Mays
Sutherland, 'White Collar Crime', in ed. Carsons, Wiles
Douglas, Ross, Hammond, 'Delinquency and Social Class', in ed. Carsons, Wiles
P. Willmott, *Adolescent Boys of East London* (Penguin)
Vaz, *Middle-Class Delinquency*
R. Roshier, *Crime and Punishment*
S. Cohen, 'Who are the Vandals?', *New Society*, 25 Feb. 1977
I. Whortley, *Soccer Violence*
A. Cohen, *Delinquent Boys* (Free Press)
R. Cloward, L. Ohlin, *Delinquency and Opportunity* (Free Press)
Shaw, McKay, *Juvenile Delinquency and the Urban Area*

Sainsbury, 'Delinquency and the Ecology of London', in ed. Carsons, Wiles

CHAPTER 18

For data relating to population you are advised to make use of the annual government
  publication *Social Trends*.
Kelsall, *Population* (Longmans)
E. Wrigley, *Population and History* (World University Library)

CHAPTER 19

D. Glass, *Education and Social Change in Modern England*
R. King, *Values and Involvement in a Grammar School*
A. Clegg, *The Challenge of Change* (NFER)
C. Lacey, *Hightown Grammar* (Manchester University Press)
D. Pidgeon, *Expectations and Pupil Performance* (NFER)
O. Banks, *The Sociology of Education* (Batsford)
M. Rutter *et al.*, *Fifteen Thousand Hours* (Open Books)
Elder, 'Life Opportunity and Personality . . .', in *Sociology of Modern Britain*, ed.
  Butterworth, Weir
P. Meddlicott, 'Streaming and the Comprehensive School', *New Society*
M. Shipman, *Sociology of the School* (Longmans)
B. Bernstein, *Class Codes and Control* (RKP)

CHAPTER 20

E. Durkheim, *Elementary Forms of Religious Life* (Free Press)
B. Wilson, *Religion in a Secular Society* (Penguin)
D. Martin, *A Sociology of English Religion* (Heinemann)
B. Wilson, 'The Anglican Church in Decline', *New Society*, 1974

CHAPTER 21

J. Rex, R. Moore, *Race, Community and Conflict* (Oxford University Press)
W. Daniel, *Racial Discrimination in England* (Penguin)
Home Office Report, *Ethnic Minorities*, 1981
W. Daniel, *Political Economic Planning Report*, 1974
Garrard, *The English and Immigration*

CHAPTER 22

A. Atkinson, *Unequal Shares* (Penguin)
A. Halsey, Reith Lectures 1978: *Change in British Society* (Oxford University Press)
J. Holman, *Poverty*

CHAPTER 23

C. Booth, *Life and Labour of the People*
P. Townsend, 'Poverty as Relative Deprivation', *British Journal of Sociology*, 1962
P. Townsend, *The Concept of Poverty* (Heinemann)
B. Abel-Smith, Townsend, *The Poor and the Poorest* (Bell & Sons)
S. Rowntree, *Poverty and Progress* (Longmans)

D. Piachaud, M. Stewart, R. Layard, *The Causes of Poverty* (HMSO)

N. Bosanquet, 'Poverty', *Spectator*, 1973

K. Caotes, R. Silburn, *Poverty, the Forgotten Englishmen* (Penguin)

Harrington, *The Other America* (Penguin)

Townsend, *Poverty in the UK* (Penguin)

H. Gans, *More Equality* (Pantheon)

Index

For a list of **Pan Study Aids** titles see page two of this book

L. E. W. Smith
English Language £1.25

The contents of this Study Aid include : composition, factual writing (including letter writing), summary, comprehension, grammar, direct and indirect speech, figures of speech and idiom, paraphrase, vocabulary, spelling and punctuation. A complete guide to preparing for O Level, School Certificate and equivalent examinations in English Language.

F. G. J. Norton
Maths £1.25

The contents of this Study Aid include : arithmetic, units, areas and volume, ratio and percentage, algebra, graphs, sets and set notion, binary operations and groups, relations and functions, statistics, probability, geometry, theorems, loci and constructions, trigonometry, sine and cosine formulae, matrices, vectors, calculus. A complete guide to preparing for O Level, School Certificate and equivalent examinations in Maths.

M. J. Denial
Chemistry £1.25

The contents of this Study Aid include : atomic structure, kinetic theory and bonding, elements, compounds and mixtures, purification, electrochemistry, acids, bases and salts, the air, gases, oxygen and hydrogen, the periodic table, the mole, formulae and equations, metals and their compounds, water, soaps and detergents, analysis, organic chemistry, energy, rates of reaction, equilibria, the chemical industry. A complete guide to preparing for O Level, School Certificate and equivalent examinations in Chemistry.

M. Nelkon and M. V. Detheridge
Physics £1.25

The contents of this Study Aid include : dynamics, statics, forces due to fluids, molecules and properties of matter, heat, waves and sound, optics, current electricity, magnetism and electromagnetism, electric charge and the structure of matter. A complete guide to preparing for O Level, School Certificate and equivalent examinations in Physics.

R. Warson
Accounts and Book-keeping   £1.25

The contents of this Study Aid include: profits and stock, profit and loss, the balance sheet, adjustments, the trial balance, final accounts, the journal, banking and petty cash, VAT, control accounts, receipts and payments, income and expenditure, partnership, limited liability. A complete guide to preparing for O Level, School Certificate and equivalent examinations in Accounting, Book-keeping and Accounts, Principles of Accounts and any course requiring an introduction of accounting practice.

D. P. Baron and J. F. Connor
Economics   £1.25

The contents of this Study Aid include: the economic problem and economic systems, organization of economic activity, population, location of industry, production, labour, unemployment, wages and trade unions, demand, supply and price, money and banking, inflation, public finance, national income, international trade, the government and the economy. A complete guide to preparing for O Level, School Certificate and equivalent examinations in Economics.

P. J. Hills and H. Barlow
Effective Study Skills   £1.25

The contents of this Study Aid include: focusing attention and concentration, reading faster and more efficiently, finding information and using libraries, making notes, essay writing, punctuation and spelling, revision and revision notes, taking an examination. A complete guide to effective study, designed to help students eliminate indecision, anxiety and time wasting and introduce to them the vital but often neglected techniques of study.

C. A. Leeds
British Government and Politics   £1.25

The contents of this Study Aid include: basic principles of government, the monarchy, prime minister and cabinet, Parliament, the civil service, the welfare state, political parties, voting and elections, public opinion, trade unions, local government, the legal system, the EEC and Commonwealth, devolution. A complete guide to preparing for O Level, School Certificate and equivalent examinations in British Government and Politics.

edited by
S. E. Stiegeler BSc and Glyn Thomas BSc Econ
A Dictionary of Economics and Commerce
£1.50

An authoritative A–Z of the terms used internationally in the
overlapping fields of theoretical economics and practical commerce.

A team of expert contributors provides a formal definition of each
word or term, followed by an explanation of its underlying
concepts and accompanied by appropriate illustrations. Special
attention is paid to such new and rapidly expanding subjects as cost-
benefit analysis and welfare economics. And the vocabularies of
banking, accounting, insurance, stock exchanges, commodity dealing,
shipping, transport and commercial law are all included.

Also available

John Daintith
A Dictionary of Physical Sciences £1.50

Stella E. Stiegler
A Dictionary of Earth Sciences £1.50

E. A. Martin
A Dictionary of Life Sciences £1.50

edited by D. C. Browning
Everyman's Roget's Thesaurus £1.95

Roget's Thesaurus is one of the English-speaking world's most valuable
and celebrated works of reference. It is a treasury of synonyms, antonyms,
parallel and related words, designed to help you find the right words or
phrase to express your ideas with force and clarity.

This edition preserves the original plan of classification and categories
(including the vast and ingenious index) and has been completely revised
to bring all words and phrases into accordance with current usage. Over
ten thousand more of these have been added, including many
technical terms, everyday neologisms, Americanisms and slang.

'Among reference books Roget's Thesaurus stands by itself . . . a treasury
upon which writers can draw'
TIMES LITERARY SUPPLEMENT

Ronald Ridout
The Pan Spelling Dictionary £1.50

The quick and easy guide to accurate spelling, designed specifically for
spelling. Clearly layed-out, with brief and straightforward definitions
of 34,000 words. A supplement to the main text identifies American
spellings where they differ from standard English. There are also lists
of proper names and abbreviations, an outline of the main principles
of English spelling, and clear instructions for using the book to find the
word you want. Ideal for the home, the classroom or the office.

Isaac Asimov
Asimov's Biographical Encyclopedia of Science and Technology £2.50

A lively and wholly absorbing reference book which traces the history
of science, from ancient Egypt to modern space flight, through 1,195
biographical sketches. Arranged in chronological order of birth, a wealth of
facts and anecdotes illuminate the contribution made by each individual
to the world of science. The index lists hundreds of scientific topics plus
the names of individuals, other than the subjects of the biographies, and
completes a book that is unique in its content, width and range.

Robin Hyman
A Dictionary of Famous Quotations £1.25

This collection took over five years to compile. Its exceptionally clear and
attractive presentation makes it a delight to read, and the lively selection
of quotations encourages the browser as well as the seeker of specific
references. The comprehensive index, with over 25,000 entries, enables
one to trace a partly-remembered quotation with maximum speed.

Ronald Ridout and Clifford Witting
English Proverbs Explained 80p

In this fascinating collection of hundreds of English proverbs still in use
the authors are concerned with proverbs as a live force and have selected
sayings which are at the same time popular, pithy and wise. Teachers,
crossword addicts and the general reader will find much to divert them,
and students of English can rejoice in an entertaining guide through a
maze of bewildering expressions.

Reference, language and information

☐	**Pan International Pocket Atlas**	£2.95p
☐	**Universal Encyclopaedia of Mathematics**	£2.95p

Literature guides

☐	**An Introduction to Shakespeare and his Contemporaries**	Marguerite Alexander	£2.95p
☐	**An Introduction to Fifty American Poets**	Peter Jones	£1.75p
☐	**An Introduction to Fifty Modern British Plays**	Benedict Nightingale	£2.95p
☐	**An Introduction to Fifty American Novels**	Ian Ousby	£1.95p
☐	**An Introduction to Fifty British Novels 1600–1900**	Gilbert Phelps	£2.50p
☐	**An Introduction to Fifty Modern European Poets**	John Pilling	£2.25p
☐	**An Introduction to Fifty British Poets 1300–1900**	Michael Schmidt	£1.95p
☐	**An Introduction to Fifty Modern British Poets**		£2.95p
☐	**An Introduction to Fifty European Novels**	Martin Seymour-Smith	£1.95p
☐	**An Introduction to Fifty British Plays 1660–1900**	John Cargill Thompson	£1.95p

All these books are available at your local bookshop or newsagent, or can be ordered direct from the publisher. Indicate the number of copies required and fill in the form below   7

....

Name..
(Block letters please)

Address..

....

Send to Pan Books (CS Department), Cavaye Place, London SW10 9PG
Please enclose remittance to the value of the cover price plus:
35p for the first book plus 15p per copy for each additional book ordered
to a maximum charge of £1.25 to cover postage and packing
Applicable only in the UK

While every effort is made to keep prices low, it is sometimes
necessary to increase prices at short notice. Pan Books reserve
the right to show on covers and charge new retail prices which
may differ from those advertised in the text or elsewhere